About This Book

Why is *The New Virtual Classroom* important?

Virtual classroom tools such as WebEx, Acrobat Connect Professional, and Centra offer powerful instructional environments while saving travel time and costs associated with traditional face-to-face classroom training. It's no surprise then that surveys show an increasing use of these synchronous technologies for training and educational purposes. However, unless virtual classroom technology is used in ways that promote learning, cost savings are only an illusion. Too often, traditional classroom courses are ported directly to virtual classrooms, failing to adapt to the features of the technology. Research shows that it's **not the delivery technology** that determines learning effectiveness. Rather, learning results from the appropriate use of media features in ways that harmonize with human memory requirements. In this book we draw on research and experience to show you how to effectively harness the power of the virtual classroom.

What can you achieve with this book?

The guidelines, research, and examples in this book and the accompanying CD show you how to take advantage of the many instructional features in the new virtual classroom in ways proven to lead to learning.

Effective use of visualization, audio, and interactive features are the main paths to effective instruction in the new virtual classroom. However, the road map to success requires more than knowing the mechanics of these features. Only by using visuals, audio, and interactions in ways proven to promote learning can you fully exploit the potential of the virtual classroom. In this book we show you how.

What this book is NOT

The New Virtual Classroom was not written to teach the mechanics of virtual classroom tools. Most tool vendors provide free training and documentation for this purpose. We have intentionally not provided tool vendor information because it would be obsolete by the time the book is printed. We have used examples from most of the major virtual classroom tools and asked our expert contributors to mention which tools they use in their work. Beyond this, we recommend consulting the Internet for the latest information. Finally, this is not a step-by-step workbook. Our goal is to provide the key guidelines for virtual classroom success, along with supporting examples and evidence. You will need to adapt our guidelines to your own unique organizational settings.

How is this book organized?

The New Virtual Classroom includes an introduction and four parts. Chapter 1 orients you to the virtual classroom with a summary of its benefits, uses, and features.

Part One, Learning and the New Virtual Classroom, focuses on our human memory systems and on the intersection between virtual classroom features and instructional events to support learning. Learner engagement is the focus of Part Two, which includes Chapters 5 through 7 on using visuals and interactions to promote active learning.

Part Three, Optimizing Your Virtual Events, focuses on key elements to address when designing and facilitating virtual classrooms including management of cognitive load, making effective introductions, packaging your program, and applying problem-based designs to virtual lessons.

Part Four, Creating Effective Learning Events in the New Virtual Classroom, includes Chapter 12, which recapitulates the guidelines described in previous chapters. Here you will read about seven principles of effective virtual classroom design plus techniques for converting face-to-face classroom courses into virtual classroom events as well as for creating virtual classroom events from scratch.

The New Virtual Classroom **Road Map**

**Chapter 1
Meet the New
Virtual Classroom**

Introduction

**Chapter 2
Learning
in the New VC**

**Chapter 3
Features to Exploit
in the New VC**

**Chapter 4
Teaching Content Types
in the New VC**

Part 1: Learning and the New Virtual Classroom

**Chapter 5
Visualize Your
Message**

**Chapter 6
Make It Active – Part 1**

**Chapter 7
Make It Active – Part 2**

Part 2: Engaging Participants in the New Virtual Classroom

**Chapter 8
Managing Mental Load
in the New VC**

**Chapter 9
Make a Good
First Impression**

**Chapter 10
Packaging Your
VC Session**

**Chapter 11
Problem-Based Learning
in the New VC**

Part 3: Optimizing Your Virtual Events

**Chapter 12
Getting Started**

Part 4: Creating Effective Learning Events in the New Virtual Classroom

About Pfeiffer

Pfeiffer serves the professional development and hands-on resource needs of training and human resource practitioners and gives them products to do their jobs better. We deliver proven ideas and solutions from experts in HR development and HR management, and we offer effective and customizable tools to improve workplace performance. From novice to seasoned professional, Pfeiffer is the source you can trust to make yourself and your organization more successful.

Essential Knowledge Pfeiffer produces insightful, practical, and comprehensive materials on topics that matter the most to training and HR professionals. Our Essential Knowledge resources translate the expertise of seasoned professionals into practical, how-to guidance on critical workplace issues and problems. These resources are supported by case studies, worksheets, and job aids and are frequently supplemented with CD-ROMs, websites, and other means of making the content easier to read, understand, and use.

Essential Tools Pfeiffer's Essential Tools resources save time and expense by offering proven, ready-to-use materials—including exercises, activities, games, instruments, and assessments—for use during a training or team-learning event. These resources are frequently offered in looseleaf or CD-ROM format to facilitate copying and customization of the material.

Pfeiffer also recognizes the remarkable power of new technologies in expanding the reach and effectiveness of training. While e-hype has often created whizbang solutions in search of a problem, we are dedicated to bringing convenience and enhancements to proven training solutions. All our e-tools comply with rigorous functionality standards. The most appropriate technology wrapped around essential content yields the perfect solution for today's on-the-go trainers and human resource professionals.

Pfeiffer
www.pfeiffer.com   *Essential resources for training and HR professionals*

Pfeiffer™

The New Virtual Classroom

Evidence-Based Guidelines for Synchronous e-Learning

Ruth Colvin Clark • Ann Kwinn

BICENTENNIAL
1807
WILEY
2007
BICENTENNIAL

John Wiley & Sons, Inc.

Published by Pfeiffer
An Imprint of Wiley.
989 Market Street, San Francisco, CA 94103-1741 www.pfeiffer.com

ISBN-10: 0-7879-8652-6
ISBN-13: 978-0-7879-8652-0

Library of Congress Cataloging-in-Publication Data

Clark, Ruth Colvin.
  The new virtual classroom : evidence-based guidelines for synchronous e-learning / Ruth Colvin Clark, Ann Kwinn.
    p. cm.
Includes bibliographical references and index.
ISBN-13: 978-0-7879-8652-0 (cloth)
ISBN-10: 0-7879-8652-6 (cloth)
1. Business education—Computer-assisted instruction. I. Kwinn, Ann, 1962- II. Title.
HF1106.C57 2007

                                                                              2006100389

Acquiring Editor: Matthew Davis   Editor: Rebecca Taff
Director of Development: Kathleen Dolan Davies   Manufacturing Supervisor: Becky Carreño
Developmental Editor: Susan Rachmeler
Production Editor: Dawn Kilgore

Printed in the United States of America

Printing   10 9 8 7 6 5 4 3 2 1

CONTENTS

CONTENTS OF THE CD-ROM

Virtual Classroom Lessons

- How to Construct a Formula in Excel
- How to Define Business Goals
- How to Plan an Interview

VC Planning and Support Documents

- Virtual Classroom Readiness Checklist
- Virtual Classroom Lesson Inventory and Script
- Virtual Classroom Welcome Letter

Designers and facilitators new to the virtual classroom often want to see good examples. This book's companion CD contains a variety of sample lessons that should give you a good feel for the virtual classroom in general and give you realistic examples of the techniques discussed in the book. If you are involved developing or delivering procedural training, such as for using software, we recommend viewing the How to Use Formulas in Excel lesson. A more principle-based or less step-by-step type of task is taught in the Defining Business Goals lesson, and the Planning an Interview lesson rethinks the same content in a problem-based structure, which you may find interesting if you want to see the difference between this and the more standard directive architecture.

You can access the samples as they are mentioned in the book, especially at the end of each chapter as you reach the On The New Virtual Classroom CD section, or you can "go to the movies" after reading a few chapters when you want a break. Or, you can leave the CD in its envelope for a while until you want some inspiration for designing your next virtual class. You may even simply enjoy seeing a virtual classroom tool that is different from your own. We have used Elluminate. Instructors can show portions of these demonstrations in either a face-to-face or virtual class.

The CD also contains Virtual Classroom Planning and Support Documents that you can use in designing and implementing your synchronous courses. The Virtual Classroom Readiness Checklist helps you to decide if the course you have in mind is appropriate for the virtual classroom and gives some of the factors that recommend the virtual classroom as a delivery media plus the elements of a synchronous-friendly organization. Once you have made the decision to move forward with this type of delivery, you can use the Virtual Classroom Lesson Inventory and Script to plan and lead your session. Finally, a sample Welcome Letter is included that you can adapt and distribute to your students to make sure *they* are ready for the great instruction you have prepared for them.

Why *The New Virtual Classroom?*

We wanted to write this book because we find virtual classroom technology a powerful medium for learning. Additionally, we see virtual classroom technology not being used as effectively as it could be. But there is more!

With all new technologies, there is a typical life cycle. At first, a new technology simply emulates older ones. For example, early television imitated live performances with opening curtains and a theatrical audience's point of view. Early computer-based training relied heavily on text. And many virtual classroom sessions have been no more than face-to-face classroom lectures ported to a new tool. As we gain experience with a new technology, we learn to exploit its features in more appropriate ways. Television producers began to shoot from several camera angles. In computer-delivered instruction, the use of visuals, audio, and simulations gave rise to new forms of media-enhanced learning. So too will synchronous e-learning come into its own as a unique instructional technology.

There is a great deal of research on human learning that transcends any particular delivery technology. We know how learning is best leveraged with text, audio, and visuals. We understand how to use examples and practice exercises to accelerate learning. *There is no need to start from scratch in designing for the virtual classroom—or any other new delivery technology!* We write this book to jump-start the evolution of the virtual classroom in ways that leverage its features to support human learning processes.

Change is a way of life. New technologies will continue to emerge. The human brain, however, is the product of eons of evolution and cannot be circumvented. This book is intended not just for the context of the virtual classroom, but also as a model for adopting all new delivery media in ways that harmonize with human learning processes.

February 2007   Ruth Colvin Clark
                                                                               Ann Kwinn

ACKNOWLEDGMENTS

OUR IDEAS HAVE benefited from suggestions and commentaries from the following instructional professionals, who have pioneered the use of virtual classroom technologies in their organizations:

Buthania Al Othman

Kim Armstrong

Heidi Bazilian

Marjan Bradesko

Mark Bucceri

Kathy Fallow

Amy Finn

Rhea Fix

Trudie Folsom

Conrad Gottfredson

Roger Hanley

Zemina Hasham

Mike Haworth

Tami Hobbs

Karin Hoffee

Karen Hyder

Sandra Johnsen Sahleen

Kristin Johnson

Stacey Keane

Chopeta Lyons

Marcus MacNeill

Julie Marsh

Sandra Morris

Bob Mosher

Brian Mulliner

Lynn Nishimura

Andrew Noell

Feroozan Noori

Diana Perney

Marty Rosenheck

Peter Ryce
Mary Schaffer
Andrew Schembri
Shauna Schullo
Rita Scott
Steve Serbun
Paul Sparks
Robert Steinmetz
Jon D. Stephenson

Pamela Stern
Rene Smith
Joe Tansey
Julia Trachsel
Eric Vidal
Lois Watson
Dawn Williams
Henry W. Willis
Mark Yeager

We also thank the following individuals who attended our demonstration virtual classroom sessions:

Jessica Ansel
Paula Cancro
Derrick L. Cogburn
Holly Fiore
Lori Funk
Ben Graff
Cynthia Jones

Bob King
Barbara Komorowski
Nisha Lopez
Feroozen Noori
Mark Templin
Michelle Verga
Andrea Wasil

Finally, we are grateful to those who helped us produce the book:

Constance Kwinn for her clever comics and illustrations

Anthony Rocha for his patience and persistence in recording the samples for the CD

Those who provided examples:

Jocelyn Dotolo
Kathy Fallow
Will Flash
Mike Haworth
Karen Hyder
Sandra Johnsen Sahleen
Tony Karrer
Taudy Mandeville

Julie Marsh
Lynn Nishimura
Andrew Noell
Becky Nutt
Peter Ryce
Ruta Valaitis
Eric Vidal
Mark Yeager

Those who helped with editing and production:

Leslie Stephen

The Pfeiffer Team

Purpose

To save travel costs and reduce time away from work, virtual classroom technologies are increasingly popular training delivery media choices. However, unless new delivery media are used in ways that promote learning, cost savings are only an illusion. In the worst case, instructors transfer poorly designed traditional classroom training directly into synchronous e-learning environments. By failing to take advantage of the powerful features of these new online tools, their potential is not realized. In this book we provide research and experienced-based guidelines of how to most effectively leverage virtual classroom technologies for learning.

Audience

We write this book for facilitators, developers, and evaluators of courses to be delivered with synchronous virtual classroom technology. We believe instructional professionals from commercial, government, and educational enterprises will find our guidelines and examples illuminating. We also recommend its use in educational technology courses as part of teacher education or instructional design university programs.

Package Components and Features

Expert Forums

Because wide adoption of synchronous technologies such as WebEx and Adobe Connect Professional for training purposes is relatively new, we called upon a number of instructional professionals who have been working with virtual classroom technologies to review our chapters and add their own experiences. Their observations appear at the end of each chapter. In addition, we incorporated snippets of practitioner wisdom throughout the chapters in our *Users Speak* inserts.

Virtual Classroom Demonstrations and Resources on the CD

We include a CD with three mini-lessons recorded with Elluminate virtual classroom software. A virtual classroom lesson on How to Use Formulas in Excel illustrates basic techniques for teaching concepts and technology-related procedures. A lesson on Defining Business Goals uses a traditional instructive approach to teach a far-transfer skill. A third virtual classroom lesson on Planning an Interview uses a problem-based learning format described in Chapter 11. At the end of each chapter we point out specific elements of these demonstrations that illustrate specific chapter guidelines.

On the CD you will also find a virtual classroom readiness checklist that you can use to guide your organization's adoption and deployment of synchronous e-learning as well as a soft copy of an e-learning facilitator's guide provided by Karen Hyder.

Glossary

Because the same terms are often used in various ways in our profession, the glossary is intended to provide a common set of definitions for the technical terms we use throughout the book.

Product Description

The book includes an introduction and four main parts as described below.

Introduction: Meet the New Virtual Classroom

In the first chapter we orient readers to the virtual classroom by describing its uses, features, and benefits.

Part One: Learning and the New Virtual Classroom

The outcomes of any new technology for training will depend on how the features of the technology are harnessed to promote human learning processes. In Chapters 2 through 4, we describe the relationships between the features of the virtual classroom and basic events of human learning. We also summarize instructional methods needed to teach five common types of content: facts, concepts, processes, procedures, and principles.

Part Two: Engaging Participants in the New Virtual Classroom

Participant dropout—physical or mental—is much more likely in the virtual classroom than in traditional classrooms. Therefore, engagement becomes a very high priority! The best path to engagement requires effective use of media features such as whiteboards and application sharing to visualize your content, in addition to the frequent and effective use of the many tool options available for active participant responses.

Part Three: Optimizing Your Virtual Events

In addition to engagement, there are several elements that will optimize virtual classroom learning. Like face-to-face classrooms, virtual classes are instructor-paced. As a result they impose higher levels of mental load than self-study environments. At the same time, the combination of managing the technology, delivering presentations, and monitoring participant responses leads to mental overload in instructors who are new to virtual classroom technology. In Chapter 8 we offer evidence-based guidelines to help participants and new instructors manage their mental load in this new environment. In Chapters 9 and 10 we offer tips for getting your class off to a good start as well as for supporting your training with surrounding elements, including handouts and welcome letters. Throughout most of the book, we assume you will use a traditional directive or instructive lesson design. However, on occasion you may want to consider adapting a problem-based learning approach to this new media. In Chapter 11 you will find the what's, why's, when's, and how's of problem-based learning in the virtual classroom.

Part Four: Creating Effective Learning Events in the New Virtual Classroom

In the final chapter, we integrate all of the guidelines offered in previous chapters into seven basic principles for success in the virtual classroom. We also suggest tips for constructing your virtual sessions, either as conversions from face-to-face classroom training or as brand-new training initiatives.

Chapter 1
Meet the New
Virtual Classroom

Introduction

Chapter 2
Learning
in the New VC

Chapter 3
Features to Exploit
in the New VC

Chapter 4
Teaching Content Types
in the New VC

Part 1: Learning and the New Virtual Classroom

Chapter 5
Visualize Your
Message

Chapter 6
Make It Active – Part 1

Chapter 7
Make It Active – Part 2

Part 2: Engaging Participants in the New Virtual Classroom

Chapter 8
Managing Mental Load
in the New VC

Chapter 9
Make a Good
First Impression

Chapter 10
Packaging Your
VC Session

Chapter 11
Problem-Based Learning
in the New VC

Part 3: Optimizing Your Virtual Events

Chapter 12
Getting Started

Part 4: Creating Effective Learning Events in the New Virtual Classroom

WHAT IS the new virtual classroom? What are its benefits, uses, and features? How is it similar to face-to-face classrooms and to asynchronous e-learning? Read Chapter 1 for an orientation to *The New Virtual Classroom.*

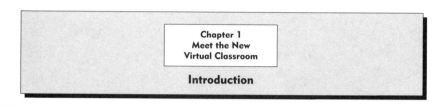

Chapter 1
Meet the New
Virtual Classroom

Introduction

Chapter 2
Learning
in the New VC

Chapter 3
Features to Exploit
in the New VC

Chapter 4
Teaching Content Types
in the New VC

Part 1: Learning and the New Virtual Classroom

Chapter 5
Visualize Your
Message

Chapter 6
Make It Active – Part 1

Chapter 7
Make It Active – Part 2

Part 2: Engaging Participants in the New Virtual Classroom

Chapter 8
Managing Mental Load
in the New VC

Chapter 9
Make a Good
First Impression

Chapter 10
Packaging Your
VC Session

Chapter 11
Problem-Based Learning
in the New VC

Part 3: Optimizing Your Virtual Events

Chapter 12
Getting Started

Part 4: Creating Effective Learning Events in the New Virtual Classroom

Meet the New Virtual Classroom

THE NEW VIRTUAL CLASSROOM is an increasingly popular alternative to face-to-face instruction due to the lure of travel savings and quick deployment of training. In this chapter we introduce the features and functions that synchronous e-learning tools make available for instruction. We describe pragmatic and instructional reasons to select the new virtual classroom as one component of your training delivery blend.

Ready or Not—Here It Comes!

Virtual classroom tools such as WebEx, Elluminate, and Live Meeting have ushered in a new age in electronic distance learning. The lure of travel savings, combined with quick deployment of training to large numbers of workers, has led to sharp increases in use of *synchronous e-learning* technologies among corporations. Survey respondents who reported participating in a synchronous event rose from 54 percent in 2001 to 87 percent in 2005 (Pulichino, 2005). According to another annual industry survey, instructor-led training from remote locations rose from 10 percent in 2003 to 16 percent in 2005 (Dolezalek, 2005; Galvin, 2003). In larger organizations of ten thousand or more, remote instructor-led training accounts for nearly one-fourth of all training delivery (Dolezalek, 2005). The growth of synchronous e-learning as a training delivery medium will likely continue, given the greater inclusion of collaborative facilities in ubiquitous tools such as Microsoft Office Version 12 and Windows Vista, which will make the functionalities of the *new virtual classroom* as accessible as today's PowerPoint or Word programs.

The benefits of the virtual classroom to workforce learning include reduced travel time and costs, less time away from the job, faster deployment of time-urgent knowledge and skills, higher completion rates compared to self-study e-learning, and the opportunity to offer training to larger numbers of workers at a lower cost. From a learning perspective, users cite opportunities for immediate interaction and feedback from instructors as well as *collaborative learning* activities as the main advantages of virtual classroom technology (Pulichino, 2005).

Still, the new virtual classrooms are not problem free. In addition to technical challenges, users report that many sessions lack interactivity and engagement with participants. Members of our virtual classroom advisory team universally mentioned poor facilitation skills as a major contributor to boring virtual classroom sessions that fail to effectively leverage the technology.

Old Wine in New Bottles?

The majority of educational uses of new synchronous e-learning technologies are simple replications of face-to-face classroom instructional techniques (Hill, Wiley, Nelson, & Han, 2004). Bob Mosher, Chief Learning and Strategy Evangelist with LearningGuide Solutions, technologies, tells us: "I almost don't like the name 'virtual classroom,' only because there is a past mindset that comes with the word 'classroom' that the virtual world just doesn't match up with. . . . Calling it a 'classroom' brings back a set of expectations and outcomes that are just different in this domain" (Clark, 2005, p. 45). Steve Serbun, an "e-learning technical manager" with Bentley Systems, concurs. He feels that the classroom label sends a misleading signal to both instructors and participants. Instead of virtual classroom, he refers to synchronous e-learning as "remote live training." Recent industry surveys use the term: "*remote instructor-led training.*"

Whatever you decide to call the new virtual classroom, the problem is not so much with the terminology or the technology as with the mindset instructors and participants alike bring to the event. Too predominant is the metaphor of learners as **meaning takers (or sponges)** rather than **meaning makers.** Instructors rely on traditional classroom "lecture" modes, assuming that learners are absorbing the knowledge they dispense. However, as summarized in Figure 1.1, learning requires sustained and relevant interactions between participants and the content, the instructor, and other learners. When that interactivity is missing, the technology gets an undeserved bad rap.

Student dropout—mental or physical—is a greater risk in the virtual classroom than in a face-to-face setting. As one instructor put it: "The main frustration with the virtual classroom environment is multitasking. No matter how engaging you are as an instructor, you must still battle the students' constant temptation to check email and multitask" (Pulichino, 2005, p. 15).

Figure 1.1. A Learner-Centered Instructional Environment.

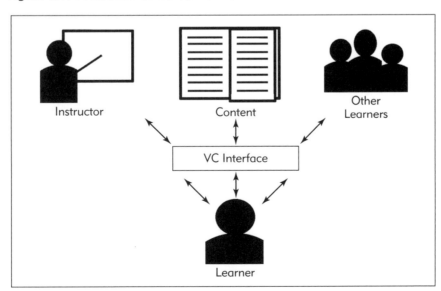

What can instructional professionals do to keep participants involved and to maximize learning from virtual classrooms? The potential of the new virtual classroom is available to those who use its features in ways that promote learning. In this book we show you how.

For readers unfamiliar with virtual classrooms, we begin with a tour. We define and describe the hybrid nature of the new virtual classroom, which on one hand incorporates features similar to a face-to-face classroom and on the other hand includes characteristics of *asynchronous e-learning.*

What Is the New Virtual Classroom?

The term virtual classroom is not new. Universities were among the first organizations to make extensive use of technologies that combined synchronous and asynchronous learning environments using tools such as Blackboard and WebCT. Thanks to the rapid spread of broadband Internet access, virtual tools that support two-way audio (voice-over IP), still and animated visuals, as well as various interactive response facilities, characterize what we call the new virtual classroom.

We define the new virtual classroom as instructor-led synchronous computer learning environments attended by participants online at the same time but in different locations. The new virtual classroom tools provide facilities for two-way communication via audio and chat; projection of visuals—both still and animated; participant interactions of various types; as well as breakout rooms for small group activities. Keep in mind that real-time instructor-led virtual classroom sessions are often recorded and therefore can be viewed in an asynchronous mode. However, we will focus primarily on the use of the new virtual classroom as a live event for workplace learning.

Features of the New Virtual Classroom

Figure 1.2 shows an *interface* typical of the new virtual classroom tools. As you can see, the *white board* consumes the largest portion of screen real estate. Instructors can project slides on the white board, which can then be annotated by participants or instructors with the use of text or drawing tools. The participant window located to the left of the white board lists the names of individuals in the session. At the top left of the interface, a series of *polling* buttons offers a facility for participants to respond to multiple choice questions. Instructors and participants can type messages in the *chat* (or *direct messaging*) area, located below the participant information window. *Icons* such as the clapping hands under the participant information window are used by

Figure 1.2. Features of the New Virtual Classroom.

With permission of Clark Training

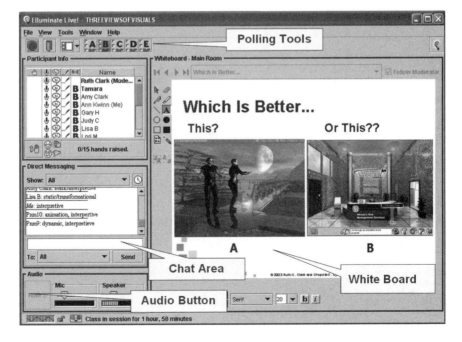

all to indicate their reactions to ongoing events in the session. Last, the audio window in the lower-left-hand corner allows any participant with a headset and microphone to speak to the group and to hear what other speakers are saying. Although the screen location of these basic features may vary among different virtual classroom software, most of the synchronous e-learning technologies offer some combination of these facilities.

In addition to these common features, most of the new virtual classrooms offer a window to show video clips or to demonstrate a computer application as well as *breakout rooms,* which offer a virtual space where a small group can access the basic features described above. Instructors can easily divide classes into small teams for discussions or assignments in breakout rooms. If you are new to the virtual classroom, review our demonstration lessons on the CD that accompanies this book to see recordings of short lessons that illustrate all of these features.

We group the various features of the virtual classroom into three main classes:

1. Features to display visual information: white board, *application sharing,* etc.;
2. Features to promote participant interactions: polling, white board tools; and
3. Features for communication between instructor and participants and among participants: chat, audio, breakout rooms.

The challenge for instructional professionals is to use these features in ways that promote the psychological processes that underpin learning. Throughout this book we will provide you with guidelines and examples to help you do just that.

The Virtual Classroom: A Hybrid Learning Environment

Like a centaur, the virtual classroom is a hybrid, in this case incorporating properties of two different delivery technologies. As summarized in Table 1.1, the new virtual classroom has some features reminiscent of a face-to-face

Table 1.1. How the Virtual Classroom Is Similar to Precursor Learning Environments.

Face-to-Face Classroom	Asynchronous e-Learning
Instructor-led—imposes high cognitive load	Requires frequent and relevant interactions to sustain attention and promote learning
Social presence is high	The screen real estate benefits from relevant visuals

classroom and in other ways is more like asynchronous e-learning. These similarities will help you apply lessons learned about what works in these two delivery environments to the virtual classroom.

Virtual and Face-to-Face Classrooms

The first obvious similarity between face–to-face and virtual classrooms is that both are instructor-led environments with all participants present at the same time. Research shows that the mental load imposed on learners is much greater in instructor-controlled than in learner-controlled environments (Clark, Nguyen, & Sweller, 2006). Under the learner control typical of asynchronous e-learning courses, the participants use navigation buttons to move from one screen to the next when they are ready. However, in classrooms, participants are subject to the pace set by the instructor. Having to assimilate new information at someone else's rate adds mental stress—especially when the student is new to the topic and/or the skills taught are relatively complex.

A second similarity between virtual and physical classrooms is the greater amount of *social presence* compared to asynchronous self-study e-learning. Social presence is the extent to which the learning environment offers opportunities for social interactions, including hand shaking, eye contact, smiles, puzzled looks, verbal exchanges, and so forth. The virtual classroom eliminates the body language social cues that we take for granted in face-to-face environments. Face-to-face classroom instructors find this loss unsettling when they first work in a virtual setting: "The lack of visual contact with learners is the most distressing issue." "It's often difficult to read body language when you are online. You don't have those subtle nuances to let you know when users are disengaged." "It is human interaction that is de-contextualized because non-verbal communication (facial expression and body language) is not shared between the instructor(s) and the learner(s)" (Pulichino, 2005, p. 15). Social cues are not only relevant to instructor comfort but are also related to learning and learner satisfaction. We will discuss social presence in more detail in later chapters.

Related to social presence is the opportunity in classroom settings for small group work as well as for on-the-spot questioning between instructors and participants. Under the right conditions, small groups working together can learn more than is possible in solo self-study environments. In Chapters 7 and 11 we discuss guidelines for when and how to set up collaborative learning environments in the virtual classroom.

Virtual Classrooms and Asynchronous e-Learning

Because instructor presence is such a predominant feature of the virtual classroom, it's easy to ignore lessons we've learned over the past twenty years from asynchronous self-study e-learning. Yet there are important similarities between the synchronous and asynchronous forms of e-learning. When learning at their work stations, participants are tempted to attend to pressing work assignments and try to divide attention between the instruction and distractions such as email or cell phones. In both synchronous and asynchronous e-learning, the main antidote to student multitasking is frequent and relevant interactions that involve all participants. The good news is that the virtual classroom is loaded with options for participant engagement! Planning and facilitating frequent and relevant interactions is the single most important thing you can do to create effective virtual classroom sessions. In Chapters 6 and 7 we show you how.

The critical necessity of frequent interactions is not the only similarity between synchronous and asynchronous e-learning. In any *e-learning* environment, the instructional interface is largely devoted to screen real estate for communicating content. In the virtual classroom, the white board serves this purpose. Too often, rather than exploiting the opportunity to display meaningful visuals, the white board is used to project a wall of words. For example, take a look at Figures 1.3 and 1.4. These before and after screens are

Figure 1.3. Less Effective Virtual Classroom Interface.

With permission from Lynn Nishimura, Sage Software

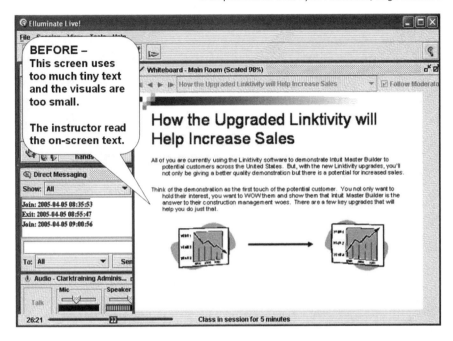

Figure 1.4. More Effective Virtual Classroom Interface.

With permission from Lynn Nishimura, Sage Software

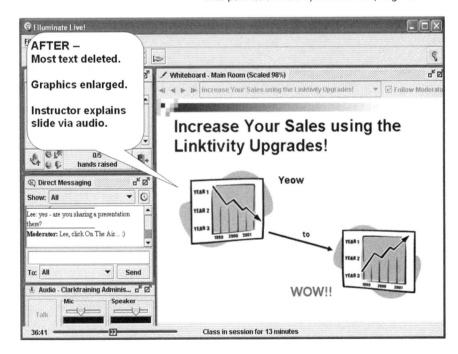

taken from student projects in our "How to Leverage the Virtual Classroom" course. The "before" sample uses a large amount of tiny text, plus two small visuals. During the presentation, the instructor read the text to the participants. In the improved version (Figure 1.4), the facilitator speaks most of the words you see in Version 1 and has enlarged the visuals, making better use of the white board. In Chapter 5 we summarize research-based guidelines for use of visuals that lead to learning in the virtual classroom.

We found it telling that among the virtual classroom experts we interviewed, everyone mentioned the importance of interactivity. Yet **not one** mentioned the need for effective visuals! Why don't we see greater emphasis on visual communication, especially in visually dominant media? We believe it's due to resources and skills. First, it's much faster to type text than to design and create an effective visual. Second, most instructional professionals have far greater verbal skills than visual literacy. Third, resource constraints often lead to reliance on clip art. The result is either slides of text or slides filled with decorative visuals that do little to promote learning. A good graphic artist is worth his or her weight in gold, especially in any form of e-learning in which the screen carries so much of the content.

Harnessing the Centaur

To summarize, the new virtual classroom embodies features reminiscent of the face-to-face classroom and asynchronous e-learning. By exploiting lessons learned from these precursor delivery media, you can make best use of the new virtual classroom. As in the face-to-face classroom, you will need to manage cognitive load carefully. In Chapter 8 we show you how. Likewise, you will want to leverage the benefits of social presence and collaborative learning activities. As in asynchronous e-learning, you will need frequent interactions to keep attention focused on the instructional event. In addition, you should exploit the visual potential of the white board to display graphics that lead to learning.

When to Use the Virtual Classroom

In Table 1.2, we distinguish between two categories of reasons that make the new virtual classroom a good training delivery media option. The reasons listed on the left are usually the driving forces behind selection of the virtual classroom in the business environment. These reasons relate to time and money. You don't have to be a whiz in finance to see the savings in travel costs when delivering training virtually (versus in person) to a geographically distributed work force. For example, Budget Rent-A-Car reduced per student training expenses from $2,000 to $156 when converting a classroom course to electronic distance learning. Boeing reported savings of more than $9,000,000 on travel alone (Burgess & Russell, 2003).

It's also faster to develop virtual classroom instruction, compared with asynchronous e-learning, and potentially faster to deploy compared to instructor-led training. It's no accident that sales and marketing departments are the leading users of synchronous e-learning (Pulichino, 2005). The need to quickly update a distributed salesforce on new products and new product features make the virtual classroom an ideal delivery vehicle. For example, Trudie Folsom, senior instructor designer at Intuit, follows face-to-face training with virtual classroom training for Intuit's channel partners. The virtual classroom sessions are used to provide short classes on special software features, sales demonstrations, and troubleshooting sessions (Clark, 2005).

A third pragmatic benefit to the virtual classroom is class completion. Compared to asynchronous e-learning, where dropout rates are high, a scheduled learning event like the virtual classroom tends to impose the discipline needed for completion.

Table 1.2. When to Use the Virtual Classroom.

Pragmatic Reasons	Instructional Reasons
Reduced travel costs	Real-time interactions between learners and instructor
Deploy training quickly	Deploying training over time
Reaching many learners	Visualization of content
Less time away from the job	Computer application demonstrations and practice
Ensuring course completion	Collaboration among participants
	Moderate social presence

However, all the time and cost savings in the world do not offset the losses incurred when the virtual classroom fails to support learning. This brings us to our second category of reasons, listed on the right hand side of Table 1.2, instructional justifications. Not all delivery media can equally accomplish all instructional goals. For example, there is no substitute for hands-on practice to learn motor skills. e-Learning is not a good choice for practice of non-computer-related motor skills.

We recommend using the virtual classroom when learning goals can be best realized by several of the following factors: (1) real-time interactions among instructors and participants, (2) real-time interactions with scarce content expertise, (3) visualization of content, (4) demonstrations and practice of computer applications, (5) collaboration among participants, and (6) moderate social presence.

If your requirements and/or resources mean that you will rely primarily on printed words, for example, text on screens with little need or opportunity for interactivity, consider an alternative delivery choice such as a website or print publication, perhaps followed by a Q&A in the virtual classroom. Virtual classrooms come alive when presenters use effective visuals and frequent, relevant interactions. When neither of these features is used, virtual classrooms gain an undeserved reputation as boring and ineffective.

The key to success in the virtual classroom is to be sure it's selected not only for pragmatic benefits, but also for the instructional opportunities it offers. And once selected, that sufficient resources are invested in course development to exploit the instructional potential of the technology.

Integrating Virtual Classrooms into Media Blends

More and more organizations are using a mix of delivery media—for the things each does best. Over 77 percent of U.S. organizations use blended learning, which accounts for 16 percent of all training in the United States (Ochoa-Alcantar, Borders, & Bichelmeyer, 2006). For example, a course designed to build interview skills for employee selection might start with a downloaded pre-reading on effective interview questions. The pre-reading is accompanied by a web-delivered asynchronous exercise on distinguishing good and bad questions, coupled with an assignment to construct several effective hiring questions. This solo pre-work is completed prior to a virtual classroom session during which participants display their questions and obtain participant and instructor feedback. The virtual classroom session might also include brief presentations and Q&A from diverse sources of scarce expertise, such as legal staff and human relations personnel. During the virtual session, participants view a video demonstration of an effective hiring interview, followed by interview role plays in breakout rooms.

In a website design class, learners might start off in a virtual classroom with a video-delivered case study requesting a website design. After viewing the case, small groups meet in breakout rooms to define their approach and instructional needs. The instructor then provides examples of website design processes as well as links to supporting resources. Following the virtual classroom sessions, teams work asynchronously to review learning resources and create a first draft design that can be shared in a subsequent virtual session. This type of blend integrates synchronous events with asynchronous opportunities for reflection and independent work.

There are as many ways to blend media as the mind can imagine. The key to success is to use each delivery medium in ways that exploit its learning features and to incorporate all the media needed to achieve the learning objective.

In the chapters to follow, you will learn proven techniques, examples, and research to help you exploit the virtual classroom in order to achieve your organization's instructional and operational goals.

The Bottom Line

The new virtual classroom offers familiar features, benefits, and uses; some are similar to face-to-face and others to asynchronous e-learning environments. We recommend that the virtual classroom be used not only for its pragmatic benefits but also for its engagement and learning features. When a virtual classroom implementation fails to support learning, return on investment may be only an illusion.

COMING NEXT:
LEARNING IN THE VIRTUAL CLASSROOM

How does the virtual classroom compare to face-to-face training when it comes to learning? In Chapter 2 we look at research reports that have compared learning from electronic distance media to classroom instruction. We introduce three major instructional components that must be addressed in any delivery medium: instructional modes, methods, and architectures. From attention to motivation, each of these components must be aligned to support basic human learning events. In the next chapter we focus on the psychology of learning in the context of the virtual classroom.

On *The New Virtual Classroom* CD

We include three recorded lessons on the CD, edited to illustrate the key features of a virtual classroom session. Each lesson illustrates different techniques appropriate to the instructional goal. If you are new to the virtual classroom, we recommend that you view one or more of these lessons as an orientation.

- How to Construct a Formula in Excel
- How to Define Business Goals
- How to Plan an Interview

For More Information

Burgess, J.R.D., & Russell, J.E.A. (2003). The effectiveness of distance learning initiatives in organizations. *Journal of Vocational Behavior, 63,* 289–303.

Clark, R. C. (2005). Harnessing the virtual classroom. *Training & Development, 59*(11), 41–45.

Long, K. K., & Smith, R. D. (2004). The role of web-based distance learning in HR development. *Journal of Management Development, 23*(3), 270–284.

Pulichino, J. (2005). The synchronous e-learning research report 2005. The eLearning Guild Research. Accessed October 2005 at www.eLearningGuild.com.

EXPERTS' FORUM

THE GROWING ROLE OF THE VIRTUAL CLASSROOM

Eric Vidal, Director, Enterprise Business Unit, WebEx Communications

I have spent the last seven years developing e-learning and marketing strategies for sales training and corporate training departments. I joined WebEx Communications in 2004 and am responsible for developing key strategies, including simplifying and accelerating online training initiatives for enterprise and government customers.

The virtual classroom allows organizations to stretch their training resources, eliminate logistical barriers, and transform their training into strategic lines of business. Both trainers and business users can rapidly train and update their dispersed audiences on the latest product updates and initiatives inside and outside the organization. They can also edit, archive, and store sessions in an online library, giving their geographically dispersed audience instant on-demand access to this valuable information. The virtual classroom gives you the tools you need to transform your existing content into highly interactive online training programs. The virtual classroom allows you to:

- Educate channel partners more frequently and cost-effectively while avoiding stale canned presentations. The virtual classroom can include trainer interaction, side conversations, and small group activities.

- Quickly update your entire organization on process changes, regulatory compliance, and new initiatives without juggling travel schedules.

- Integrate tests, quizzes, and polls into your online training curriculum and assess the impact of your training material and presentation. Track performance and offer encouragement and support using a variety of online testing and collaboration tools.

- Generate revenue or help with resource accounting with self-service registration and e-commerce payment features. Offer paid-on-demand training classes in a secure, reliable environment with no additional capital expenditures. Can you imagine turning your cost center into a profit center?

When trainers and business professionals first started implementing the virtual classroom a few years ago, it was mainly to reduce costs (save time and money on travel). Next, people started to use it to expand their reach and do more with less. The e-learning leaders using WebEx solutions are constantly pushing the virtual classroom to not only save time and travel, but to embed the virtual classroom into actual business processes in order to impact the way the organization works. These leaders are not only using the virtual classroom inside the training organization, but with groups like product management, marketing, sales, customer support, services, legal, and much more. For example, at Philip Morris the approval time for a manufacturing process improvement change was reduced from nine months to nine days. Similarly, Fidelity National increased mortgage application-to-close ratios by reducing the process for closing transactions by over forty-eight hours. At Kraft Foods, supplier training process duration was compressed from six months to three days.

A recent survey of 341 WebEx customers told us how the virtual classroom is impacting their businesses and bottom lines inside their organizations:

- Get products to market faster

- Create more effective channel partners

- Develop more effective and efficient sales teams

- Shorten sales cycles by educating prospects and customers faster

- Improve customer service and satisfaction

- Reduce support costs by training customers

- Protect company by staying compliant

- Create revenue-generating opportunities with customers and partners

- Shorten the time for application rollouts

- Provide access of subject-matter experts to dispersed audiences

POSITIONING THE VIRTUAL CLASSROOM IN THE ORGANIZATION

Andrew Noell, Learning Manager–Virtual Classroom
Lead for the Consulting Function, Deloitte Inc.

At Deloitte Consulting LLP, we are always looking for innovative ways to provide high quality training in the most cost-effective manner. As a professional services firm, our practitioners are working on client engagements and it is difficult for them to travel for training. Additionally, as a knowledge-driven organization it is critical that we keep our practitioners up-to-date on key consulting topics. Five years ago, we started exploring the virtual classroom as an option. We have had great success with virtual classrooms. We are currently using Centra. But we also recognize that the virtual classroom has some challenges that need to be addressed. The three main challenges we have with virtual classrooms are:

- Awareness of the platform

- Preparing instructors to deliver training virtually

- The lack of interaction and engagement with participants

Awareness of the Platform   One of my first assignments as virtual classroom lead for Deloitte Consulting LLP was to create a communication tool we could distribute to increase awareness of virtual classroom learning. We came up with a one-page document called "Virtual Classroom Learning in a Nutshell," (See Figure 1.5.) In this document, which we circulated to our internal learning champions who were interested in understanding more about this platform to deliver learning, we defined virtual classroom as a real-time, instructor-led, online learning opportunity, explained when and why you would use it, and described the benefits and features of the solution. We also highlighted sample offerings from some of our successful deliveries as a reference.

Preparing Instructors to Deliver Training Virtually   Our instructors typically fall into two categories: (1) they are hesitant to work with the new technology or (2) they significantly underestimate what it takes to deliver learning in a virtual classroom environment. It can be very challenging to schedule time with our instructors to help them prepare. Over the years, we have had to find creative ways to do this. Some of the strategies we use include:

Figure 1.5. Communication Tool to Increase Awareness of the Virtual Classroom.

With permission of Andrew Noell, Deloitte Inc.

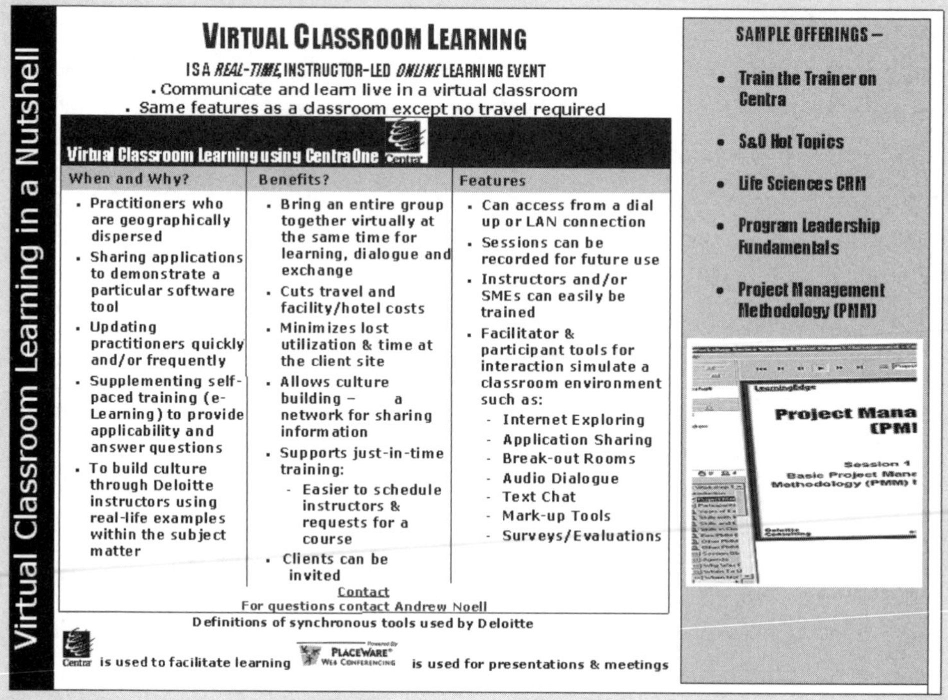
Virtual Classroom Learning in a Nutshell
VIRTUAL CLASSROOM LEARNING
IS A REAL-TIME, INSTRUCTOR-LED ONLINE LEARNING EVENT
. Communicate and learn live in a virtual classroom
. Same features as a classroom except no travel required
Virtual Classroom Learning using CentraOne
When and Why?
. Practitioners who are geographically dispersed
. Sharing applications to demonstrate a particular software tool
. Updating practitioners quickly and/or frequently
. Supplementing self-paced training (e-Learning) to provide applicability and answer questions
. To build culture through Deloitte instructors using real-life examples within the subject matter
Benefits?
. Bring an entire group together virtually at the same time for learning, dialogue and exchange
. Cuts travel and facility/hotel costs
. Minimizes lost utilization & time at the client site
. Allows culture building – a network for sharing information
. Supports just-in-time training:
- Easier to schedule instructors & requests for a course
. Clients can be invited
Features
. Can access from a dial up or LAN connection
. Sessions can be recorded for future use
. Instructors and/or SMEs can easily be trained
. Facilitator & participant tools for interaction simulate a classroom environment such as:
- Internet Exploring
- Application Sharing
- Break-out Rooms
- Audio Dialogue
- Text Chat
- Mark-up Tools
- Surveys/Evaluations
Contact
For questions contact Andrew Noell
Definitions of synchronous tools used by Deloitte
Centra is used to facilitate learning
PLACEWARE WEB CONFERENCING is used for presentations & meetings
SAMPLE OFFERINGS –
• Train the Trainer on Centra
• S&O Hot Topics
• Life Sciences CRM
• Program Leadership Fundamentals
• Project Management Methodology (PMM)
Project Mana (PMI
Session 1
Basic Project Mana Methodology (PMM)

1. *Conference call.* Set up a conference call over lunch or after hours to provide an orientation of the virtual classroom, discuss the technical requirements, and review design and delivery strategies.
2. *Train-the-trainer.* In the virtual classroom, demonstrate the tool and how it is used from an instructor's perspective.
3. *Dress rehearsals.* In the virtual classroom, run through the delivery from start to finish, practicing the interactive features, reviewing what was learned during the train-the-trainer session, and become comfortable with delivering their content in a virtual environment.

The Lack of Interaction and Engagement with Participants   When we started delivering virtual classroom sessions, we noticed that there was some confusion between an informational webinar and a virtual classroom learning opportunity. We needed to help our instructors design strategies to engage our participants.

We group the virtual classroom features into three categories when training our instructors:

1. Participant and instructor interface orientation

2. Event participation—dialogue, white board tools, and surveys

3. Virtual classroom capabilities—file sharing, application sharing, web views, and breakouts

Additionally, during the instructor training we use classroom analogies when describing some of the features. For example:

- Describe the white board as a "virtual" flip chart where participants can brainstorm ideas. Instead of tearing off a full sheet and taping it to the wall, in the virtual classroom you save it (for reference later) and start with another blank white board.

- Refer to file sharing as a "virtual" handout. Similar to a classroom, if an instructor passes around a document for you to keep, you can choose to take it with you or leave it on the table. With file sharing, you have a choice to accept or decline the automatic download initiated by your instructor.

- Set up breakout rooms similar to a classroom with instructions and the assignment. Allow time for participants to orient themselves to their new "room" in addition to the time allotted for the assignment. Have coaches assigned to each breakout room to assist.

As we overcame the challenges associated with the virtual classroom, our best practices made it easier for instructors to determine when to add different interactions to engage the participants. Virtual classroom is now one of our key learning solutions within Deloitte Consulting LLP.

ADOPTING THE VIRTUAL CLASSROOM

Dr. Kim Armstrong, Engineering Learning, Training and Development Enterprise Curriculum Lead, The Boeing Company, and Department of Professional Studies, California State University

At Boeing we are faced with an ever-growing population of students who are virtual and global. There has been a major shift over the past two years to reduce the Boeing footprint in terms of office/factory space, and many employees are enticed to become part of our virtual office program. We also have an ever-expanding presence globally, moving employees to all corners of the globe.

As we see more and more of our employees "virtual" and global, we were faced with how to include them in learning and development opportunities. We looked at our current delivery methods, which were primarily instructor-led, and determined that we must include the virtual classroom in order to stay competitive and to motivate our employees.

For example, we created a program for developing future chief engineers. The program is multi-phased and includes several weeks of virtual classroom learning through three elements—virtual simulation (each student independently completes a virtual simulation during the program), virtual team learning (where the students are teamed up in smaller groups to discuss the virtual simulation), and a concept we designed called "leaders teaching leaders." The leaders teaching leaders concept uses WebEx and telecon, a virtual facilitator, and a virtual instructor to teach lessons based on the virtual simulation and team discussions that they had completed. In addition to cost savings, some benefits of the virtual classroom included the opportunity to bring together a large number of geographically, organizationally, and globally diverse groups of students. These students benefited from each other's experiences and knowledge and allowed us to extend the classroom and the learning experience over a longer period of time. When we completed an ROI study on this program, we found that the virtual element added to the impact on knowledge transfer and the ultimate ROI was greater than 540 percent.

One of the key lessons learned when using the virtual classroom is employing a skilled virtual facilitator for each session, in addition to the instructor. The facilitator, just as in a classroom, sets the stage for the participants, handles the technology aspects (runs the Webex and PowerPoint slides, videos, and so forth), introduces the instructor, provides the protocol for the class session (such as how to be recognized to ask a question, ensuring that students stay engaged, ask questions, keep time on the agenda, protocol about muting phones, etc.), and keeps the virtual session interesting and engaging. We also use the virtual facilitator as a coach to our leaders who will be presenting virtually prior to their sessions.

Another key lesson learned is using photographs to introduce the facilitator, instructor, and each of the participants. It is very helpful for the participants to "see" what their instructors and fellow classmates look like. We use photos at the start of the session. We also bring up the photos from time to time when someone is asking a question. It really adds a personal touch. Many of our participants, when surveyed after the class, noted that the photos made the virtual class feel more like a regular classroom-based class.

Chapter 1
Meet the New
Virtual Classroom

Introduction

Chapter 2
Learning
in the New VC

Chapter 3
Features to Exploit
in the New VC

Chapter 4
Teaching Content Types
in the New VC

Part 1: Learning and the New Virtual Classroom

Chapter 5
Visualize Your
Message

Chapter 6
Make It Active – Part 1

Chapter 7
Make It Active – Part 2

Part 2: Engaging Participants in the New Virtual Classroom

Chapter 8
Managing Mental Load
in the New VC

Chapter 9
Make a Good
First Impression

Chapter 10
Packaging Your
VC Session

Chapter 11
Problem-Based Learning
in the New VC

Part 3: Optimizing Your Virtual Events

Chapter 12
Getting Started

Part 4: Creating Effective Learning Events in the New Virtual Classroom

PART ONE

Learning and the New Virtual Classroom

ANY LEARNING EXPERIENCE, regardless of delivery media, is effective only to the extent that basic human learning processes are supported. The following content is covered in this part of the book.

Chapter 2: The effectiveness of learning in the virtual classroom compared to face-to-face classroom. Human memory and the events of learning.

Chapter 3: How to leverage the unique features of the virtual classroom to support learning.

Chapter 4: How to teach five basic content types in the virtual classroom: Facts, concepts, processes, procedures, and principles.

**Chapter 1
Meet the New
Virtual Classroom**

Introduction

**Chapter 2
Learning
in the New VC**

**Chapter 3
Features to Exploit
in the New VC**

**Chapter 4
Teaching Content Types
in the New VC**

Part 1: Learning and the New Virtual Classroom

**Chapter 5
Visualize Your
Message**

**Chapter 6
Make It Active – Part 1**

**Chapter 7
Make It Active – Part 2**

Part 2: Engaging Participants in the New Virtual Classroom

**Chapter 8
Managing Mental Load
in the New VC**

**Chapter 9
Make a Good
First Impression**

**Chapter 10
Packaging Your
VC Session**

**Chapter 11
Problem-Based Learning
in the New VC**

Part 3: Optimizing Your Virtual Events

**Chapter 12
Getting Started**

Part 4: Creating Effective Learning Events in the New Virtual Classroom

2

Learning in the New Virtual Classroom

DOLLARS SAVED BY CONVERTING SOME OR ALL of a face-to-face event into a virtual event are an illusion when learning suffers. What do we know about the instructional effectiveness of new virtual classroom technology? How does learning in the new virtual classroom compare with learning from traditional face-to-face classes? In this chapter we review:

- Research on media effectiveness
- Three instructional components that make up any learning environment
- How to support human learning processes in the virtual classroom

Which Technology Is Best for Learning?

Imagine you have to take a statistics class. You could take the class in a traditional classroom setting, take it via asynchronous e-learning self-study, or take it in a virtual classroom. Where would you learn most effectively? When we ask this question during our seminars, typically about 75 percent of participants vote for a face-to-face classroom session, while the other 25 percent prefer some form of e-learning. Individuals opting for an instructor-led environment want to ask questions of the instructor and to interact directly with others taking the class. Those who lean toward asynchronous e-learning prefer to work at their own pace and have the opportunity to review topics as needed. A third group comments that their choice would depend on the instructor and the e-learning program.

Media Comparison Research

Over the past sixty years, hundreds of media comparison experiments have been done to determine the best technology for learning purposes. Usually these experiments compare learning from a classroom version of a lesson with a second version of the lesson delivered via the latest technology. The earliest experiments, conducted in the 1940s, compared learning a skill in the classroom with learning the same skill from film. More recent experiments have contrasted classroom learning with various types of e-learning. The results of all of the media comparison research are pretty consistent. The potential for learning is more or less equivalent from all delivery media! Why? Because what causes learning **is not** the delivery media per se, but the *instructional components* used to teach.

We've all attended classroom sessions that were not effective. Likewise, we've seen many examples of e-learning that Kirschner (2005) calls CSPT (Computer-Supported Page Turning). What determines learning effectiveness is not whether the instruction is delivered in a physical classroom or on a computer. Rather, it's the building blocks—what we call instructional components—that shape the effectiveness of any learning event, regardless of delivery medium.

Electronic Distance Learning vs. the Classroom

A recent synthesis of media comparison research—known as a *meta-analysis*—summarized the results of over two hundred different experiments that compared classrooms with various distance learning technologies (Bernard, Abrami, Lou, Borokhovski, Wade, Wozney, Wallet, Fixet, & Huang, 2004). Learning, student satisfaction, and course completion data were compared. Figure 2.1 shows a histogram of the learning effect sizes from all of the studies. *Effect size* is a statistic that indicates the relative advantage of one experimental condition

Figure 2.1. Comparisons of Learning from Face-to-Face with Distance Learning Show No Practical Differences.

Adapted from Bernard et al. (2004).

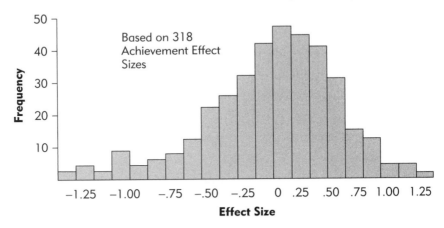

(in this case delivery media) over another. Effect sizes lower than .20 indicate little practical advantage of one condition over another. Effect sizes of .80 and above suggest considerable practical advantage of one condition over the other.

The histogram of achievement effect sizes shows two main findings. First, the bars are broadly spread across the graph. This indicates a lot of variation in the learning results among the various comparisons. Some distance learning classes led to much better learning than the physical classrooms, and vice versa. The histogram also shows that the majority of effect sizes fall between plus or minus .30. The low effect sizes tell us that most of the comparisons did not show much difference in learning between classroom courses and electronic distance learning.

Based on an extensive review of research comparing online with face-to-face courses, Tallent-Runnels, Thomas, Lan, Cooper, Ahern, Shaw, & Liu (2006) concluded: "Learning in an online environment can be as effective as that in traditional classrooms. Second, students' learning in the online environment is affected by the quality of online instruction. Not surprisingly, students in well-designed and well-implemented online courses learned significantly more, and more effectively, than those in online courses where teaching and learning activities were not carefully planned and where the delivery and accessibility were impeded by technology problems. This finding challenges online instructors to design their courses in accordance with sound educational theories" (p. 116).

Stonebraker and Hazeltine (2004) asked corporate participants in a production and inventory management virtual classroom course to compare their experience with the face-to-face classroom. The research team also compared test passing rates between individuals taking training in a physical classroom with those completing virtual classroom training. The participants rated their sense of cohesion, social interaction, and task interaction in the virtual class significantly less than in a live class. However, in spite of this, they perceived their ability to learn as about the same in either environment. Course satisfaction in the virtual class depended primarily on perceived level of learning, perceived job relevance of the class, and the perceived sense of connection with others. The test passing rate reported among participants in the virtual class fell within the same range as for students attending traditional classroom sessions.

These recent research summaries confirm once again that learning can occur whether instructor-led training is held in a classroom or via a computer. Much more important to learning than the delivery medium is the instructional quality of the course. And instructional quality depends on how effectively the three main components illustrated in Figure 2.2 are used.

Instructional Modes, Methods, and Architectures

Whether you are preparing lessons for asynchronous e-learning, synchronous e-learning, or classroom delivery, it is the decisions you make regarding communication *modes,* instructional *methods,* and course *architectures* that determine learning effectiveness. Here we will summarize the options you have for each of these instructional components.

Communication Modes: The Atoms of Instruction

The smallest instructional component includes the three basic communication modes: text, audio, and graphic representations. We think of these three

Figure 2.2. Three Components of Instruction.

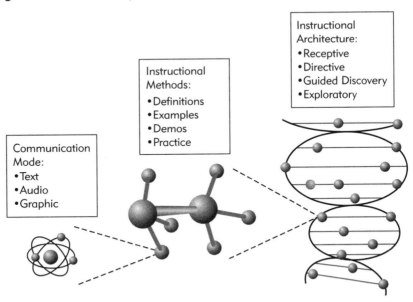

modes as the atoms of instruction that combine to make up the larger components. Your delivery technology will influence which communication modes you can use. For example, books are limited to text and still graphics. In contrast, the new virtual classroom supports all three communication modes.

Instructional Methods: The Molecules of Instruction

Text, audio, and graphics are used individually or in combination to make up the instructional methods. Instructional methods are the psychologically active ingredients of any learning environment. By that we mean they must support essential learning processes. Some common and important instructional methods include definitions or descriptions, examples and demonstrations, and practice exercises with feedback. We think of instructional methods as the basic molecules of instruction. In the virtual classroom, you can deploy a wide range of instructional methods to support learning.

Instructional Architectures: The DNA of Instruction

At the highest level, we identify four basic lesson or course design plans—what we call architectures. Since architectures determine many important components of courses and lessons, we refer to them as the DNA of instruction. Architectures vary according to: (1) the amount and type of interactions available to learners, (2) the degree and source of learner guidance offered in the course and lessons, and (3) the organization of content and instructional methods. Four prevalent design architectures, summarized in Table 2.1, are *receptive, directive, guided discovery,* and *exploratory* (Clark, 2003).

A *receptive architecture* is a lesson that primarily delivers content. A traditional college lecture and a video documentary are two common examples. In a receptive lesson, the instruction provides information that the learners (hopefully) absorb. Receptive learning environments can incorporate text, audio, and visuals as well as a variety of instructional methods. Receptive learning environments include little or no opportunity for explicit learner interactions.

A *directive architecture* is characterized by short lessons that provide a small amount of information, followed by examples and practice with corrective feedback. Most lessons designed to teach technology skills use a directive approach. Typically, the instruction demonstrates the steps to complete a procedure, followed by a practice exercise accompanied by feedback that corrects errors or confirms correct responses.

Guided discovery architectures require learners to engage with a problem or goal as a conduit for learning. For example, a lesson begins with a video of a nurse-patient interview and a group of learners works collaboratively to design a treatment plan for the patient. Unlike directive architectures, which are *instructive,* guided discovery learning is more *inductive.* The premise of guided discovery is that learning occurs in tandem with solving problems or performing work-related tasks. As the learner solves the problem or completes the assignment, she is learning new knowledge and skills. Some forms of guided discovery learning include problem-based learning and scenario-based learning.

Our fourth architecture is *exploratory.* The Internet is a good example. Exploratory environments may incorporate a multitude of instructional

Table 2.1. Four Instructional Architectures Based on Clark (2003).

Architecture	Features	Learning Assumptions	Examples	Best Used for
Receptive	• Content delivery • Few interactive opportunities	• Passive absorption of knowledge	• Some classroom lectures • A video	• Learners with prior content knowledge • Building awareness • Briefings vs. skill building
Directive	• Bottom-up sequences • Short lessons • Frequent questions • Immediate feedback • Rule-example-practice approach • Instructive learning	• Gradual building of knowledge through progressive sequences of questions and feedback • Based on behavioral psychology • Avoidance of errors	• Programmed instruction • Much software training	• Teaching procedural skills • Teaching novice learners
Guided Discovery	• Problem- or task-centered lessons • Inductive learning • Learning from experience • Instructors are coaches	• Authentic job problems foster learning • Learning by experience is more effective • Mistakes are learning opportunities	• Problem-based learning • Case or scenario-based learning	• Experienced learners • Principle-based tasks • Focus on problem-solving skills
Exploratory	• High degree of learner control • Rich repository of instructional resources • Good navigation	• Learners should have many choices • Learners make the best decisions about when and how to learn	• The Internet	• Experienced learners • Self-directed learners • Diverse learning outcomes

resources, but it is up to the learners to access and make use of these resources based on their perceived needs. Exploratory learning environments offer the greatest amount of learner control over which content and instructional methods to access. Exploratory environments are learner-driven and hence are rare in an instructor-led setting. Electronic environments that include clear navigation and a rich bedrock of alternative resources characterize the majority of exploratory courses.

Throughout this book we will focus primarily on directive architectures. However, in Chapter 11 we discuss ways to adapt the virtual classroom for guided discovery lesson designs.

Which Instructional Components Work Best?

When is it better to use text for explanations and when is it better to use audio? When is it better to provide examples rather than assigning practice? Which of the four architectures is most effective? Research comparing the effects of these components on learning tells us that the best combinations are those that support essential psychological learning events. In the next section we summarize what we know about our memory systems and the processes that convert new knowledge and skills into mental models stored in memory. We begin with a quick tour of working and long-term memory.

Working Memory and Long-Term Memory and Learning

They say that opposites attract. When it comes to our two memory systems—*working memory* and *long-term memory*—they are just about opposite in every way. However, working memory and long-term memory complement one another during learning. While working memory has a very limited capacity and duration for information, long-term memory has a very large capacity and serves as a permanent storehouse of knowledge. We know that working memory has a capacity of around five to nine chunks or pieces of information.

As its name implies, working memory is the active member of the pair. Working memory is the center of our conscious thoughts and processes. Learning actively takes place in working memory. In contrast, long-term memory is relatively inert. It serves as a repository, not as a processor. The successful outcome of any learning activity is processing of new content in ways that result in the storage of new knowledge and skills in long-term memory.

Working memory and long-term memory cooperate. Working memory capacity for information is shaped by the amount of knowledge stored in long-term memory. Although all of us have a working memory capacity of five to nine chunks of information, a chunk for one person is not the same as a chunk for another. Chunk size depends on your knowledge residing in long-term memory. When novice chess players view a mid-play chess board, they see each chess piece as a separate piece of information. For them, the board consists of about twenty-four chunks of data. When a master-level chess player looks at the same mid-play chess board, he perceives about eight to ten chunks of information because the chess expert groups four or five individual pieces into small clusters based on play patterns familiar to him or her. Experienced learners have more related knowledge in long-term memory, which gives them a greater virtual working memory capacity. In contrast, novice learners are more easily overloaded and profit from communication modes, instructional methods, and design architectures that minimize load on working memory.

Working memory includes separate storage areas for visual and for auditory information. By selecting communication modes that use the visual and auditory centers in complementary ways, the capacity of working memory can be extended. In Chapters 5 and 8, we will offer specific guidelines on how to use the communication modes of text, audio, and graphics most effectively.

Harnessing Learning Processes in the Virtual Classroom

The instructional modes, methods, and architectures you create or select will only be effective if they support several important instructional events. All of these events accommodate the features of working memory and long-term memory and the exchange of information between them. The main events, illustrated in Figure 2.3, include supporting attention, activating prior knowledge from long-term memory into working memory, managing *cognitive load* in working memory, aiding construction of new *mental models* to be stored in long-term memory via encoding, encouraging *transfer of learning* via retrieval, and guiding the management of the learning process via *metacognition.* All of these events are fueled by learner motivation. A demotivated learner may not invest the effort needed for successful learning. In the next section we offer a few examples of ways to support these events in the virtual classroom.

Support Attention in the Virtual Classroom

Because working memory is limited, instructional professionals must focus learner attention and discourage divided attention in all learning environments. Given the temptation for students to multitask during virtual classrooms events, supporting attention is especially critical. To focus

---

Figure 2.3. Effective Instruction Supports Critical Psychological Events of Learning.

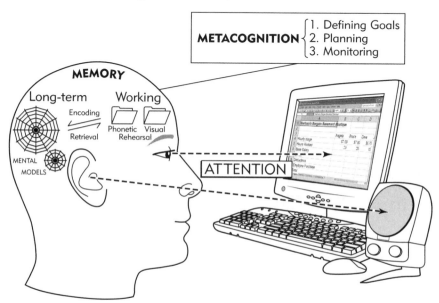

attention in the virtual classroom, use the various white board signaling tools to draw the eye to important elements of graphics as they are explained. In addition, maintain a lively pace seasoned with frequent interactions in varied formats.

In our classes, we display an average of one slide each 1.5 minutes. At some points in the lesson, we might show three to four slides in a minute. During exercises, a single slide may remain in place for several minutes. Our main recommendation is to limit the number of ideas expressed on one slide and maintain a lively pace, while at the same time offering many opportunities for learners to actively respond.

Discourage divided attention by setting ground rules regarding use of the virtual classroom facilities and multitasking, and by minimizing extraneous instructional elements. For example, when explaining a complex visual on the white board or during application sharing, don't add a web-cam image of the instructor.

Activate Prior Knowledge in the Virtual Classroom

Learning is a process of integrating new incoming data with relevant prior knowledge that is active in working memory. Moving that prior knowledge from long-term memory into working memory is an important early event in any lesson. Often this is accomplished with an interactive review. For example, in a lesson on formulas in Excel, the instructor may review a prior lesson on cell references. Alternatively, an analogy can serve as a bridge from existing mental models to new ideas. For example, when learning the concept of peristalsis in a biology class, the analogy of squeezing ketchup from a small packet improved learning (Newby, Ertmer, & Stepich, 1995).

Manage Cognitive Load in the Virtual Classroom

We devote all of Chapter 8 to proven techniques you can use to manage cognitive load in the virtual classroom. Because working memory has such a limited capacity, you must utilize it in the service of your instructional goals—not for processes extraneous to those goals. We know that instructor-driven media such as the virtual classroom are already prone to overload because the learner has little control over the pace of the class. Therefore, managing cognitive load is especially important in both physical and virtual classroom environments.

One way to manage cognitive load is through the judicious use of the communication modes of text, graphics, and audio. For example, if you explain a visual with text and redundant narration that repeats the text, you overload working memory. Instead, you should explain visuals with instructor narration alone. This makes best use of the visual and auditory centers in working memory.

Regarding instructional methods, providing a mix of step-by-step examples along with practice exercises is more efficient than providing only one example followed by lots of practice problems. This is because having to work problems imposes a high load on working memory compared to reviewing examples.

Either a receptive or a guided-discovery lesson design tends to impose more cognitive load than a directive approach. Directive architectures chunk instruction into short segments interspersed with interactions that build skills gradually. In contrast, guided-discovery designs use a problem as a mechanism for learning. Having to solve problems and learn complex new skills at the same time can easily overload novice learners. In Chapter 8 we describe many other proven techniques you can use in the virtual classroom to manage cognitive load.

Help Learners Construct New Mental Models in the Virtual Classroom

When you successfully reduce cognitive load, you free working memory to process new content in ways that build new mental models in long-term memory. Mental models are the memory structures stored in long-term memory that incorporate all our knowledge and skills.

In the virtual classroom, use a combination of graphics and words. We all have two ways to encode new knowledge, one for visuals and one for words. When words and visuals are used in a coordinated fashion and are linked to the instructional goals, better learning occurs than when using a visual alone or words alone.

Examples and practice exercises are two effective instructional methods that promote building of new mental models. Learners can mentally process new information when you provide a good example for them to study. Learners also mentally process new information when they are overtly engaged in responding to relevant practice exercises.

Avoid the use of a receptive architecture in your virtual classroom sessions. Receptive architectures usually result in passive participants whose attention soon wanders. Instead, make use of lesson designs that incorporate frequent and overt participation that will promote learning.

Encourage Transfer of Learning in the Virtual Classroom

Getting new knowledge stored in long-term memory is a necessary but not sufficient condition for success. The new information has to be retrieved into working memory later when needed on the job. This is what we call *transfer of learning.*

Context is your best route to learning transfer. Lessons in the virtual classroom should incorporate the relevant contexts of the workplace. Graphics, examples, and practice exercises should reflect real-world environments. For example, in our Excel demonstration lesson on the CD, we show different spreadsheet calculations and formulas to help learners build a job-relevant and robust mental model. In addition to using real-world examples, ask participants to bring their own work contexts to the training. For example, in our Excel demonstration lesson, learners develop their own spreadsheets as a follow-up project assignment.

Guide Learning Management in the Virtual Classroom

Good learning management skills help learners set instructional goals, plan the best learning methods, and monitor their progress toward those goals. Some learners have good management skills. However, many do not. For example, many learners do not know how best to tackle an instructional goal on their own. In addition, many cannot determine what set of subgoals or skills they need in order to reach a larger goal. Your virtual classroom environment can provide management support. Valid pretests are one good method to define which virtual classroom sessions individuals should attend. For example, in our Excel course, a pretest is used to assign learners to specific virtual classroom sessions. Providing frequent practice checks also helps learners (and instructors) confirm whether students have attained the learning goal or need more instructional time. Stonebraker and Hazeltine (2004) reported that perceived level of learning was a major satisfier for corporate virtual classroom students.

Promote Motivation in the Virtual Classroom

Like physical classrooms, virtual classrooms, with their synchronous group events, impose an external discipline that drives course completion (and hopefully learning). Many learners yield to competing demands for their time and attention and consequently fail to complete self-study learning events. Are you surprised that, in many doctoral programs, among the candidates who complete all of their course work, less than half finish their dissertations? Why? Attending classes is a relatively short-term goal, which is driven externally. In contrast, dissertation work puts the responsibility back on the candidate to set up, complete, and write up his or her research. One pragmatic value to the virtual classroom is the tendency of scheduled events to drive the learning process. The chances of completing a synchronous instructional event are significantly greater, compared to self-study asynchronous learning environments that rely to a greater degree on individual motivation and discipline (Bernard et al., 2004).

In the context of the virtual class, support motivation through social presence, by incorporating job-relevant examples and interactions into the class, by maintaining a brisk pace, and by offering focused, frequent, and job-relevant interactions.

Avoid extrinsic motivators such as games or themes that are not relevant to the training goals. Although these attempts to spice up a dull topic can add interest, at the same time they run the risk of overloading memory with information that is not relevant to course goals (Mayer, 2005b).

The Bottom Line

Three instructional components—communication modes, instructional methods, and design architectures—determine learning effectiveness. It is the effective use of these components, not the instructional delivery medium, that leads to learning. For best results in the virtual classroom, harness the features of the technology to support the key learning events of attention, activation of prior knowledge, management of cognitive load, processing of new content, transfer of learning, management of learning, and motivation.

COMING NEXT: EXPLOITING FEATURES IN THE NEW VIRTUAL CLASSROOM

Before we leave the topic of media comparisons, we need to acknowledge that media differ regarding the instructional components they can support. For example, a book cannot deliver audio, animations, or simulations. To fully exploit any delivery technology, use its functionalities in ways that support the learning events reviewed in this chapter. In Chapter 3 we focus on the key features of new virtual classrooms that you should harness for most effective learning.

On *The New Virtual Classroom* CD

Our recorded virtual classroom lessons reflect two of the four architectures we discuss, directive and guided discovery.

Directive Architecture The demonstration lessons, How to Use Formulas in Excel and How to Define Business Goals, use a directive architecture. In both lessons the instructor presents some content, illustrates with some examples, and asks learners to practice applying the content in small chunks. In both lessons, prerequisite concepts such as What is a formula? and What is a business goal? are presented prior to the steps or guidelines that make up the main objective of the lesson.

Guided Discovery Architecture How to Plan an Interview uses a problem-based learning format. Early in this lesson, learners are given a video-delivered problem and placed into breakout rooms to brainstorm. Following small group discussions, participants define their learning issues and are provided instructional resources to use to complete their assignment.

For More Information

Clark, R. (2003). *Building expertise.* Silver Spring, MD: International Society for Performance Improvement.

Bernard, R. M., Abrami, P. C., Lou, Y, Borokhovski, E., Wade, A., Wozney, L., Wallet, P. A., Fixet, M., & Huang, B. (2004). How does distance education compare with classroom instruction? A meta-analysis of the empirical literature. *Review of Educational Research, 74*(3), 379–439.

Stonebraker, P. W., & Hazeltine, J. E. (2004). Virtual learning effectiveness. *The Learning Organization, 11*(3), 209–225.

Tallent-Runnels, M. K., Thomas, J. A., Lan, W. Y., Cooper, S., Ahern, T. C., Shaw, S. M., & Liu, X. (2006). Teaching courses online: A review of the research. *Review of Educational Research, 76*(11), 93–135.

EXPERT'S FORUM

INFORMATION IS NOT TRAINING

Dr. Rob Steinmetz, President, Training Systems Design

Both traditionally and currently, a vast number of corporations and organizations rely on subject-matter experts to design, develop, and deliver both face-to-face and distance learning events. The underlying assumption is *if you know the subject, you can impart that knowledge efficiently and effectively to others.* Unfortunately, all of us in this field know this notion is simply a common misperception. Popularity does not make it true.

With apologies to Marshall McLuhan, while the media may impact the message, it is not the primary determinant of effectiveness in instilling new knowledge and skills. Rather, it is the skillful utilization of the different modes and means of communication within a well-designed architecture that wins the day.

My professional mantra has always been *"Information Is Not Training."* Training is the building of cognitive engrams (or as Clark and Kwinn call them, "mental models") that link external stimuli or conditions with predictable, correct, and repeatable behaviors. To achieve this end, one must strategically employ such techniques as partial redundancy through alternate modes; repetition in alternate forms (such as verbal explication, modeling, simulation, and so forth); knowledge of results; corrective feedback; delayed practice; variable pacing; and a host of other significant instructional devices.

For example, my company built a number of equipment simulators set in the context of real-work scenarios in which the equipment was used. The Windows-based training programs were connected to equipment keyboards and provided a realistic point of view of the work environment. Users were presented with step-by-step guided demonstrations via text and audio directions. Incorrect actions were given corrective feedback to get users back on the right path. For practice, users were given the name of the procedure and asked to complete it without step-by-step prompting.

This chapter distills the myriad of variables and their non-linear interactions involved in learning into a simplified set of instructional components. While I would ultimately hold that mission-critical learning (and any learning involving the safety of human beings) demands a thorough understanding of exactly how perceptual systems function, how working memory functions, and how mental models are built, sustained, modified over time, and go into extinction, the models presented in this chapter provide an excellent introduction for the "rest of the world."

Chapter 1
Meet the New Virtual Classroom

Introduction

Chapter 2
Learning in the New VC

Chapter 3
Features to Exploit in the New VC

Chapter 4
Teaching Content Types in the New VC

Part 1: Learning and the New Virtual Classroom

Chapter 5
Visualize Your Message

Chapter 6
Make It Active – Part 1

Chapter 7
Make It Active – Part 2

Part 2: Engaging Participants in the New Virtual Classroom

Chapter 8
Managing Mental Load in the New VC

Chapter 9
Make a Good First Impression

Chapter 10
Packaging Your VC Session

Chapter 11
Problem-Based Learning in the New VC

Part 3: Optimizing Your Virtual Events

Chapter 12
Getting Started

Part 4: Creating Effective Learning Events in the New Virtual Classroom

3

Features to Exploit in the New Virtual Classroom

ALTHOUGH A COURSE'S DELIVERY MEDIUM will not determine instructional effectiveness, the way specific media features are used and combined will promote or hinder learning. Unfortunately, more often than not, media—new and old—are abused. Media features that lead to learning are ignored as instructional professionals fall back on the ubiquitous lecture. Alternatively, technophiles overuse media features in ways that exceed human mental capacity to learn from them.

Four important virtual classroom features to be leveraged for learning include:

- Facilities for communication modes: audio, text, and visuals
- Response options for overt learner engagement
- Instructor-paced delivery of content
- Social learning facilities

All Training Media Are Not Equivalent

Learning is never about the media! Or is it? We saw in the previous chapter that when **the same lesson** is delivered in two different media, say classroom and web-based training, the learning is more or less the same. But this is not to say that all media are equivalent. In fact, some psychologists argue that the media research comparisons are irrelevant because they do not fully utilize the capabilities that different media offer. For example, computer-delivered training can provide simulations that are difficult if not impossible to deliver in a book.

When faced with any instructional goal, ask yourself: "What instructional modes, methods, and architectures will best achieve my goals?" In Chapter 2 we defined modes as the communication vehicles of audio, visuals, and text. Instructional methods include techniques proven to promote learning, such as examples and practice exercises. And we defined architectures as the design framework for the lessons, the DNA that defines the structure of a lesson.

For example, if your goal is to teach a new software application, a demonstration followed by hands-on practice would help participants learn the new procedures. You need to determine what mix of media can best deliver these instructional modes and methods. For example, you could deliver a demonstration with step-by-step visuals in a workbook accompanied by text explanations, or in most e-learning environments, with static or animated visuals and audio explanations.

As you consider your instructional requirements, you need to also factor in pragmatic constraints related to the technology and resources of your organization. These constraints may limit your media options. For instance, you might be told that, to save travel costs, all of the training must be delivered using virtual classroom technology. In this situation, you must identify and exploit the features available in the virtual classroom to best achieve the intended goals.

Features That Matter

In the ideal world, you can use the mix of delivery media that best matches your instructional goals. In reality, you will face technological and resource constraints that may limit your options, as Ruth experienced not too long ago:

> I was invited to teach a university distance learning course. Since I was unfamiliar with the e-learning tool the university used, I viewed some sample courses.

To my dismay, I found that, for synchronous class sessions, the technology could only support text—mostly in the form of chat. The instructor "lectured" using text chat, and learners asked questions with chat. There was no media capability for display of graphics or use of audio. I found these instructional tools too limiting and, fortunately, had the option to bypass the assignment.

What are the most important features to consider in any learning environment? No matter what mix of media you use, your goal should always be to harness whatever features are available to you in the service of learning. Based on research evidence on learning, we propose four fundamental features (see Figure 3.1):

1. Communication modes

2. Overt rehearsal options

3. Control over pacing

4. Social learning facilities

Figure 3.1. Four Media Features That Influence Learning.

Communication Mode	 abc
Rehearsal	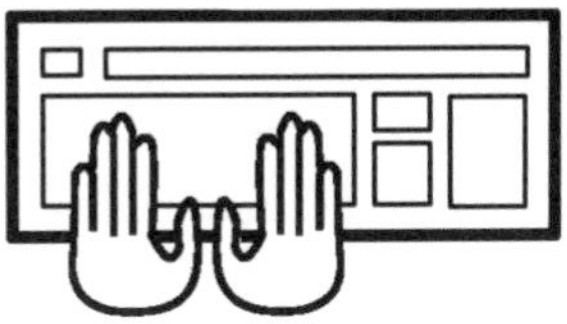
Pacing	 NEXT
Social Learning Facilities	

Let's take a look at the evidence relating to each of these features and see how the virtual classroom supports each, compared to other delivery media such as the face-to-face classroom or asynchronous e-learning.

Communication Modes

First you need to consider the extent to which various media alternatives can deliver three basic modes of communication: audio, text, and visuals. A podcast can only deliver sound, whereas the distance learning technology Ruth described in her university assignment could only deliver text. Generally speaking, the more communication modes a technology can support, the greater potential that technology has to promote learning.

The Power of Visuals

Research shows that a **relevant** visual can dramatically improve learning. Notice that we emphasize "relevant." In fact, we have evidence that visuals added for the sake of interest or engagement—in other words visuals not directly relevant to the instructional goal—can actually depress learning!

Mayer and his colleagues prepared several lessons to teach processes, including how lightning works, how a bicycle pump works, and how brakes work. Some lesson versions included only a textual explanation, while comparison versions included both relevant visuals and text. Participants who studied from lessons that included both text and visuals on average learned 89 percent more than those studying from text alone (Mayer, 2001). The reason is that the combination of a relevant visual and words offers a double opportunity for learners to build a mental model.

However, not all visuals are equally effective. In fact, the wrong type of visual can be downright ineffective! Using the lightning lesson, Harp and Mayer (1998) found that adding related but unessential vignettes, such how lightning affects aircraft, added interest to the lesson but depressed learning. No doubt the unessential information detracted attention from the main points and disrupted the building of a cohesive mental model. We refer to e-learning courses that spice up technical content with extraneous visuals and activities such as irrelevant games as the "Las Vegas" approach to instruction.

In addition, learners who have background knowledge regarding the lesson topics often **do not benefit** from visuals. Having two representations—one in words and one in visuals—can be redundant for these learners and can even depress their learning. Mayer and Gallini (1990) found that visuals illustrating how a braking system works improved learning outcomes of students with little prior knowledge of brakes, but not of students with experience maintaining brakes.

Visuals have great potential to improve or to detract from learning. Therefore, media that can display visuals have the potential to improve learning when the visuals are relevant to the content and appropriate to the audience.

Visuals in the Virtual Classroom

In many e-learning interfaces, both synchronous and asynchronous, much of the real estate is available for visual representations. Most modern virtual classroom interfaces, such as the one in Figure 3.2, devote considerable space to the white board, which can be used to project or create visual representations. Therefore, the virtual classroom has high potential for projecting visuals that can improve learning. Our challenge is to exploit that potential appropriately. You will learn more about how to use visuals effectively in the virtual classroom in Chapter 5.

The Power of Audio

Presenting words in audio can lead to better learning than presenting words in text. This guideline is based on the *modality principle*—one of the most widely confirmed findings in recent instructional research. According to the

Figure 3.2. The White Board Offers Large Screen Real Estate for Graphics.

With permission from Trudy Mandeville, TechComm Partners Inc.

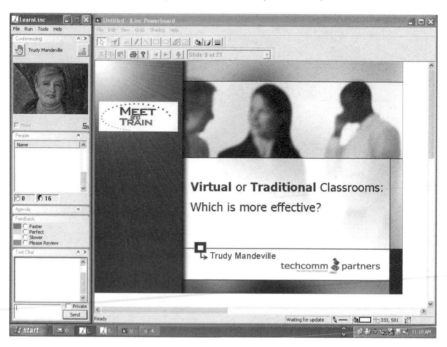

modality principle, learning is better when a complex visual is explained by audio narration than when a visual is explained by text. Many research experiments involving learners of different ages and lessons on diverse topics support the modality principle. For example, Tindall-Ford, Chandler, and Sweller (1997) trained trade apprentices how to conduct electrical tests of appliances using a volt meter. One group learned the procedure by studying a diagram explained with text. The second group learned the same procedure by listening to an audio presentation of the same words while they viewed the diagram. As you can see in Figure 3.3, the version using audio led to better learning.

The reason for the modality principle is that working memory has two storage areas—one for visual information and one for auditory information. Lessons that explain visuals with text overload the visual center with two visual sources. These lessons do not use the auditory center at all. In contrast,

Figure 3.3. Better Learning from Visuals Explained by Audio Than by Text.

From Tindall-Ford, Chandler, and Sweller, 1997

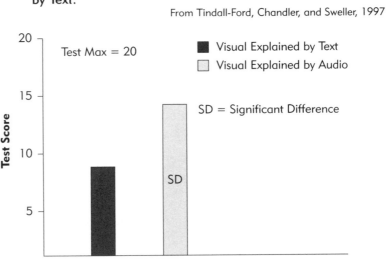

lessons that explain visuals with audio narration balance the content across both centers and in that way maximize the use of limited working memory capacity.

Audio and Social Presence

Another benefit of audio is that human speech adds a personal element to instruction that activates our inherent social responses. To respect social conventions, we tend to pay attention when someone is talking directly to us. In contrast, when reading a book or watching TV, we often find ourselves out of touch with the message. We read the words but realize we did not process any of the meaning. We were thinking about something else. We heard the sounds on the TV, but our attention was elsewhere.

The power of *social presence* may explain the benefits of *learning agents*. A learning agent is an on-screen character often used in asynchronous e-learning to communicate with the learner. Moreno, Mayer, Spires, and Lester (2001) compared learning from several versions of learning agents. They found their agent was equally effective in the form of a cartoon bug, a human video image—or, in fact no image at all! However, they found that learning was best when the agent communicated by audio rather than by text and when the agent's voice was human rather than machine generated. Research we have to date points to the power of **the voice,** rather than the image of learning agents.

Audio and the Virtual Classroom

Most virtual classroom interfaces offer the potential for two-way audio. The instructor can explain visuals on the white board using audio. Students can also take control of the microphone to ask or respond to questions. Some virtual classroom tools support multiple simultaneous speakers, while others limit audio to one person at a time. Since human capacity to process multiple auditory messages is limited, restricting talk to one speaker at a time might actually promote learning!

When instructors explain a visual projected on the white board using audio narration, they apply the modality principle. Likewise, when seminar participants, including the instructor, use the microphone to communicate, social presence is increased.

The Power of Text

Although audio has proven to be the most efficient mode for explaining visuals, a drawback to audio is its transience. Once spoken, there is no record of the words. In many cases learners need to reference words over a period of time. For example, when completing a practice exercise, learners need to refer back to the directions as they work through the activity. In the same way, when performing a procedure on the job, a working aid with directions in text provides a more persistent reference than one with directions in audio.

Some types of content cannot be displayed visually. Written words are the best method to convey this type of content. For example, learning objectives and abstract concepts such as "integrity" are best presented in text. We know that text-dominant media such as books supplemented with occasional visuals can effectively communicate knowledge and skills.

Text and the Virtual Classroom

Most virtual classroom interfaces offer a text chat facility. If a participant mentions a website or a telephone number, she can type it into the chat window—making it easy for everyone to copy. Text chat is useful when the instructor would like all participants to respond, in contrast to using audio for a single response.

The white board has a text typing tool that allows participants to type words on the white board. For example, in Figure 3.4 participants in a virtual classroom type in their responses on a grid created on the white board. This display allows everyone to see all of the responses and comment on them, as appropriate.

Communication Modes and the Virtual Classroom

As we have seen, the virtual classroom interface offers opportunities for instructors and for learners to communicate via visuals, audio, and text. These alternative modalities, when effectively used, have great potential to increase learning. At the same time, more modalities call for more care in their planning and coordination. For example, if learners use the chat facility to

Figure 3.4. Participants Type Responses into White Board.
With permission of Kathy Fallow, Vertex Solutions.

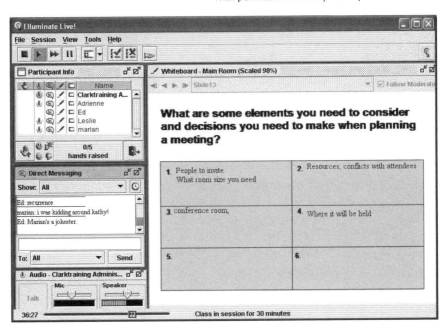

correspond with other participants during an instructor presentation, divided attention will diminish learning. The instructor must orchestrate the various communication facilities to maximize learning from them.

Overt Rehearsal Options

Another essential aspect of effective synchronous training is the opportunity for rehearsal, during which the learner can actively respond to practice exercises such as multiple-choice questions, case studies, role plays, or hands-on tasks. Some delivery media, such as self-study books or video, offer limited opportunities for learners to make overt responses in ways that can be reviewed and assessed by others. In contrast, the face-to-face classroom equipped with computers or other equipment offers a wide range of overt rehearsal opportunities. In traditional classrooms, learners can work alone or in groups to complete a paper-and-pencil practice exercise, or they can try out new computer skills with the guidance of an instructor. Alternatively, role-play exercises can provide a context to practice communication skills involved in sales, customer service, or supervision.

In general, the more facilities a medium offers for rehearsal, the greater the potential for learning. However, it is up to the instructional professional to exploit those facilities. The mere availability of diverse interaction options does not necessarily mean they will be used—or used effectively. In spite of the rich opportunities for learner activity, many classroom sessions are little more than instructors lecturing and showing slides to learners who remain passive. This is not a fault of the classroom, but rather of the instructional professional who fails to exploit the interactive opportunities available to him.

As summarized in Figure 3.5, research on the structure and placement of interaction opportunities gives us three universal principles:

1. Practice should mirror job requirements.

2. Distributed practice leads to better learning than practice assigned all at once.

3. During initial learning, faded examples should evolve into practice assignments.

Figure 3.5. Three Universal Principles of Interactions.

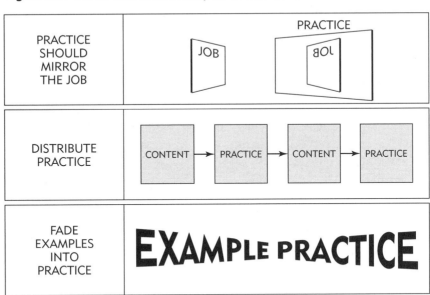

Principle 1: Mirror Job Requirements in Practice Exercises

A common mistake in construction of practice exercises is to ask learners to merely regurgitate content presented by the instructor or in the workbook. For example, a question might ask participants to list the four steps of an effective performance appraisal meeting. However, on the job, workers do not list steps. Rather, they apply steps to perform the task effectively.

Application rather than recall practice is essential to support transfer of learning. This is because retrieval cues must be implanted in memory at the time of initial learning. For example, suppose you are asked to list the months of the year? No problem. But suppose you were asked to list the months of the year in alphabetic order? This would be a more challenging task. Why? Because you learned the months of the year chronologically, the retrieval cues embedded in memory are similarly organized.

To ensure that you embed job-relevant cues at the time of learning, you need to conduct a job analysis to identify the psychological and physical context in which new skills will be applied. Then you write learning objectives and design practice to mirror the tasks that workers perform on the job (and you identified in the job analysis). So for example, rather than asking learners to list the steps to conduct a performance appraisal, better learning transfer will result from practice that asks participants to practice those steps in a case study or role-play exercise.

Mirroring Job Requirements in the Virtual Classroom   The virtual classroom offers a variety of response options for interactivity. It is up to the instructional professional to construct practice exercises that are job relevant. The **format** of the practice—whether it involves a polling question or typing text into the chat window—is not as important as the **context** of the practice. Regardless of response options used, construct practice exercises around work-related tasks in the form of realistic case scenarios. For example, the practice exercise incorporated into the application sharing window in Figure 3.6, taken from our CD Excel lesson, requires learners to construct the appropriate spreadsheet formula to achieve the desired calculation result. Although, in this example,

Figure 3.6. An Application Practice in an Excel Virtual Class.

From *The New Virtual Classroom* CD.

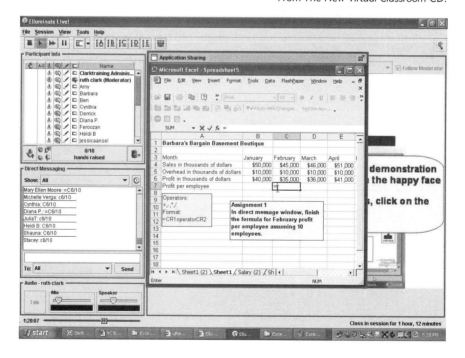

the instructor used the chat response option, she could have used the audio facility to call on a participant or run a multiple-choice polling question.

Principle 2: Distribute Practice Throughout Learning Events

Two lessons may have exactly the same number of interactive opportunities. However, the lesson that spreads those interactions throughout the session rather than grouping them into one or two practice assignments leads to better learning in the long run. If, for example, you have eight practice interactions, it's better to distribute them at the beginning, middle, and end of the lesson, rather than all at the end.

When all of the practice is assigned at one time, working memory can temporarily retain the information from practice 1 as it moves to practice 2. Therefore, less mental effort is needed to process practice 2. However, if practice 2 is placed, say five minutes or so after practice 1, working memory will have to process from scratch, leading to increased encoding work and a better chance for learning.

Frequent practice supports learner attention. Lacking the physical presence of an instructor, student attention in the virtual classroom tends to drift. It's not uncommon for participants to respond to email, review unrelated documents, or even leave their computers during the session. Inserting frequent interactions will discourage these kinds of multitasking activities. Frequent interactions are an important technique to keep your audience engaged!

Distributed Practice and the Virtual Classroom   The virtual classroom offers a multitude of overt response facilities, including polling buttons, icons, chat, and audio. It is up to the instructional professional to exploit these opportunities with frequent interactions. How frequent? Avoid inflexible guidelines such as "include an interaction every third slide." Instead, a more general rule of thumb is to include interactions frequently, for example, try not to let more than two or three minutes elapse without some form of learner involvement.

Face-to-face classroom instructors new to the virtual classroom find the lack of body language disconcerting. A whole new set of skills to "read the audience" is needed to determine who is getting it and who is confused.

By closely monitoring individual responses to frequent and effective interactions, the instructor can quickly identify evidence of confusion or confirm understanding. Instructors must learn to substitute polling or chat responses for body language cues of individual learner progress. To effectively monitor individual participant responses, maintain an instructor-participant ratio that is relatively low—around ten to fourteen participants to one instructor. Low participant-student ratios are important in skill-building virtual classroom sessions. In contrast, for briefings or sessions not focused on individual skills, larger groups are fine. We've conducted webinars with groups of one hundred or greater. We keep webinars interactive, but are not as concerned with individual responses to questions as with general response patterns. For example, in Figure 3.7, a bar graph summarizes responses to a polling question to communicate trends, but not individual responses.

In Chapters 6 and 7 you will learn in greater detail the many different types of learner involvement you can generate in the virtual classroom.

Figure 3.7. A Bar Graph Summarizes Large Group Responses to a Polling Question.

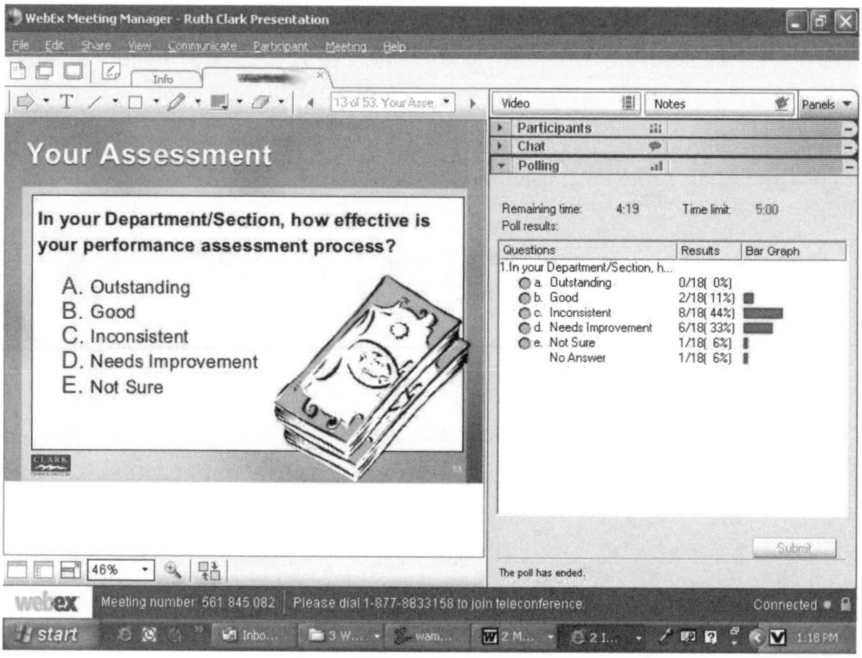

Distributed Practice and Blended Learning   One of the major advantages to a course that blends a combination of virtual classroom sessions with self-study media is the opportunity to distribute learning over a longer period of time than is possible in most face-to-face classroom sessions. We offer our "How to Leverage the Virtual Classroom" course in either a two-day instructor-led session or in four two-hour weekly virtual sessions with project assignments in between. Overall, we find that projects from participants in the virtual classroom sessions are more elaborate and complete as a result of the spaced distribution of the instructional event over a month, rather than compressed within two days.

Principle 3: Replace Some Practice with Faded Worked Examples

As useful as practice is for learning, having to work multiple extensive skill-building practice exercises adds a considerable load to working memory. A number of research studies have documented the time efficiency and learning benefits of substituting a series of worked examples for practice exercises, so that the learner gradually assumes more and more of the work (Clark, Nguyen, & Sweller, 2006). In Chapter 8, we show you how.

Control Over Pacing

Some delivery media allow the learner to determine the rate at which he or she will progress in the course. High learner control over pacing is typical of asynchronous computer training designed for solo learning. Self-paced media such as asynchronous e-learning or self-study workbooks allow learners to study at their own rate and to easily review information. In contrast, instructor-led training either in the face-to-face or virtual classroom is paced by the instructor. The delivery pace will be too fast for some and too slow for others and, unlike videotape, there are generally few opportunities to stop, pause, or rewind the class.

There is increasing evidence that instructor-paced training tends to impose greater cognitive load than self-paced classes. For example, Mayer and Jackson (2005) prepared lessons on how waves form. They presented the same content either in a paper version that allowed learner control of pacing or in a multimedia version using narrated animation. The paper version resulted in significantly more learning.

As you consider your delivery media options, keep in mind the tradeoffs. Clearly, instructor-delivered training provides opportunities for participants to engage in social exchanges, as they ask questions and discuss ideas. At the same time, instructor-driven delivery is likely to impose greater cognitive load than is self-paced media. Some learning activities such as projects benefit from reflection time not readily available in instructor-paced environments. If your instructional goals include some complex content elements as well as a need for individual reflection, you may want to deliver them in a self-paced medium, followed by an instructor-led session to discuss, practice, and clarify the content.

Pacing in the Virtual Classroom

Most virtual classroom sessions are presented under instructor control and therefore are likely to impose greater cognitive load than self-paced media such as books or asynchronous e-learning. As a result, the instructional professional must mitigate the negative effects of cognitive overload. We mentioned the modality principle earlier. By using instructor narration to explain a complex visual, limited working memory capacity is maximized. In addition, when explaining a complex visual, the instructor should use one of the many cueing devices, such as a highlighter or pointer, available to focus attention on the important elements of the visual being explained. The virtual classroom may not be the best place for activities that require reflection. Extending the virtual classroom with self-paced individual assignments using asynchronous media can compensate for the pacing constraints of an instructor-led environment. In Chapter 8, we describe many proven techniques you can adapt to the virtual classroom to avoid cognitively overloaded sessions.

Social Learning Facilities

Under the right conditions, learners who work together on a lesson can achieve more than learners who work on the same lesson by themselves

(Cohen, 1994; Lou, Abrami, & D'Apollonia, 2001). Group activities reap learning benefits when:

- Assignments involve design or problem-solving tasks, rather than applying procedures.
- Group sizes are small, in the range of three to five participants.
- Assignments are sufficiently complex to benefit from the perspectives of several individuals.
- Assignments and group processes are clearly defined and structured. Structured group learning techniques such as *jig saw* or *structured argumentation* offer proven methods for *collaborative learning* (Clark & Mayer, 2003).

Training delivery media that can accommodate collaborative activities in general offer more learning opportunities than media that cannot. The face-to-face classroom offers a variety of flexible arrangements for small group work. Unfortunately, many instructional professionals fail to exploit those opportunities. It's not uncommon to leave a classroom session with minimal or no exchanges with other participants. Other media—especially media designed for self-study—are quite limited in opportunities for collaborative work, unless they integrate additional opportunities for social exchanges such as discussion boards, chat sessions, or email.

Collaborative group activities can lead to greater learning because they offer more opportunities for overt learner involvement than is possible in a larger group. The exchange of ideas and preparation of assignments maximize opportunities for individual learner rehearsal and consequent learning.

Social Learning in the Virtual Classroom

One important feature in the virtual classroom is the breakout room. A breakout room, like its physical correlate, allows small groups of learners to work together on an assignment or hold a discussion in which everyone has ample opportunity to participate. The breakout room typically has all of the facilities of the main interface, including a white board, polling, audio, and so forth. Spending a few minutes in a breakout room allows a group of three to five participants to actively engage with each other in ways that can lead to greater individual participation and consequent learning. Since Stonebraker and Hazeltine (2004) found that group cohesion is one of the satisfiers in the virtual classroom, breakout rooms should be used on a regular basis in virtual classroom training. You will learn some specific guidelines on the use of breakout rooms in Chapter 7.

Media and Learning

We cannot say definitively that delivery media have NO effect on learning. The more features offered that can be used to support the core psychological learning events, the greater the learning potential of a given medium. For example, the new virtual classroom offers opportunities to communicate in all three modalities, whereas books are limited to text and visuals. The virtual classroom offers numerous interactive response options, while other media offer only a few. Instructional professionals must exploit the features available in a given medium to optimize its potential. More often than not, media features are ignored. Even in a face-to-face classroom, which offers many powerful opportunities to promote learning, instructors resort to a lecture in order to "cover the material" in the time allowed. By so doing, they perpetuate the illusion that "material covered" equates to material learned!

Alternatively, media features are overused. Technophiles are seduced by the allure of a Las Vegas approach by including rotating visuals, frequent animations, and background music, using them in ways that overload human cognitive capacity.

Often an emerging delivery medium such as the new virtual classroom gets a bad reputation when used to merely deliver content, rather than teach. As with any new medium, the promise of the virtual classroom lies in taking advantage of its features in ways that promote human learning processes.

The Bottom Line

Learning can be effective from a variety of delivery media as long as you harness your media features in ways that support human learning. Virtual classroom technology offers a number of facilities to communicate in multiple

---

USERS SPEAK

The advisory team talks about the important features of the virtual classroom

The most important tool features are application sharing, collaboration, annotation tools, chat, being able to control interaction easily, including passing control between participants.

Bob Mosher, Chief Learning and Strategy Evangelist with LearningGuides Solutions

Trainers need to be able to share their desktops with the students so they can watch demonstrations. We currently do not have a lot of interactivity because the classes can have 35 people attending at once. That's a lot to manage for the trainers!

Trudie Folsom, Senior Instructional Designer, Intuit, Inc.

The polling functions were used for several purposes. Because we had audiences that varied by role, function, and location, we often used polls at the beginning of each session to determine who was participating. This helped the facilitator determine which scenarios, activities, and examples to use during the session to make the session as "real world" as possible. We also used polls to check for understanding, kick start discussion, etc.

  Text Chat: We found that many participants prefer using the text chat feature over raising their hands and waiting to speak.

Jon D. Stephenson, Instructional Designer, and Kristin Johnson, Project Manager,
Learning & Development, Wells Fargo Home Mortgage

---

modes, to elicit overt participant responses, and to promote social presence. It is up to you as a developer or facilitator of virtual classroom sessions to orchestrate these various features effectively!

COMING NEXT: TEACHING CONTENT TYPES IN THE VIRTUAL CLASSROOM

Success in the virtual classroom depends in part on aligning the most appropriate instructional methods to your instructional objectives and associated content. In the next chapter, we illustrate how to teach five basic content

types in the virtual classroom. These are facts, concepts, processes, procedures, and principles.

For More Information

On Communication Modes and Learning

> Clark, R. C., Nguyen, F., & Sweller, J. (2006) *Efficiency in learning.*
> San Francisco: Pfeiffer. (See Chapters 3 and 4.)

On Design of Effective Practice

> Clark, R. C. (2003). *Building expertise.* Silver Spring: MD: ISPI.
> (See Chapters 8 and 9.)

> Clark, R. C., & Mayer, R. E. (2003). *e-Learning and the science of instruction.*
> San Francisco: Pfeiffer. (See Chapter 9.)

> Clark, R. C., Nguyen, F., & Sweller, J. (2006) *Efficiency in learning.*
> San Francisco: Pfeiffer. (See Chapter 8.)

On Social Learning

> Clark, R. C., & Mayer, R. E. (2003). *e-Learning and the science of instruction.*
> San Francisco: Pfeiffer.

EXPERTS' FORUM

LEARNING TO EFFECTIVELY USE THE VIRTUAL CLASSROOM

Joe Tansey, Learning and Development Consultant,
Wells Fargo Corporate Human Resources

In the late 1990s, increased Internet connection speeds and improved virtual classroom technologies began to provide companies with an alternative to classroom
training. At that time, I was working in a small training department at a large financial services company that was struggling to find a way to train geographically dispersed bankers. I promoted the idea of single virtual classroom system to be shared
by training groups enterprise-wide and was hired by our corporate learning and

development group to manage its rollout and ongoing use. Many factors influenced our choice of a virtual classroom tool. Chief among them were ease of use, participant feedback tools that were both effective and added warmth to the online environment (for example: active laughter and applause tools), and an underlying architecture that could ensure maximum uptime and ease of support.

In my new role supporting the virtual classroom, I had to learn how to make effective use of it to support learning in the classes I designed and facilitated. I also had many opportunities to observe content developed and delivered by others. Initial reactions to the virtual classroom among instructors and learners new to it included fear, skepticism, and enthusiasm. Comparisons to the traditional classroom abounded. Many decried the limitations of the virtual classroom (for example: the absence of eye contact and body language) and characterized it as a poor substitute for classroom training. Others reveled in the new opportunities it embodied. One facilitator in another part of the company told me how it had changed his life. He was able to greatly reduce his travel schedule and spend a lot more time with his family.

In spite of initial trepidation felt by many, in retrospect, it's amazing how so many facilitators and learners, young and old, made the transition to the virtual classroom in such a short period of time. Similarly, easy-to-use authoring tools greatly reduced the technical barriers to content development used for synchronous and asynchronous content development. It has been remarkable to observe how the culture of training has changed. The tools are here, and better ones will follow. The challenge now is to catch up and hone the facilitation and content development skills of our training professionals.

We have found some effective ways to use the three modes of audio, text, and video. For example, a useful feature of text chat is that it can provide learners with a non-threatening way to pose questions or communicate other needs with the instructor. Questions on the mind of one learner are often on the minds of others. If instructors aren't able to answer all questions during the allotted class time, they can usually save the text chat and respond to questions after class. Instructors can also use text chat to allow all learners to respond to a question or exercise. Participants can view all responses instantly. This is a valuable way for participants to share a wealth of ideas and information. Text chat can be more efficient for some exercises than using the virtual classroom white board tool. Text chat makes it easy for all involved to match responses with contributors, and no responses are overwritten or erased—which can be a risk with some white board tools.

In the virtual classroom, participants can be required to raise their hands before being granted the "mic" to speak. Even when this is not a technical requirement, hand-raising can be a useful etiquette. It can help to ensure that more learners' voices are heard, which can lead to greater sharing of ideas and experiences. This can be an advantage over the physical classroom, in which a few outspoken individuals can dominate discussions.

10,000 STUDENT HOURS OF INSTRUCTOR-LED DISTANCE LEARNING: LESSONS LEARNED

Steve Serbun, eLearning Technical Manager, Organization,
Bentley Systems, Incorporated

At Bentley System, Incorporated, we have been delivering instructor-led distance learning to AEC (architecture, engineering, and construction) professionals since 2005. We teach engineering software applications for the lifecycle of the world's infrastructure, transmitted via synchronous distance learning technology. In the past eighteen months, we have provided in excess of ten thousand student hours of training to over nine hundred participants.

Our challenge is to integrate instructional design with the application's features to create an effective and engaging interactive environment for the participants. Experience has shown that success is due to a combination of the presenter's experience with the tool and a feel for the session dynamics—how participants prefer to communicate.

Our delivery is unique in the live distance learning training environment in that our sessions are typically in four-hour increments. Our classes are offered on consecutive days for a total of eight to forty hours. This scheduling provides the flexibility of offering sessions in smaller chunks, as opposed to the typical full day, which we believe optimizes learning.

Some keys to success:

- Promote the medium by demonstrating its effectiveness.

- Certify instructors on the technology and best practices in distance learning, which are especially important in the early adoption stage.

- Utilize verbal and visual feedback to optimize participant interaction.
- Preparation, practice, and experience are the recipe for success.

As the person responsible for training colleagues globally, my thought process about the most effective distance learning training environment has evolved over time. I have conducted distance learning application and soft skills training worldwide to Bentley colleagues in China, Japan, India, Australia, New Zealand, the Middle East, and South America. The most common delivery method for training our instructors is synchronous technology.

Following are some lessons learned:

Lesson 1 Distance learning delivery is being driven by market demands for a more convenient way to learn collaboratively without geographical boundaries. Effective training programs must include this method of learning.

Lesson 2 Content presentation structure and technical proficiency are even more important to master in distance learning because they allow the instructor to be more flexible in handling the vagaries associated with this new medium.

Lesson 3 Although distance learning is effective, there are advantages to teaching instructors distance learning techniques face-to-face:

- Accelerates the learning curve
- Overcomes language barriers
- Accommodates localization issues

Is distance learning as effective as in-person training? Not yet. Is it an effective alternative? Absolutely!

Convenient access to learning, combined with participant learning motivation, mitigate any real or perceived issues with the instructional delivery method.

Chapter 1
Meet the New
Virtual Classroom

Introduction

Chapter 2
Learning
in the New VC

Chapter 3
Features to Exploit
in the New VC

Chapter 4
Teaching Content Types
in the New VC

Part 1: Learning and the New Virtual Classroom

Chapter 5
Visualize Your
Message

Chapter 6
Make It Active – Part 1

Chapter 7
Make It Active – Part 2

Part 2: Engaging Participants in the New Virtual Classroom

Chapter 8
Managing Mental Load
in the New VC

Chapter 9
Make a Good
First Impression

Chapter 10
Packaging Your
VC Session

Chapter 11
Problem-Based Learning
in the New VC

Part 3: Optimizing Your Virtual Events

Chapter 12
Getting Started

Part 4: Creating Effective Learning Events in the New Virtual Classroom

4

Teaching Content Types in the New Virtual Classroom

LEARNING IS SUPPORTED BY instructional methods such as examples, analogies, and practice exercises. But how do you know which instructional methods to use when? The types of instructional content associated with your learning goals or objectives will guide your selection of effective teaching methods. Five types of content commonly found in workplace training are facts, concepts, processes, procedures, and principles. For each of these types, we summarize the main instructional methods you can use to help students learn them, including specific guidelines for implementing those methods in the virtual classroom.

Match Teaching Methods to Content

In *Developing Technical Training* Clark (2007) describes instructional methods to teach five common types of content found in most organizational training programs. The content types (see Table 4.1) are *facts, concepts, processes, procedures,* and *principles.* Whether you are using self-study workbooks, e-learning, or classroom PowerPoint presentations, the same instructional methods are needed to teach these content types. What differs is how you implement an instructional method—which in turn depends on the

Table 4.1. Five Types of Instructional Content.	
Knowledge	*Skills/Tasks*
Concepts	Procedures
Facts	Principles
Processes	

features of your delivery medium. For example, let's consider the instructional method of demonstration. With print media, you can display visuals of the equipment or screen captures with text callouts. Alternatively, on a computer, a demonstration can be presented with animated visuals explained by audio narration.

In this chapter we define and give examples of each of the content types summarized in Table 4.1. We also show how to implement the instructional methods recommended for each type in the virtual classroom.

Two Types of Tasks: Procedures and Principle-Based

Cost-effective workforce training identifies and teaches work tasks that, when performed correctly, contribute to bottom-line organizational goals. For example, an important task in a customer service center is accurately applying company credit policies to new service plans. Effective completion of this task pays off directly in the financial health of the company with fewer defaulted payments.

Organizational work tasks are of two main types: *procedural* and *principle-based*. Procedural tasks, also known as *near-transfer* tasks, are step-by-step activities that are completed pretty much the same way each time. Sending an email and completing a customer order form are two common examples. Principle-based tasks, also known as *far-transfer* tasks, are made up of guidelines that are implemented a different way each time, depending on the context in which the task is performed. Handling a sales inquiry or conducting an employee performance review are two examples. When completing tasks such as these, workers will need to adjust task guidelines to the specific circumstances of the sales discussion or performance review.

Teaching Procedural Tasks

Procedural tasks are best taught by a step-by-step demonstration of how to perform the task, followed by guided hands-on practice with feedback. If your training includes a large number of procedures and practice time is limited, provide step-by-step working aids to guide performance after the training. If working aids are already available, trainers should help learners make use of them during the practice sessions to ensure their use in the workplace.

In some situations, the job requires procedures to be performed quickly, accurately, and without reference to working aids. Landing an airplane is one example. Touch typing is another. Learners will need to practice these types of skills until the steps are automatic. Automaticity requires hundreds of practice sessions. Once automatic, these tasks can be carried out quickly and accurately with almost no conscious effort, allowing the performer to use working memory capacity for other tasks. For example, as I type this page using my automated typing skills, I can devote working memory to expressing my ideas effectively.

Teaching Procedural Tasks in the Virtual Classroom

The virtual classroom is an excellent tool for teaching new computer procedures. A feature called *application sharing* allows the instructor to project a running application in a window and demonstrate step-by-step how to interact with the application screens. At the same time, participants can hear the instructor's explanations of the actions she is taking. In Chapter 3, Figure 3.6, we illustrated application sharing taken from our CD lesson on entering a formula into Excel.

The virtual classroom facilitator should perform the first demonstration by narrating each step she carries out in the application sharing window. It's often a good idea to add memory support to the application screen to guide the demonstration. For example, in our Excel demonstration shown in Figure 3.6, we placed a brief text summary of the calculation goal and a reminder of formula formatting rules on the spreadsheet.

After the first demonstration, involve your participants in a second demonstration. For example, you might call on different learners to direct your steps via audio or you might ask everyone to type into the chat window what steps you should take next. Alternatively, the facilitator can turn control of the application over to different participants, each of whom will perform one or two steps of the procedure. The other participants can critique the steps of the active participant using direct messaging. For example, in Figure 4.1, taken from our CD demonstration lesson on Excel, the instructor has given control of the application to Cynthia, who walks the class through the procedure.

After the demonstration phase, each participant needs individual hands-on practice with the application. If the application resides on each participant's desktop, the facilitator can ask participants to complete an assigned task on their own computers. For example, in the Excel training, spreadsheets with data already entered were emailed to each participant. Multiple pages in the spreadsheet included diverse data along with calculation assignments. Participants were asked to calculate specified values and write down the formula they used. They were directed to return to the virtual classroom at a specified time and to type their answers into direct messaging. For individuals with questions or incorrect answers, the facilitator demonstrated the correct procedure by giving control of the application to the participant while providing guidance.

Figure 4.1. Control of the Application Is Passed to a Participant.
From the Excel lesson example on *The New Virtual Classroom* CD.

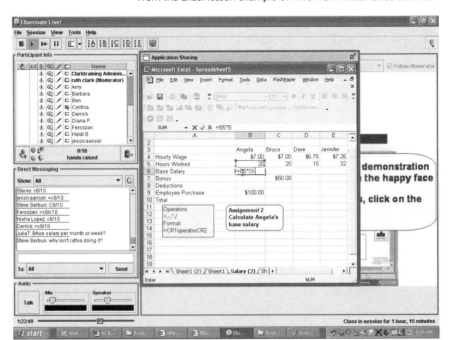

To demonstrate gathering customer information in a telephone interview, the facilitator can ask one of the participants to play the role of the customer while the facilitator interviews the "customer" and enters the information into the shared application. For practice, the facilitator can set up breakout rooms in which pairs take turns playing the customer and the customer service representative.

If fast and accurate performance is needed before tackling real work assignments, learners need drill-type practice to build automaticity. *Asynchronous* e-learning programs offer the best learning environment for drill and practice. Software simulations offer individual learners multiple opportunities to practice until their responses are both fast and error-free.

Procedures that involve learning to operate equipment other than computers can be demonstrated in the virtual classroom. For example, line drawings, photographs, or video clips supplemented with facilitator explanations can illustrate procedures. However, in most cases hands-on practice with the actual equipment will be needed. Until virtual reality technology is more widely available, learning to manipulate devices other than computers is best reserved for face-to-face learning environments.

Teaching Principle-Based Tasks

Principle-based or far-transfer tasks require a different instructional approach than procedural tasks. Since the guidelines of far-transfer tasks must be adapted uniquely to each work situation, learners need to see demonstrations of how far-transfer tasks are performed in diverse circumstances. In addition, they will need practice applying the guidelines to different scenarios. Unlike procedural tasks, there will rarely be a single correct approach to a far-transfer task. Instead, the instructor will have to make a judgment about whether the learner's actions or task outcomes fall within an acceptable range.

Because there is a range of potentially effective approaches to far-transfer tasks, these tasks are especially amenable to practice in group settings. Working in a group offers opportunities for multiple perspectives that can be integrated into the solutions. This work can be accomplished in breakout rooms and/or outside the virtual classroom. In some cases, far-transfer tasks require considerable time and reflection to complete and to debrief. Designing a web page is one example. Preparing a financial investment plan for specific clients is another. When time and reflection will benefit learning, asynchronous self-paced media permit learners to work independently at their own rates to complete assignments.

Teaching Principle-Based Tasks in the Virtual Classroom

Begin teaching far-transfer tasks by describing and illustrating the guidelines of the task. To make the lesson most interactive, consider an inductive teaching sequence. Start by showing demonstrations of the task being executed or examples of task products. Imagine, for example, that you are teaching some kind of design task—designing a website perhaps. Begin the lesson by assigning small groups to visit three to five designated websites and in the process make a list of effective and ineffective features. Students could do this activity in the virtual classroom using breakout rooms and the web tour facility. Alternatively, participants could view the websites individually as a pre-class activity and discuss their findings in breakout rooms during the virtual classroom session. As each team summarizes its findings in the main room, the facilitator synthesizes common guidelines by typing them on the white board. At this point, the facilitator can present guidelines or a process for website design, asking participants which guidelines or phases were applied to the various sites they visited. Finally, teams would be assigned a scenario for designing a website. Since this activity is likely to require time and reflection, it is best completed partially or entirely outside of the virtual classroom. The instructor provides each team with a website design case study and a worksheet with a design process and assigns a specified time to post the product. Prior to the next virtual classroom meeting, teams post their products and critique one or two other teams' products. In a subsequent virtual classroom session, teams are responsible for providing a critique of a different team's product. If time permits, each team could then revise its draft products based on the feedback received.

Although we used the example of website design, you can apply these techniques to any far-transfer task and task outcome. If your focus is on interpersonal skills, then your samples can be provided using video or audio recordings and your practice will be role plays that can be recorded and reviewed by the entire class. If your focus is on problem solving such as troubleshooting, your samples can be recordings of talk-aloud diagnostic sequences and your practice will be case-study problems.

You can see an example of a far-transfer virtual classroom lesson on identifying business goals during needs assessments on our CD. In Figure 4.2, we illustrate the definitions of a business goal participants typed into the chat window after viewing some valid and invalid business goals. Following this introduction to business goals, participants prepare for an interview by using private chat to discuss with a partner questions they would ask. Participants then view a video interview displayed in the multimedia window and work in breakout rooms to identify the business goals described during the interview.

Teaching Processes

A process is a flow of activities among different individuals, business units, or equipment components. A hiring process, for example, typically involves managers who define job skill requirements, HR personnel who advertise and screen

Figure 4.2. Following a Series of Examples, Participants Define Business Goals in the Chat Window.

From the Defining Business Goals sample on *The New Virtual Classroom* CD.

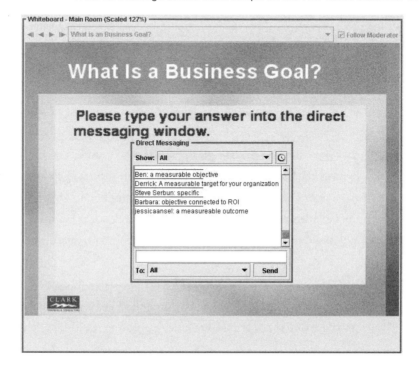

applicants, and supervisors or HR specialists who interview and make hiring decisions. A mechanical process involves the different components of a piece of equipment and the state changes of those components from initiation to completion of the mechanical activity. How a hydraulic braking system works is an example of a mechanical process. Scientific processes focus on events in the natural world, such as photosynthesis, digestion, and evolution.

Process knowledge is needed by anyone involved in part of a process or anyone responsible for maintaining or improving a process. For example, managers need to know their organizations' performance appraisal process so they understand how their roles fit into the larger picture. Repair technicians need to understand how their equipment works under normal conditions in order to link symptoms to probable failures.

Instructional Methods for Processes

Present processes with a series of visuals showing the flow of activities from start to finish. The visuals may be still pictures, animations, or video clips. Explain the process stages with audio narration. After the process is explained, ask participants to practice by applying process knowledge in ways that it would be applied on the job. For example, equipment failure scenarios could be presented and participants could be asked what internal components are likely to have failed. Or "What if?" scenarios can be used to prompt participants to identify what stages of a process may have failed or been omitted. For example, in teaching a hiring process, the instructor might ask: "What if Sally files a discrimination lawsuit because she was not hired for the position? What specific aspects of the hiring process might have been deficient?"

Depending on the complexity of the process and the degree of detail needed by workers, lessons may begin with high-level processes, followed by lessons that zoom into each stage in more detail. For example, a lesson on the entire instructional design process might be followed by individual lessons on each stage, such as a lesson on needs analysis, a lesson on task analysis, and so on.

Teaching Processes in the Virtual Classroom

Use the white board to show diagrams that illustrate the process. Explain the flow and outcomes at each stage with audio narration while using the cueing tools to focus attention to the particular stage you are discussing. For example, in Figure 4.3, pulled from our CD demonstration lesson, the instructor uses a box to draw attention to one stage in a needs assessment process. If participants are familiar with the process, ask them to describe their own experiences with various stages. You might ask, for example, "In your organization, who is responsible for conducing needs assessments? Mark, how about in your organization?"

Following the presentation and discussion, post some "What if?" questions on the white board and use polling, chat, or audio for responses. Invite discussion and alternative points of view.

Teaching Supporting Knowledge

There are two main types of knowledge that workers need in order to perform tasks or to understand processes. These are *facts* and *concepts*. Several recent research studies have shown that, to avoid overloading learners with all of the

---

Figure 4.3. The Instructor Uses a Flow Diagram to Explain a Needs Assessment Process.

From the Business Goals Lesson on *The New Virtual Classroom* CD.

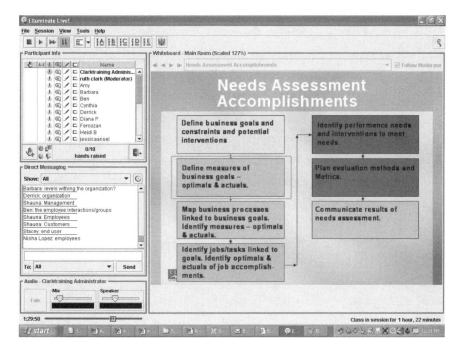

content at once, it is best to teach major supporting knowledge topics separately from the task steps, task guidelines, or the process stages (Clark, Nguyen, & Sweller, 2006). For example, if you are teaching the process of how a hydraulic brake works, before explaining the process flow, teach the name and actions of each component in the braking process. Or if you are teaching a task such as how to construct a hiring interview questionnaire, teach related knowledge such as "what is a legal question" before presenting the interview guidelines.

What Are Facts and Concepts?

Facts are unique, specific information needed to perform a task. For example, to log onto a system, a specific user name and password are commonly needed facts. When learning a new computer program, the appearance of the screens and fields are factual information. When teaching a mechanical process, the name of each component involved is a fact.

In contrast, concepts are single words that represent classes of items—all of which share common core features but differ on irrelevant features. For example, the term "chair" is a concept. Just about all chairs share the following features: (1) a back, (2) a seat, (3) a support to the floor, and (4) intended for one sitter. Some of the variable features of chairs include color, presence of arms, and type of support to the floor, such as rocker, legs, and so on. Table 4.2 shows examples of concepts and related facts.

Most task steps and guidelines, as well as process stages, reference many concepts. Concepts that are new to participants should be explained separately from the task itself. For example, if a step in a credit establishment procedure states: "Determine whether the applicant has a good payment record," the learner would need to know the concept of a payment record and what distinguishes a good record from a poor one.

Table 4.2. Examples of Facts Versus Concepts.

	Examples	
Concepts	Historical Figures	Fictional Characters
Facts	George Washington	The Easter Bunny
	Rosa Parks	Luke Skywalker

Presenting Factual Information

In most cases, facts that are essential to complete a task or understand a concept can be presented "just in time" when the learner is about to perform the step. Often, facts need not be memorized but can be provided in some type of reference support. For example, in an Excel demonstration, the instructor posts a small box on a spreadsheet that summarizes the correct operator symbols to use in an Excel formula. If, in contrast, workers need to access facts from memory, they can memorize them on the job through repeated use or in training through drill-and-practice exercises.

Teaching Concepts

Concepts linked to job tasks or processes, in general, should be taught separately from the task or process. For example, before learning a hydraulic braking process, present the names and actions of each component. In a research study, students studying a lesson that taught **concepts first** learned more than another group of students studying a lesson that presented concepts and process stages together (Mayer, 2005b).

To teach a concept, provide a definition that includes the key attributes of that concept and then illustrate the concept with several examples. Use text and visuals on the white board to display the definition and examples. For example, when teaching the concept of a formula in Excel, the facilitator places two examples on the white board and explains that all formulas start with an equal sign and can include cell references (a separate concept), numbers, and mathematical operators (another concept). As the facilitator presents the concept, she uses white board cueing tools to point out key attributes in the two examples.

As with far-transfer tasks, concepts lend themselves to an inductive teaching approach. Rather than simply stating the attributes of a concept, the facilitator can show several examples and ask participants to identify common attributes. For example, in our Excel lesson on the CD, the instructor shows two examples of Excel formulas and asks participants to type into chat what they notice about how all formulas begin.

After presenting definitions and examples, assign practice exercises to help learners identify new instances of the concept. Concept exercises present several new valid and invalid instances of the concept and ask learners to identify the valid examples. In our sample lesson on identifying business goals on *The New Virtual Classroom* CD, the definitions of a business goal typed into chat (shown in Figure 4.2) were based on several sample goals that had been previously shown by the instructor. You may want to include practice after teaching each concept or present several related concepts and then assign practice that includes multiple concepts.

Teaching Concepts in the Virtual Classroom

Begin your lesson with an overview of the process or task you will be teaching. Follow the overview with topics that teach key concepts needed to perform the task or understand the process. Use the white board to display concept features and show examples. Concrete concepts, which have parts and boundaries, can be illustrated with graphics. Some examples of concrete concepts include website navigational schemes, tool bars, and Excel formulas. More abstract concepts such as "operational goal" or "integrity" will likely require text-based illustrations. Follow the definitions and examples with a practice session that asks learners to identify valid instances of the concept. You could use polling, chat, circling, or matching on the white board for this type of exercise.

Pulling Your Lesson Together

Many virtual classroom lessons are designed to teach participants how to perform a new task or how to apply a new process to their work routines. In your job analysis, begin by writing out the steps for procedural tasks and the guidelines for principle-based tasks. As you review the main tasks, identify any processes that would help learners to perform the tasks more effectively. For example, if the main task is to "troubleshoot equipment X," a related process is "how equipment X works" in normal operations.

Your next step is to identify important supporting facts or conceptual topics. Teach important related concepts before teaching the tasks or processes. Following your virtual classroom session introduction, teach important concepts by presenting the attributes along with examples, or alternatively by asking participants to derive attributes from several examples. Follow with practice that requires participants to identify new valid instances of each concept. Next teach the key tasks of the lesson—presenting demonstrations followed by task practice. Teach most facts just in time—providing reference support when and where those facts are needed to perform a task. End your lesson with a summary.

Some task practice may be best reserved for asynchronous individual or group work outside of the virtual classroom. For example, if procedures need to be performed quickly and accurately from memory, assign individual drill-and-practice sessions in an asynchronous environment. Practice assignments that require time and reflection are also often better tackled outside of the virtual classroom environment. A summary of these methods is provided in Table 4.3.

The Bottom Line

No matter what medium you are using, the methods for teaching the five common content types of facts, concepts, processes, procedures, or principles are the same. You will need to adapt these instructional methods to the features of your delivery medium, as we illustrated with the virtual classroom. We will build on these ideas in the next chapters on graphics and interactions.

Table 4.3. A Summary of Methods to Teach Content Types.

	Procedure	*Principle*	*Process*	*Concept*	*Fact*
Present content	Steps	Guidelines	Stages	Definition	Data
Give real-life example	Demonstration	Demonstration in varying scenarios	Example of how to use process knowledge on the job	Multiple examples	Illustration of fact
Let student practice	Hands-on application of steps	Hands-on application of guidelines	Trouble shoot process-related problems	Identify valid examples	Apply as needed with other types of content

COMING NEXT:
VISUALIZE YOUR MESSAGE

The virtual classroom, with its predominant white board, cries out for visuals to illustrate content. Too often virtual classrooms project only walls of words, thus failing to harness the potential of graphics for learning. Alternatively, they present irrelevant visuals, which may depress learning. In Chapter 5 we offer evidence-based guidelines for selection, treatment, and presentation of visuals in the virtual classroom.

On *The New Virtual Classroom* CD

The CD includes three lessons: one that focuses on a procedure and two that focus on principle-based tasks.

The lesson on How to Construct a Formula in Excel illustrates how to teach a procedure, preceded by teaching of major related concepts and facts such as formulas and formula formatting rules.

The lesson on How to Define Business Goals focuses on teaching of guidelines applied in interviews as part of a needs assessment. This lesson illustrates how to teach principle-based guidelines preceded by teaching of major related concepts, including business goals.

The third demonstration focuses on another far-transfer (principle-based) skill—how to plan an interview. This lesson uses a guided-discovery architecture introduced in Chapter 2 and discussed in detail in Chapter 11.

For More Information

Clark, R. C. (2007). *Developing technical training.* San Francisco, CA: Pfeiffer.

Foshay, W. R., Silber, K. H., & Stelnicki, M. B. (2003). *Writing training materials that work.* San Francisco, CA: Pfeiffer.

Mayer, R. E. (2005). Principles for managing essential processing in multimedia learning: Segmenting, pretraining, and modality principles. In R. E. Mayer (Ed.), *The Cambridge handbook of multimedia learning.* New York: Cambridge University Press.

EXPERT'S FORUM

MIXING LEARNER BACKGROUNDS IN THE VIRTUAL CLASSROOM

Pamela Stern, Learning and Performance Consultant

I was first exposed to virtual work through participating in my doctoral program in 2003 and first designed for the virtual classroom in 2004. At the same time, I began to design for clients using the virtual classroom blended with e-learning. In my various assignments, I have worked with HP's Virtual Classroom, Macromedia's Breeze platform, and NetMeeting and have successfully experienced Icohere's virtual learning community/classroom, but I have not used it to design learning.

The virtual classroom enables people who are not co-located to learn together. Participants can learn together as well as model others' behaviors while remaining in their own work context. This communal behavior promotes learning and, as in a face-to-face classroom, gives meaning to working with others who have similar goals for learning—whether the learner is new to a job and learning the tasks for the first time or is considered an expert.

When working with a group of distributed computer technicians, I learned that the virtual classroom can allow a mixed audience of experts and less-skilled workers to learn successfully together. The experts were initially unhappy because they were expected to attend a computer maintenance course whose content they felt they already knew. They complained because they thought the course was not designed with them in mind. However, when the expert technicians joined the virtual class and the facilitator used the course to promote work group projects, rather than delivering a straight lecture, their opinions changed. The course allowed the expert participants to work together and share their experiences with the novices. The course materials included both procedure and principle-based tasks. The course exercises called on the higher-level customer communication skills of the experts, allowing their experience to provide a model for the less-skilled participants.

When sharing their learning experiences with others, both expert and less-skilled participants reported that, as a result of the training, they were better able to collaborate on problem solving with their co-workers. Their satisfaction increased, as did their ability to mentor others.

Chapter 1
Meet the New
Virtual Classroom

Introduction

Chapter 2
Learning
in the New VC

Chapter 3
Features to Exploit
in the New VC

Chapter 4
Teaching Content Types
in the New VC

Part 1: Learning and the New Virtual Classroom

Chapter 5
Visualize Your
Message

Chapter 6
Make It Active – Part 1

Chapter 7
Make It Active – Part 2

Part 2: Engaging Participants in the New Virtual Classroom

Chapter 8
Managing Mental Load
in the New VC

Chapter 9
Make a Good
First Impression

Chapter 10
Packaging Your
VC Session

Chapter 11
Problem-Based Learning
in the New VC

Part 3: Optimizing Your Virtual Events

Chapter 12
Getting Started

Part 4: Creating Effective Learning Events in the New Virtual Classroom

Engaging Participants in the New Virtual Classroom

ENGAGEMENT IS at the heart of successful virtual classroom learning. In this part, we will discuss the following topics.

Chapter 5: The research and guidelines to harness the visual features of the virtual classroom.

Chapter 6: The research and guidelines to harness the response features of the virtual classroom.

Chapter 7: How to maximize participant engagement in the virtual classroom by involving more participants more of the time.

Chapter 1
Meet the New
Virtual Classroom

Introduction

Chapter 2
Learning
in the New VC

Chapter 3
Features to Exploit
in the New VC

Chapter 4
Teaching Content Types
in the New VC

Part 1: Learning and the New Virtual Classroom

Chapter 5
Visualize Your
Message

Chapter 6
Make It Active – Part 1

Chapter 7
Make It Active – Part 2

Part 2: Engaging Participants in the New Virtual Classroom

Chapter 8
Managing Mental Load
in the New VC

Chapter 9
Make a Good
First Impression

Chapter 10
Packaging Your
VC Session

Chapter 11
Problem-Based Learning
in the New VC

Part 3: Optimizing Your Virtual Events

Chapter 12
Getting Started

Part 4: Creating Effective Learning Events in the New Virtual Classroom

5

Visualize Your Message

THE WHITE BOARD PREDOMINATES in the virtual classroom inter-face. When the white board is underutilized, valuable instructional opportu-nities are lost. Presentations that rely predominantly on text fail to engage and teach as effectively as appropriate visual representations. Alternatively, slides that incorporate too many decorative or unrelated thematic visuals do not contribute to learning and may even depress learning.

In this chapter we offer proven guidelines for selection, treatment, and pre-sentation of visuals in the virtual classroom to include:

- Virtual classroom facilities to display visuals
- Seven communication functions of graphics
- Visual treatments to support seven psychological learning events
- Design guidelines for adapting visuals to the virtual classroom interface

Visualizing Content in the Virtual Classroom

Modern virtual classroom technology offers you multiple features to present still and animated graphics, summarized in Figure 5.1.

In previous chapters, you have seen a number of examples of the white board displaying PowerPoint slides. The application sharing feature shown in Figure 3.6 launches a window in which the facilitator can demonstrate desktop applications. Video clips can be projected through a multimedia window. For example, Figure 5.2 from our business goals lesson on *The New Virtual Classroom* CD shows a screen shot from our video interview. Web tour facilities offer another visual resource in the virtual classroom. When the instructor launches a web tour, all participants can see websites of interest, as shown in Figure 5.3.

Unlike the face-to-face classroom, where physical presence pervades the learning environment, e-learning—both synchronous and asynchronous—is much more dominated by screen images. Visuals are one of your main tools to engage learners, communicate content, convey instructional methods, and promote active learning!

Working in any highly visual medium such as video or e-learning requires greater visual literacy skills than working in traditional text-based

---

Figure 5.1. Virtual Classroom Features to Display Visuals.

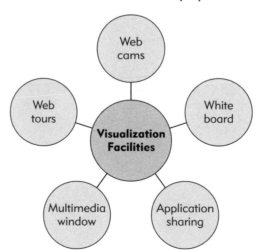

Figure 5.2. The Multimedia Window Is Used to Display Video Clips.

From the Business Goals lesson on *The New Virtual Classroom* CD.

Figure 5.3. The Web Tour Feature.

With permission of © Microsoft Corporation—Microsoft is a
registered trademark of Microsoft Corporation.

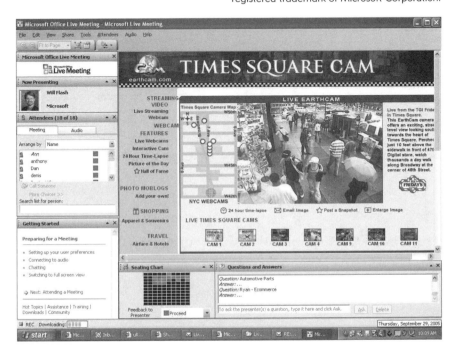

media. Most instructional professionals have devoted years to developing and refining their verbal skills—both written and oral. But typically, they have devoted little or no time to expressing ideas visually. Therefore, using the visualization features available in the virtual classroom may challenge those who are inexperienced with highly visual media. In this chapter, we offer some research-based guidelines on the best kinds of visuals you can use to promote your instructional goals.

Visuals and Learning

In Chapter 3 we presented evidence that visuals carry psychological clout. Visuals immediately attract attention and can either significantly promote or depress learning. Fletcher and Tobias (2005) and Clark and Mayer (2003) summarize research proving that multimedia images relevant to the instructional goal greatly improve learning, while visuals added for entertainment or interest can depress learning. What kinds of visuals are most relevant for learning purposes?

Three Views of Visuals

Clark and Lyons (2004) describe three different ways you can categorize visuals based on their *surface features, communication functions,* and *psychological functions.* We recommend that you look beyond a visual's surface features, such as whether it is a photograph, a line drawing, or a video, and consider its functional features. In the next section, we illustrate the communication functions of visuals in the virtual classroom, as summarized in Figure 5.4.

The Seven Communication Functions of Visuals

A very large proportion of visuals in instructional materials serve no useful learning function (Mayer, Sims, & Tajika, 1995; Woodward, 1993). Many

Figure 5.4. Communication Functions of Visuals.

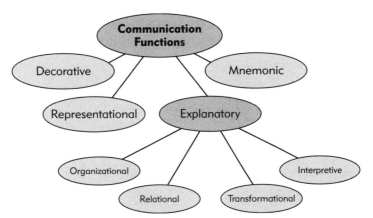

useless visuals fall into the category of *decorative*. Decorative visuals are used either for "aesthetic" purposes or to add interest or humor to a screen or page. Decorative visuals overly predominate in instructional materials because (1) they are easier to plan and access from clip art sources than other types of visuals, which often require customized art, and (2) viewers find screens or pages that contain visuals more attractive, even if the visual is irrelevant to the learning purpose. We recommend that you minimize the use of decorative graphics in lieu of the other communication types summarized in the next paragraphs.

Representational visuals show learners what an object looks like. Examples include software screen captures, photographs of equipment, and/or line drawings of products. These kinds of visuals are common in training designed to teach operations or troubleshooting of equipment or computer applications. The visual in Figure 3.6 incorporates a representational graphic of a spreadsheet as part of a demonstration using application sharing.

Mnemonic visuals are designed to aid memory. Most of us recall verbal mnemonics such as Every Good Boy Does Fine to represent the notes on the treble staff lines in sheet music. Visual mnemonics are also powerful tools to aid recall of factual information. In many corporate training programs, factual information can be accessed from physical or online memory aids. Therefore, memorization of facts is not necessary and there is often less need for mnemonic visuals in workforce learning.

The remaining four communication types fall under the general heading of *explanatory* visuals. These include *organizational, relational, transformational,* and *interpretive* visuals. Explanatory visuals are especially powerful for learning purposes because they help learners form relationships among lesson topics.

Organizational graphics illustrate qualitative relationships among content topics and are very useful as overviews and orienting visuals. Figure 5.4 is an organizational visual designed to show the relationships among the seven communication functions of visuals. Use organizational graphics to show coordinate (peer) and subordinate (child) relationships among related content topics in your courses or lessons.

Relational graphics illustrate quantitative relationships in the form of pie charts, bar graphs, and other diagrams that summarize numeric data. As a lead-in to our lesson on business goals on *The New Virtual Classroom* CD, we use a pie chart to illustrate the distribution of annual training expenditures. Many virtual classroom tools allow the facilitator to display the results of a polling question in a bar graph format. This is an excellent way to visually illustrate overall trends in polling responses from large groups. You can see an example in Figure 3.7.

Transformational visuals show changes over time or space. In our Excel demonstration lesson on the CD, you will see a transformational visual in the application sharing window used to demonstrate how to work with a spreadsheet. The application sharing and multimedia features in virtual classrooms are useful to show animations that illustrate a mechanical, business, or scientific process as well as procedural demonstrations.

However, you do not necessarily need animations to convey transformational content. Research has shown that a series of still diagrams with arrows can promote learning of mechanical systems as effectively as an animation (Hegarty, Narayanan, & Freitas, 2002). Hegarty (2005) summarizes over twenty studies that compared learning from static and animated graphics, concluding that "there was no advantage of animations over static graphics" (p. 456). The key to effective use of animations lies in matching the functions and features of the animation (for example, use of effects such as cueing, slow motion, and so on) to your instructional content (for example, procedures versus principle-based tasks) and to your learner's background knowledge (Hegarty, 2004). We are still learning about the conditions under which animations are most effective for learning.

One of the drawbacks to animated visuals is the amount of mental load they impose on learners because they convey a great deal of visual information in a transient manner. You may want to consider a series of still shots in place of or before using an animation. For example, consider the transformational visual shown in Figure 5.5. The instructor has used a series of still screen shots to show a navigation sequence through the Outlook application. Although she could have used application sharing, several still visuals offer a comprehensive view of the inter-relationships among the screens, as well as ample time to review the sequence. If you would like to employ this technique, start by describing a series of cued screen captures, as shown in Figure 5.5, and follow up with an animated demonstration using application sharing.

Figure 5.5.　Use of Several Still Shots in Place of Animations.
With permission from Kathy Fallow from Vertex Solutions.

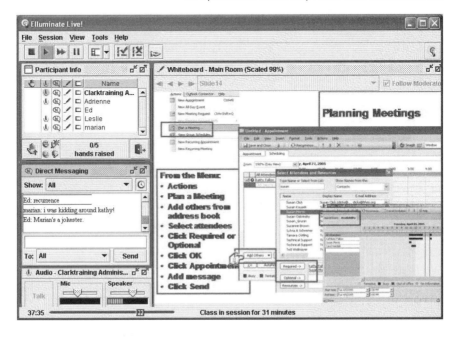

Interpretive visuals illustrate a theory or cause-and-effect relationships. Often interpretive visuals are used to make invisible or abstract processes or relationships concrete. Interpretive visuals are common in lessons teaching scientific content. Research summarized by Clark and Lyons (2004) shows that interpretive visuals improve learning of cause-and-effect relationships more effectively than do representational visuals of the content elements. In Figure 5.6 we show an interpretive visual illustrating a statistical probability formula. By

---

Figure 5.6. An Interpretive Illustration to Represent a Statistics Formula.
From Renkl, 2005.

1. Bicycle

You and your friend take part in a two-day mountain bike course. For each day of the course the instructor brings five helmets, with each one having a different color (green, blue, yellow, red, and silver). The helmets are handed out randomly and given back to the instructor at the end of each day. On both of the days, you are the first and your friend is the second one to get a helmet.

What is the probability that you get the blue helmet and your friend gets the green helmet on the first day of the course?

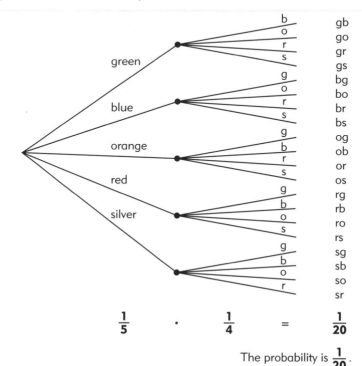

providing a visual and a mathematical representation, learner understanding is improved. Use interpretive visuals for concepts and principles.

The seven communication functions are not mutually exclusive. A transformational visual usually includes a number of representational graphics. A transformational visual may also serve an interpretive function. Use the communication categories as a tool to enable you to plan more powerful visuals for your virtual classroom lessons.

Use Visual Treatments That Support Learning Events

Use the instructional components (modes, methods, and architectures) in the virtual classroom to support one or more of the learning events summarized in Chapter 2. The six basic learning events include support for attention, activation of prior knowledge, management of cognitive load, building of new mental models, transfer of learning, and motivation. Here we show you how to use visuals in the virtual classroom to support these events.

Support Attention with Graphic Treatments

When displaying a complex visual, focus attention by using any of the cueing tools available in the white board. A complex visual may be a representational graphic with several elements, such as a diagram of a car engine. Animated visuals and video are almost always complex because they involve multiple visuals displayed quickly over time. Most virtual classroom tools offer a number of white board facilities for cueing of still visuals. These tools include boxes you can draw around elements of your graphic, highlighting, and movable pointers in various shapes. In Figure 5.5 the instructor shows a series of screens to illustrate a navigational sequence. As she describes each phase of the navigation, she uses a red box and hand pointer to direct attention to the relevant part of the screen.

When using visual features other than the white board, such as application sharing, you will typically not have access to the white board cueing tools and will need to look into the application itself for cueing resources. For example, when demonstrating formulas during application sharing of Excel, we used the mouse pointer in Excel as a cueing device.

Use diverse cueing elements liberally when displaying complex visuals such as the one in Figure 5.5, since cognitive load is greater in instructor-paced environments than in self-study venues, where learners can review visuals at their own pace.

In addition to focusing attention, you should discourage divided attention in your graphic treatments. Divided attention occurs when related content is physically separated in the instructional interface, such as when a visual and text related to that visual are in different locations on the screen. Instead, place text labels or descriptions close to their visual referents.

Activate Prior Knowledge with Visuals

Learning is based on the integration of new content into existing knowledge structures activated from long-term memory into working memory. Course and lesson introductions facilitate this process when they provide activities or content that brings relevant information out from long-term memory into conscious awareness. Lesson reviews serve this purpose, as do introductory metaphors and analogies that link new knowledge to existing mental models.

Interpretive visuals that concretize abstract ideas or theories may activate prior knowledge when they use images familiar to the participants. For example, in a biology lesson on peristalsis (movement of digested food through the intestines), the instructor used a visual of an individual ketchup packet in which the ketchup was being extruded by a thumb exerting pressure from one end of the packet toward the opening.

Representational or transformational visuals drawn from prior participant experience—either from previous lessons or from the work environment—can also activate prior knowledge. For example, our Excel lesson on the CD starts with a brief interactive review of cell references using screen captures of spreadsheets.

Use Visual Treatments That Minimize Cognitive Load

As we've stated previously, any instructor-paced learning environment, such as the virtual classroom, imposes greater cognitive load than self-paced media.

In *Efficiency in Learning* (2006) Clark, Nguyen, and Sweller explain a number of cognitive load principles that should be applied to all learning environments. Here we summarize two of these as they apply to visuals in the virtual classroom.

Use Audio to Explain Visuals   Learning is better when a complex visual, especially moving images, are explained with audio rather than with text. Instructional psychologists call this the *modality principle.* The modality principle works because dividing content between the auditory and visual centers of working memory optimizes limited memory capacity. In the virtual classroom, the instructor applies the modality principle when she verbally explains a (visual) demonstration displayed with the application sharing facility.

Less Is More   Provide learners only the minimum needed for understanding. It's a still prevalent myth that it's better to explain visuals with a combination of text and audio. In fact, offering content in redundant modes overloads working memory and slows learning. According to the *redundancy principle,* when you display a visual, you should explain it with audio only. Do not add redundant text that is a repetition of the audio.

In keeping with the less-is-more principle, omit extraneous visual noise in your graphics. Often a simple line graphic will be more effective than a photograph, for example. As we mentioned previously, avoid a Las Vegas approach to learning by minimizing decorative visuals that attract attention but do not contribute to learning.

Use Graphics That Build Mental Models

Developing new mental models in long-term memory is the goal of all instruction. Explanatory graphics are especially useful for building mental models, since they illustrate relationships among content elements. For example, the interpretive visual shown in Figure 5.6 helps learners understand the mathematical formula for calculating probability. As another example, in Figure 5.4 we used a concept map to show qualitative relationships among the communication functions of visuals.

Engage participants in your visuals! For example, when showing bar charts of polling data, don't interpret the charts for your participants. Instead, ask them to type their conclusions into the chat window or to discuss their ideas with audio. Figure 5.7, taken from the business goals demonstration lesson on the CD, illustrates the use of a white board visual to promote active learner processing of a video clip. A screen grab from the video interview is displayed on the white board. After viewing the video, participants have typed into the bubbles what the interviewer and respondent are thinking at the stopping point in the interview. Research shows that learning from visuals is greater when learners actively work with the visuals in meaningful ways. In Chapter 7 you will learn more guidelines on ways to engage learners in the virtual classroom.

Use Visuals That Transfer Learning

All resources invested in training are wasted when transfer fails. For factual and procedural content, transfer is best when you use representational visuals that mirror the work environment. When teaching a computer

Figure 5.7. Plan Visuals That Engage Learners.
From the Business Goals lesson on *The New Virtual Classroom* CD.

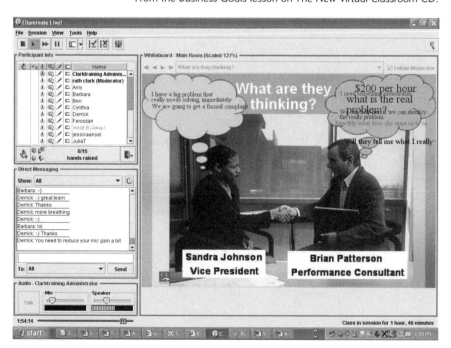

application, learners need to see and practice with the screens in job-realistic scenarios.

For concepts and principles, the transfer challenge is more complex. The most important transfer technique for concepts and principles is multiple diverse contexts to serve as examples as well as for practice exercises. For example, when teaching how to construct formulas for spreadsheets, show a variety of formulas used to calculate diverse work-related scenarios, such as sales totals by region, take-home pay after taxes, and inventory changes over time.

Use Graphics That Motivate and Don't Detract

As a countermeasure to high dropout rates in e-learning courses, instructional professionals often fall into a trap of relying on decorative visuals or exotic thematic graphics to add interest. Research by Harp and Mayer (1997, 1998), described in Chapter 3, underscores the dangers of these types of visuals. They may be motivational. However, decorative visuals can detract from learning by distracting learners from the core instructional content, by loading working memory with irrelevant data, or by interfering with the building of the right mental models in long-term memory.

You need to use visuals that motivate but at the same time do not disrupt the other psychological events we've discussed. First, select visuals that communicate the relevance of the lesson content. Second, use visuals that facilitate the psychological learning events we have summarized in Chapter 2. For example, an organizational visual such as the one shown in Figure 5.4 or an interactive visual such as Figure 5.7 will aid learners in building of mental models. As Harp and Mayer (1997) conclude: "The best way to help students enjoy a passage is to help them understand it" (p. 100).

Design Visuals That Work in the Virtual Classroom Interface

Keep in mind that the interface real estate devoted to your visual is smaller in the virtual classroom compared to the face-to-face classroom or even most asynchronous e-learning, in which much of the computer screen can be filled with an image. Synchronous participants are typically viewing your visuals in a white board that uses only a fraction of the interface. Therefore, a visual that might project effectively on a screen in a physical classroom may not display as well in your virtual classroom environment.

Plan visuals that are simple, and avoid slide templates that consume a great deal of screen real estate, leaving little room for your meaningful images. If you have complex graphics, split them among several slides using a build or overlay technique. This change of scenery will have the additional advantage of holding learner attention. When you show text on the white board, the font size should be no smaller than 16 points. For instance, the visual in Figure 5.8 is too complex and uses too much tiny text.

The Bottom Line

A visual can be worth a thousand words when well conceived and effectively designed for the content and the delivery medium! When planning virtual classroom presentations, think visually and emphasize explanatory

Figure 5.8. Too Much Tiny Text and Small Visuals Are Ineffective on the White Board.

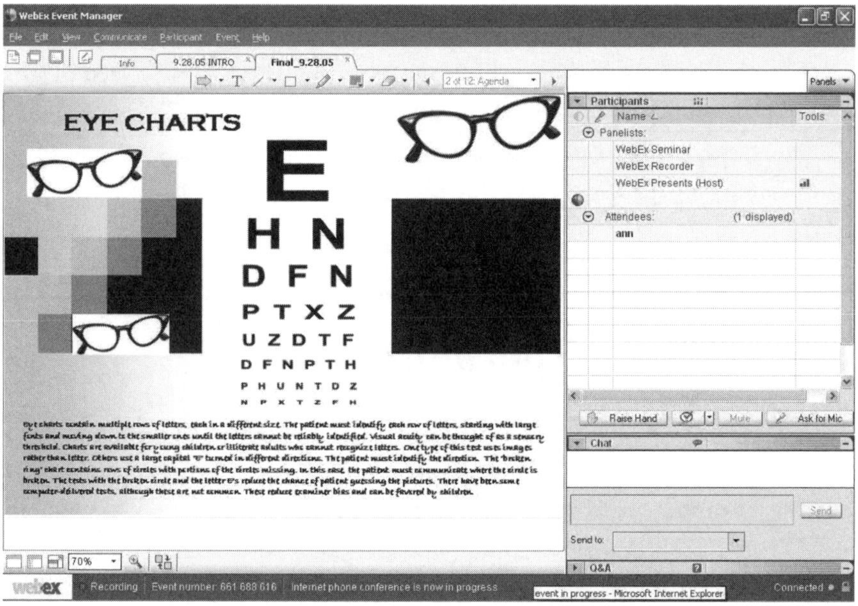

graphics in lieu of decorative visuals that do not serve any instructional purpose.

COMING NEXT:
MAKE IT ACTIVE: PLANNING INTERACTIONS
IN THE NEW VIRTUAL CLASSROOM

No matter how you approach your virtual classroom sessions, if you do nothing else, be sure to make your sessions learner-centered! Active learner participation is so critical to success in the virtual classroom that we devote the next two chapters to techniques and examples for productive interactivity. In Chapter 6 we overview the response options available to you in the virtual classroom, discuss tradeoffs among them, and describe four basic types of interactions you can use: demographic, behavioral, attitudinal, and knowledge.

On *The New Virtual Classroom* CD

The demonstration lessons use most of the visual categories we have discussed in this chapter. The Excel formula lesson uses the white board and application sharing to project representational and transformational visuals of formulas and spreadsheets. The principle-based lessons (Defining Business Goals and How to Plan an Interview) make use of the white board and the multimedia player to project explanatory visuals and an illustrative video.

For More Information

Clark, R. C., & Lyons, C (2004). *Graphics for learning*. San Francisco: Pfeiffer.

EXPERTS' FORUM

DESIGNING EFFECTIVE VISUALS FOR THE VIRTUAL CLASSROOM

Chopeta Lyons, e-Learning Consultant

As a consultant with over twenty-five years of working with numerous companies and organizations to build training solutions, I have witnessed the many iterations of tools promising to lower the barriers to technology-delivered training. This latest wave, however, really delivers on that promise. In the past three years, many of my clients have eagerly adopted the virtual classroom, either alone or as part of a blended package, as the ideal solution for their distance learning needs. The relative simplicity of use in tools such as WebEx, Breeze, and Elluminate lets instructors embrace as much or as little of the power these tools offer as needed.

However, the number of PowerPoint presentations currently used in corporations, organizations, and education settings is mind-numbingly huge. Unfortunately, when setting up virtual classrooms, an all-too-common practice is to load these preexisting presentations into a web-based synchronous tool without a thought to adapting the visual content. As can be imagined, the results are rife with unintended consequences. Nowhere is this more apparent than in the overall graphic design and use of illustrations. Although tool vendors offer tips on the technical aspects of using graphics, such as increasing efficiency in display and speed, they naturally do not address best practices for using graphics to support instruction.

By employing the tips below, my clients have dramatically enhanced the effectiveness of their virtual classroom training materials:

- Build the habit of asking before clicking on the "insert clip art" button if the content could benefit from a flowchart, diagram, or graph. Push beyond the use of graphics as mere decoration.

- If a content-specific graphic is important or complicated, consider creating it as a series of overlays that the virtual classroom instructor can explain as he or she "builds" to the finished illustration.

- When creating dynamic graphics, consider the instructor who delivers the content. The current crop of tools provide functions (highlighter, text entry, pointer shape) that can aid learners to interact dynamically with graphics but, depending on the confidence and the expertise of the presenter, sometimes simple builds and overlays may work just as well to engage the learner with the content and reduce the presenter's stress over managing the tools.

- Avoid complicated backgrounds or graphic "noise" that detracts focus from key content. This is not to say that the graphic presentation should be amateurish, dull, or boring, only that it should not overwhelm the learners' cognitive capabilities. While a polished, attractive background adds to the credibility of the material presented, overly ornate or loud interfaces can draw attention away from the instructional content. One client's organization required that the bold corporate standard template be used for all company PowerPoint presentations. In order to reduce the "noise," we successfully made the case that, in a virtual classroom, the slides function as a white board, not as a corporate presentation.

- Limit the amount of text displayed whenever possible to key points.

- Increase size of text. Many virtual tools display the slides inside a smaller area, with boxes for participant rolls, chats, and other areas of the screen display devoted to the virtual classroom itself. Text that is easily readable on a full-screen display may dip beneath the legibility index when displayed in the shared document or presentation area.

- Avoid the seduction of "glossy" or glitzy decorative graphics that compete for the learner's attention. As one quick example, a white board presentation devoted two-thirds of the display area to decorative head shots and used 8-point type for the instructional text. The designer's intent was to "keep the learner interested," but the net effect was frustrated participants straining to read text.

- Consider the cursor or pointer as a dynamic part of the overall graphic design that the learner experiences. It can focus or distract. If you want the learner to focus on one part of the white board, avoid jiggling or causing other eye-catching movement of the pointer in another.

- Whenever there is a choice, use simple, relevant graphics that are professional, clean, and easy to comprehend and quick to display.

GUIDELINES FOR VISUAL DESIGN

Andrew Schembri, President and Owner, Independent Design
Group Los Angeles, Inc. (IDGLA Inc.)

I founded my company, IDGLA, Inc., sixteen years ago. My team is comprised of designers, technologists, and business strategists with years of experience in providing successful products and services to many industries. I am very experienced in the corporate training field, having worked closely with instructional designers and subject-matter experts to deliver many online, print-based, and stand-up training experiences.

Here are some observations relevant to this chapter:

- Visuals are not just images, drawings, etc., but also include screen layout, color, text, and functionality that can enhance or distract from learning.

- Delivery platforms impose limitations on visuals used for the virtual classroom and the software it is created in.

- All users see things differently, which means there is no one standard that can be applied to visuals.

This chapter's authors imply that visuals for entertainment or interest depress learning. In my experience, this is not always the case. People are inundated with high-quality entertainment images such as in video games and DVD menus and therefore have high entertainment expectations, regardless of the purpose of the medium (entertainment or education). One example that stands out is a course on dairy products for a major grocery client for whom we introduced an animated illustrated cow and used transitional animations of the cow to show the users that they had completed a section and were ready to "MOOve" on. The animation was not relevant to the course per se, but on review, it enhanced interest, as the user was encouraged to progress to get to the next surprise animation.

Regarding the functions of visuals, I have found that customizing visuals for a particular course and for the audience are key factors to enhance the experience and the learning for the user. Representational visuals should be aimed at and designed directly for the user. For example, a group of IT professionals may not appreciate a cartoon-like illustration that looks like it was designed for children.

Representational visuals should be enhanced by use of design. A screen capture of software or line drawings of products can be confusing and uninteresting. A more focused approach (honing in on a section of an illustration) may be clearer to some viewers. Simplifying a diagram by showing key elements can eliminate unnecessary clutter, thus reducing confusion. Breaking down visuals into a sequence that is instructor- or viewer-controlled also helps in learning. 3D animations of complex objects can be simplified to the key elements.

Organizational, relational, and transformational visuals are often poorly designed. For example, an organizational hierarchy may be better displayed as a graphic incorporating elements of the subject matter, rather that a simple flow chart. Same with pie charts. Incorporating subject-matter elements into the visual or diagram will be more useful than an uninteresting pie chart. Conversely, moving away from the subject matter, such as by using metaphors, needs to be done carefully to avoid confusion. Overall, visuals need to reinforce the topic.

Chapter 1
**Meet the New
Virtual Classroom**

Introduction

Chapter 2
**Learning
in the New VC**

Chapter 3
**Features to Exploit
in the New VC**

Chapter 4
**Teaching Content Types
in the New VC**

Part 1: Learning and the New Virtual Classroom

Chapter 5
**Visualize Your
Message**

Chapter 6
Make It Active – Part 1

Chapter 7
Make It Active – Part 2

Part 2: Engaging Participants in the New Virtual Classroom

Chapter 8
**Managing Mental Load
in the New VC**

Chapter 9
**Make a Good
First Impression**

Chapter 10
**Packaging Your
VC Session**

Chapter 11
**Problem-Based Learning
in the New VC**

Part 3: Optimizing Your Virtual Events

Chapter 12
Getting Started

Part 4: Creating Effective Learning Events in the New Virtual Classroom

6

Make It Active

PLANNING INTERACTIONS IN THE NEW
VIRTUAL CLASSROOM

DEVELOPING INTERACTIVE VIRTUAL CLASSROOM SES-
SIONS is the single most important investment you can make for successful events! From attention to motivation, all of the major learning events
described in Chapter 2 are aided by effective interactions. Make frequent and
relevant participant interactions a top priority! In this chapter and Chapter 7 we
show you how.

In this chapter we overview the interactive features available in most virtual
classroom tools and highlight some tradeoffs among them. You will learn how to
plan interactions that support each of the psychological events of learning as well
as four types of interactions: demographic, behavioral, attitudinal, and knowledge.

Interactive Options in the Virtual Classroom

Virtual classroom software tools actually offer instructors **more opportunities** for frequent learner interactions than do most traditional classroom settings. Frequent and effective use of these response facilities is the single most
important technique for successful virtual events. Figure 6.1 summarizes the
major response facilities available in most virtual classroom tools, including

Figure 6.1. Response Facilities in the Virtual Classroom.

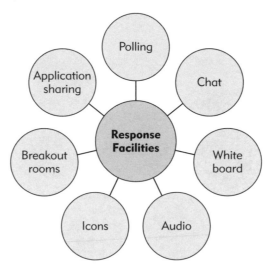

polling options for multiple-choice-type questions, text chat, the white board for text and graphic input, audio for verbal responses, icons such as a happy face to communicate feelings, breakout rooms for small group work, and application sharing for software practice.

Polling

The polling feature provides buttons that participants click to indicate their selection of two to five response options for a multiple-choice or yes-no option question posted by the instructor. In some virtual classroom tools, the polling options are accessed through a separate window or pod. Typically, the instructor sets up these polls ahead and activates the polling window at the appropriate time in the session. Figure 6.2 shows an example of this type of poll. In other tools, the polling buttons are always available as a part of the interface. The instructor will display a multiple-option question on a slide in the white board, and participants respond in the polling area in the interface. An example of this type of poll is shown in Figure 6.3. The polling buttons A through F are located in the upper-left corner of the

Figure 6.2. A Polling Question in Microsoft Live Meeting
Aggregates Results with Bar Graphs.

With permission from © Microsoft Corporation—Microsoft
is a registered trademark of Microsoft Corporation.

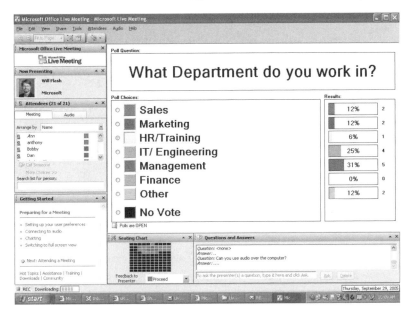

Figure 6.3. A Polling Question Uses Visual Response Options.

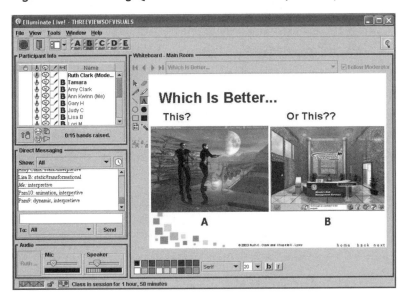

interface. The instructor can choose to let everyone see all of the responses in the participant information window, as in Figure 6.3, or can keep individual responses hidden from the participants if greater anonymity is desired. Some tools automatically display polling results aggregated in chart form, such as the bar chart in Figure 6.2.

Some advantages of polling include the speed and ease of administration of questions, the opportunity for all participants to respond, and the ability to display responses, either by individual participant and/or in an aggregated format. Polling options work best for structured interactions—such as questions with two to five response options. As instructors, we easily fall in the habit of writing multiple-choice questions with text, but keep in mind that the white board also supports visual question alternatives, as shown in Figure 6.3.

Chat

Virtual classroom interfaces incorporate a chat window in which the instructor or participants can type short text statements. Each participant's name appears next to his or her statements, allowing easy identification of communicators. Like the polling option, the chat facility allows responses by all participants at the same time. Chat is a good option for questions requiring brief open-ended responses, for questions that require a brief constructed response rather than recognition of a multiple-choice option, or for multiple-choice questions with multiple correct answers. For example, in Figure 6.4 the instructor asks all participants to state one thing they already know about synchronous online learning. To maximize participation, we sometimes ask everyone to type in their answers but **not to press send** until the instructor says "Send." In that way, reflective learners have more time to consider their answers without the distraction from the first answers to appear in the chat window.

Chat also offers an opportunity for participants to ask questions during an instructional presentation in a less obtrusive manner than using the hand icon to ask a verbal question.

A disadvantage of chat is the limited amount of screen real estate dedicated to text messages in most virtual classroom interfaces. When the

Figure 6.4. Instructor Asks Participants to Respond in the Chat Window.
With permission of Sandra Johnsen Sahleen—Univar USA Inc.

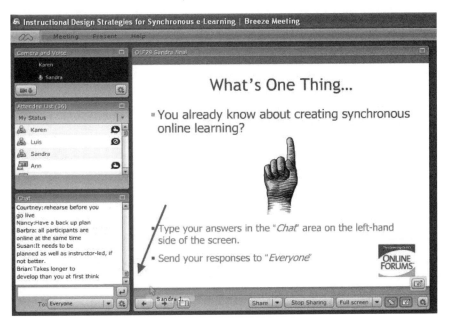

response box fills, new text messages cause older responses to scroll up. If you have a large class, you may want to use some crowd control mechanisms to limit who sends messages. For example, you might ask everyone to type in an answer but only the women or only a certain division to actually send their answers. Alternatively, you may provide a workbook in which everyone responds and then, after a pause, call on only some participants to type in their answers. In skill-building training, use the chat feature when your class size is relatively small and you would like participants to respond with brief open-ended answers. This allows the instructor to readily track the accuracy of each person's response and make corrections as needed.

Most virtual classroom software tools allow participants to send public messages that everyone can see, as well as private messages visible only to those the sender selects. One way to use private messaging is to pair participants up to discuss an exercise or question by sending messages back and forth to each other. You can see how we used paired chat in a discussion assignment in *The New Virtual Classroom* CD demonstration lesson on identifying business goals.

Because chat offers a seductive opportunity for participants to communicate with one another privately at any time during a session, we recommend setting some ground rules regarding its use. For example, we ask participants to use chat for on-task communication only during instructional activities—no passing notes in class!

White Board Input

Many instructors find clever ways to get participants engaged with the white board. Virtual classroom software allows instructors and participants to type onto the white board and to mark it with highlighters, pens, lines, boxes, and symbols. In Figure 6.5, participants use the marking and typing tools to show

Figure 6.5. Virtual Classroom Participants Mark Locations on a Map.

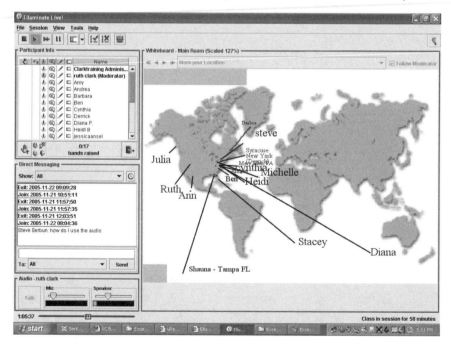

their physical locations on a map. This is a great icebreaker to use in your course introduction because it gives everyone a fun opportunity to gain experience with the white board tools and it helps to establish social presence. You can use the white board to reinforce discrimination of parts of a complex diagram by asking participants to highlight the equipment part where troubleshooting should begin or to identify the likely source of a fault. Of course, if you have a large class and everyone is marking on the white board, it soon becomes cluttered.

Unlike some of the other interaction facilities such as chat, the white board can allow anonymous input. If you want to pose a sensitive question or issue, ask participants to type short responses on the white board. At the end of each of our class sessions, we have an instant feedback white board divided into two sections headed with pluses and minuses. We ask participants to type their session comments anonymously into both sections.

Audio

Questions posed by the instructor either on the white board or verbally can be answered verbally by individual participants. The instructor can pose a question and ask participants to raise their hands, or the instructor can call on a participant. Calling on participants on a regular basis is as good a technique in the virtual classroom as it is in the physical classroom to ensure participant attention. A limitation of audio is that some tools allow only a single individual to talk at a time. In addition, unlike the previously mentioned response facilities, audio responses are transient, leaving no visual record. On the other hand, audio participation increases social presence and is the best option for longer open-ended responses (or participant questions) that would require too much typing to express in chat. We recommend using audio in conjunction with other response facilities. For example, after participants select their preferred visual options, shown in Figure 6.3, the facilitator asks participants to use audio to explain the reasons for their choices.

Icons

Most virtual classroom software offers various icons, such as a smiley face, applause hands, confused face, and many others, which allow instructors to get instant feedback regarding understanding or feelings. These are useful to identify understanding or confusion. For example, instructors can say: "Now that I've demonstrated this feature, let's go on to a practice. Click on the happy face if you are ready for practice or on the hand icon if you have questions." Or, if participants have been working on an exercise in a workbook, the instructor might say: "Work the exercise on page 32, and when you are done, click on the happy face."

Encourage participants to use the icons spontaneously as well. If participants agree with a statement or like an activity, they can click on the applause icon to show approval. For example, on our Excel demonstration lesson on *The New Virtual Classroom* CD, you can see spontaneous use of the applause option following a participant attempt to solve a problem in application sharing.

Breakout Rooms

A breakout room offers all or many of the above interaction features in a small group setting. With two to five participants in a breakout room, audio time is much more accessible to everyone. Breakout rooms can be used just as you would use them for any small group activity in the face-to-face classroom. For example, structured short case scenarios can be discussed and responses entered on the white board by the group scribe. The group spokesperson can summarize team discussions when everyone reconvenes in the main room. Or role-play exercises can be conducted in trios with one person serving as an observer. Guidelines for conducting the role play can be posted on the white board, and the observer can take notes in chat as the role play proceeds and give feedback via audio or white board following the role-play exercise.

We use breakout rooms in two of our CD demonstration lessons (business goals and interviewing) for small group discussions following a video case study. Participants in the interviewing lesson scribed some questions regarding the video case study on the white board during their breakout room discussion. The instructor copied the breakout room white board responses and pasted them into the main room. This helped team spokespersons summarize their results during the debriefing in the main room.

Application Sharing

Most virtual classrooms allow instructors to launch a computer application in an "application sharing" window. If you use application sharing only for instructor-presented demonstrations, participant attention will soon drift. Instead, make demonstrations interactive by creating a series of completion examples that lead to a full practice exercise. In our Excel lesson on the CD, after giving a demonstration of formula use in the spreadsheet, the instructor starts an example by selecting the correct cell and typing in the equal sign. The instructor then asks the participants to use chat to type in the remainder of the formula.

Instructors can pass control of an application to individual participants. For example, in our Excel demonstration lesson, the instructor turns the spreadsheet over to one of the participants, asking her to demonstrate her solution. As the participant takes control of the application, her actions and explanations are seen and heard by everyone.

Interactions and Learning

In Chapter 2 we introduced the main psychological learning events that transform information from the instructional environment into long-term memory. One reason that interactions are such a powerful instructional method is that they can enable **all of the learning events**: support participant attention, activate prior knowledge, manage cognitive load, promote rehearsal and encoding, support transfer of learning, and promote learning management and motivation. In the next section we summarize how you can create interactions that maximize their psychological impact.

Support Attention with Frequent Interactions

Having to respond frequently to varied types of interactions in the virtual classroom in and of itself will promote learner attention. If every one to three

---

USERS SPEAK

Our advisory team reflects on interactivity in the virtual classroom

I've added increased activities to (a) keep participants' attention, as they tend to multi-task, and (b) to assess whether they are "getting it" or not—as I don't have the benefit of seeing their faces (and seeing the light bulbs or confusion). When appropriate (and when budget allows), I add multimedia to provide more pizzazz and to provide opportunities for interaction with content.

Mark Bucceri, Principal Education Specialist, Centra Software

We have designed courses to be more interactive and provide more opportunities for students to learn from each other. I have set up many sessions where users are presenting content and their findings rather than having me lead the discussion.

Zemina Hasham, Director, Customer Development, Elluminate Inc.

To accommodate the virtual classroom, we conduct more team teaching— collaboration with other teachers. We are more specific when giving directions. I have to find virtual resources. I don't limit myself. I need to think outside the box.

Diana Perney, Lead Teacher, Pennsylvania Virtual Charter School

---

minutes learners are asked to select a polling option, type into direct messaging, or are called on for an audio response, they will be less likely to multitask or drift. In addition, if your event includes one or two breakout rooms in which individuals work together in a small group, participation and attention will increase. Frequent interactions are the most important technique you can use to sustain attention in the virtual classroom.

Activate Prior Knowledge with Interactions

In Chapter 2 we reviewed the process whereby new incoming knowledge is integrated with existing mental models in long-term memory. Since this integration takes place in working memory, prior knowledge in long-term memory must be brought into consciousness in working memory. Interactive reviews of previous lessons or experiences related to new content offer an excellent route to activation. For example, in our Excel sample lesson, the instructor interactively reviews cell-reference notations by asking participants to type into chat the location of spreadsheet data. In a class on employee performance management, the instructor asks each supervisor participant to summarize a recent problem he or she has faced. Interactions to activate prior knowledge are best placed at the start of a lesson or lesson topic.

Manage Cognitive Load with Interaction Staging

According to cognitive load theory (Clark, Nguyen, & Sweller, 2006), there are wasteful and useful forms of cognitive load. Load is wasteful when it does not lead to learning, such as when working memory is filled by irrelevant work or data. As a consequence, less capacity is available for learning. In contrast, useful cognitive load leverages limited working memory capacity for processes that lead to learning. In Chapter 8 we summarize a number of techniques you can use to manage cognitive load in the virtual classroom. In this section, we summarize a few techniques as they pertain to design and display of interactions, including (1) orienting participants to response tools, (2) providing clear and visible directions, (3) offering memory support, (4) avoiding extraneous interactions, and (5) gradually progressing from examples to practice.

Orient Participants to Response Tools   During your first class session, display some quick introductory interactions that require all participants to use the most common response options in order to become comfortable with the virtual classroom environment. Introductory interactions can include such activities as: select a polling option to indicate your experience with the topic, type your class expectations onto the white board, use a marker tool to show your location on a map on the white board, type your software version into direct messaging, and/or introduce yourself via audio. These types of interactions can serve the primary purpose of introducing participants to each other and the secondary purpose of building familiarity with all of the virtual classroom response features.

Give Clear Written Directions   Write directions that are simple and clear. Along with the question, provide response directions in text on the white board, as shown in Figure 6.4. For a multiple-choice polling question, place written directions in a consistent location on the white board, somewhat like this: *Respond by clicking on A, B, C, or D on the polling buttons.* Use audio for very simple directions, such as: *Raise your hand to explain the reason for your response.* For breakout room work, write out directions on the white board and copy them into each breakout room. If you are looking for certain categories of responses during breakout room work, put a template on the white board to guide the discussion and record team responses.

Provide Visual Memory Support   If an exercise requires factual information or steps, display that information in text in a visually accessible format. For example, in Figure 3.6 a small box was drawn on the spreadsheet to display formula formatting rules. The formatting rules remain visible during the exercise as participants construct their first formula. As the lesson progresses, you may want to fade or remove the memory support—especially if the skill needs to be applied from memory on the job.

Avoid Extraneous Interactions   Extraneous interactions require learners to respond in ways that do not directly support one of the learning events we have discussed. For example, some instructors try to liven up a lesson with a Jeopardy® type game. These may be fun, but in most cases, they merely require participants to respond from rote and fail to support the deeper mental processing that leads to job-relevant learning. The problem is not the use of a game but the use of a game that does not promote the type of knowledge and skills needed on the job.

Ease into Practice of Procedures Gradually   Research has shown that learning of procedural steps is faster and better when the instructor starts with a demonstration, followed by several examples in which the instructor works part of the example and the participants complete it. As the lesson progresses, the instructor assigns more and more of the work to the learners. This technique, called *faded worked examples,* is described in detail in Chapter 8.

Promote Rehearsal and Encoding with Your Interactions

Mental rehearsal in working memory leads to learning. Learners can rehearse mentally without any overt activity. For example, while viewing an effective visual, learners mentally process it in ways that lead to learning. Learners rehearse explicitly when they respond to questions and engage in activities such as case studies in breakout rooms. Use interactions that lead to explicit rehearsals to ensure appropriate rehearsals and to help the instructor monitor participant understanding.

Some types of explicit rehearsal are better than others. Rehearsals that merely ask learners to repeat content or to identify previously presented content are low-level and do not lead to acquisition of job-relevant knowledge and skills. In a communications class, asking learners to type in the three stages of communication that the instructor presented **is not** an effective interaction because it merely asks participants to regurgitate information. Instead, plan interactions that emulate what learners will have to do on the job. Rather than list stages of communication, participants will need to apply those stages to diverse work scenarios. Providing participants with an interaction in which they must complete a dialog by responding to an audio or video statement is a more effective type of interaction because it builds job-relevant skills. Using breakout rooms for role-play exercises in which all participants take turns applying communication guidelines is another effective interaction.

When you review our CD lesson samples, you will see that all of the interactions are application level and that none require participants to respond from rote memory. Application level interactions help participants build job-relevant knowledge.

Promote Transfer with Effective Interactions

Transfer of learning means that knowledge and skills have been acquired in long-term memory in ways that allow participants to access or retrieve them back on the job. To ensure transfer success during training, instructors must embed the appropriate retrieval hooks or cues in the exercise.

For procedural tasks that are performed more or less the same way each time, provide practice environments that are very similar to those participants will use on the job. For example, if they are learning to fill in a customer order screen, they should practice with screens that are identical to those they will use in the workplace.

In contrast, for principle-based tasks that will require judgment and adjustment to each work situation, promote transfer by giving learners a variety of different interactive experiences that require them to try out guidelines in diverse settings. For example, better learning transfer in a sales class will result from examples and practice exercises that incorporate varied product and customer scenarios.

Guide Learning Management with Interactions

Many research studies show that most students **are not good judges** of what they know and what they should study. Some students overestimate what they know, while others underestimate their skills. If you have a group of learners with diverse experience and skills, you can use a pretest to guide them to the most appropriate virtual classroom lessons. Pretests can be quite informal. You can direct potential students to a website with a pretest that includes both traditional test questions as well as job requirements' questions. The combined results can be used to provide recommendations regarding which virtual classroom sessions would be most appropriate. For example, those learners who indicate that their jobs require them to construct graphs and charts in Excel and who are unable to perform this task in a test question would be assigned to the lesson on graphs and charts.

Frequent interactions also help the instructor assess learner progress. The virtual classroom actually offers more opportunities to assess individual learner progress than is possible in the face-to-face classroom. Lacking the body language cues in face-to-face events that signal either understanding or confusion, virtual classroom instructors must learn to use participant responses to frequent interactions to "read" audience progress.

Four Types of Interaction

Most experienced instructors gravitate naturally to knowledge-type questions in the virtual classroom. However, we recommend three additional types of questions you can use to make your sessions active events. These are *demographic, behavior,* and *attitude.*

Demographic Interactions

In any learning setting, it is useful for instructors to know about the relevant background of their participants as well as for participants to be introduced to their class colleagues. Learning about participants is especially critical in the virtual classroom, where instructors don't have the usual physical cues they use in face-to-face learning environments to know their participants. Demographic interactions reveal relevant attributes about participants, such as their work assignments, their job titles, their physical locations, their industries, and so forth. Use demographic interactions during session introductions to obtain relevant background on participants and to establish social presence. For example, in Figure 6.2, participants are polled regarding their department assignments. In Figure 6.5 participants identify their physical locations on a map.

Behavior Interactions

Behavior interactions ask about what participants have done, are doing, or will do. Like demographic questions, these types of questions are useful ways to learn about the participants' backgrounds. For example, in Figure 6.6 from

---

Figure 6.6. A Behavior Interaction Using Polling.
From the Excel lesson on *The New Virtual Classroom* CD.

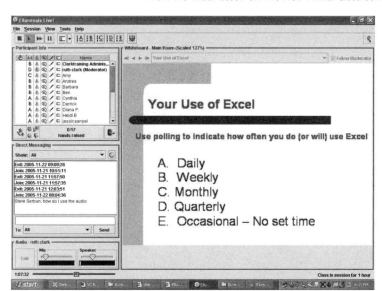

our Excel demonstration lesson on the CD, we ask participants to indicate how often they are (or will be) using spreadsheets as part of their work assignments. If your class is going to include a follow-up project, the white board or chat can be used for participants to indicate what type of project they are planning. At the end of the class, a breakout room discussion can focus on how participants will apply new knowledge and skills on the job. All of these interactions are examples of behaviors that participants have done or will be doing related to course content.

Attitude Interactions

All too often, instructional professionals focus exclusively on knowledge and skills and neglect attitudes. Yet it is often attitudes that get in the way of learning or obstruct application of new skills on the job. Attitude questions reveal the opinions or feelings of your participants. For example, you might post three or four visual samples on the white board. These could be website samples, screen samples, product samples, etc. Then you could ask participants to indicate which samples they like best or to rate their preferences using symbols to "vote" for each option. We use a white board session satisfaction rating activity at the end of each of our virtual classroom events. Participants type anonymously what they perceived as effective or ineffective.

Knowledge Interactions

Most instructional professionals are well versed in constructing and administering knowledge-type questions. You can use knowledge interactions in the form of pretests to guide participant selection of the appropriate virtual session and as lesson lead-ins to activate prior knowledge or assess entry knowledge of your audience. Include knowledge interactions frequently throughout a training session to help the instructor and participants assess their learning progress. If the instructor sees that several participants are making errors, this is a signal to review the content. If the instructor detects one or two participants having problems, this is a signal to work with those participants individually to clarify misconceptions.

One way to make your knowledge interactions more engaging is to ask one participant to respond and ask other participants to give feedback on the response. Obtaining participant feedback is especially useful when you use response facilities that only support a single participant response, such as audio or application sharing. Learner feedback is also a good engagement strategy for small group practice sessions in which one or two individuals are trying out a skill and other participants in the room comment via text chat.

The Bottom Line

There are tradeoffs among the various virtual classroom interaction options. However, for learning purposes, the specific response feature you use is less important than constructing interactions that lead to learning. Construct interactions that mirror the job to give your organization the best return on investment in the virtual classroom. Supplement knowledge questions with demographic, behavioral, and attitude interactions in order to establish social presence, learn about class participants, and acknowledge feelings and opinions as important correlates associated with applying new knowledge and skills.

On *The New Virtual Classroom* CD

In our How to Construct a Formula in Excel demonstration lesson, you will see the use of attribute, behavior, and knowledge questions using polling, chat, application sharing, and white board input.

In our Defining Business Goals and How to Plan an Interview sessions, you will see use of behavior and knowledge questions using audio, chat, polling, white board input, and breakout rooms.

For More Information

Clark, R. C. (2003). *Building expertise.* Silver Spring, MD: International Society for Performance Improvement.

Hofmann, J. (2004). *Live and online: Tips, techniques, and ready-to-use activities for the virtual classroom.* San Francisco: Pfeiffer.

COMING NEXT:
MAXIMIZING ENGAGEMENT IN
THE NEW VIRTUAL CLASSROOM

Interactivity in the virtual classroom is the number-one predictor of successful synchronous e-learning. In Chapter 7 we continue our discussion of interactivity by emphasizing techniques that will keep more of your participants engaged more of the time. These techniques include use of inductive questions, lead-in questions, breakout rooms, and emphasis on inclusive response options.

EXPERTS' FORUM

CREATIVE INTERACTIONS IN THE VIRTUAL CLASSROOM

Sandra Johnsen Sahleen, Instructional Designer/
Technical Writer, Univar USA Inc.

I have over fifteen years' experience in learning design and development, most recently working in the virtual classroom environment with learner adoption of and creation and facilitation of virtual collaborative events.

Interactivity in a virtual classroom is the most important thing you can do to ensure your events succeed. Exploiting the features available in the classroom is key to keeping your audience engaged, challenged, and wanting more. Polling features are not the only way to ask questions and gauge audience knowledge. Try posting a question on a slide, supply answers, and ask the audience to use the annotation tools to select a response on the screen. This allows users to answer anonymously, and the presenter can provide additional input as required.

Depending on your familiarity with the virtual classroom features and your ability as a presenter to multitask, using the chat facility may or may not be a good option for you. Audience size should be a consideration when planning this type of feedback method. We've discovered that having another facilitator or production assistant available to help support direct messaging (chat) is a valuable asset when managing the event's conversation flow.

White boards are another great way for your audience to interact in the classroom. Encourage users to play with drawing tools. Let artists create masterpieces, provide a dialog with text, or draw lines connecting information your audience has supplied. Additionally, avoid the "blank white board screen" provided by so many virtual classroom tools. Instead, use your presentation template as the background. A darker background is easier on the eyes when viewed on a PC monitor.

In my experience, using breakout rooms during an event may be an area for thoughtful reflection as you plan your content. Some tools provide your audience with easy access to breakout areas; however, you should seriously consider audience composition during development. Based on technical skill levels, moving among breakout rooms may become a challenge for the inexperienced facilitator, as well as for presenters who are monitoring breakout activities.

If the virtual classroom tool you are using allows event recording, make use of it as an option to attending a live class. Your audience will appreciate this additional opportunity if unexpected business challenges prevent "live" participation.

You're only limited by imagination and the desire to make your audience comfortable and confident using the virtual classroom. The more comfortable the audience becomes, the better their acceptance of interactions and their desire for more.

START INTERACTING RIGHT AWAY

Diana Perney, High School English Teacher, the Pennsylvania
Virtual Charter School

Currently, I work for the Pennsylvania Virtual Charter School. This is an exciting and innovative educational choice families have in Pennsylvania—cyber schooling! As a lead teacher, I am responsible for the hiring, mentoring, and training of the other high school teachers in the virtual setting. At our school we use Elluminate, and the Online School (OLS).

We have all experienced being bored silly while attending a class or a meeting! The presenter talks at you and nothing sinks in. You can't multitask, so you sit there tapping your pencil and thinking of all the things you could be doing. Since this is happening in face-to-face situations, imagine what happens in the virtual setting. The participants answer email, listen to messages, or leave to get coffee—and you have no clue. Using the interactive options in the virtual classroom maximizes learning.

We all have different learning styles, and by utilizing the response tools, you meet the learners' varied needs. For example, when beginning a session, I review how to use the response tools. I ask the learners to show me a smiley face if they can hear me; or I activate the white board tools and ask them to write their names and choose clip art icons that represent them. This enables the learners to use the tools, to ask how to use them, and it creates an open atmosphere where learning can begin. The learners hear me, see the screen, and complete an action.

Another way to engage learners is by using the polling tool. I use this tool throughout a session. I create on the white board a multiple-choice question to start the session and ask the learners to respond, choosing A, B, or C. The polling results give me a sense of the class and activates prior knowledge for the learner. I will repeat this process throughout the session to engage the learners and to keep my finger on the pulse of the class. It often catches the participants off guard—they don't know when I will ask the next question. The polling tool also meets the needs of visual, auditory, and kinesthetic learners. I ask the question, they see the question, and a button needs to be clicked to indicate a response.

Breakout rooms are the most successful response tool. The room enables the learners to utilize the tools. It also makes the learner responsible for his or her own learning. However, it can be the most difficult for the presenter. When using breakout rooms, you are a facilitator and have to give up the control! Planning ahead is the most effective way to use this tool. Breakout rooms can be created prior to the session so the participants can be moved to the appropriate rooms quickly. Also, all information can be posted to the white board before the session. When the learners are working in small groups, assign them jobs. Everyone has equal responsibility. While in the room, the learners can use the direct messaging, the audio, and the white board and its tools. You have created an environment in which interaction is key to success. When the task is complete, all groups return to the main room and report back to the larger group. This creates accountability. As the facilitator, you have the ability to move from group to group, assisting each as needed.

My best advice is to start slow. Introduce the response tools one at a time. You need to be comfortable with the tools before giving control to the group. I would not recommend using the breakout rooms the first time you teach virtually—ease into that. If you are comfortable using the tools, then learners will be, too!

USE ROLE PLAY IN THE VIRTUAL CLASSROOM

Rhea Fix, Red Pepper Consulting

The sample shown in Figure 6.7 is from my colleagues Joey Dotolo and Becky Nutt. The role-play approach has been used for several things, such as call demonstrations,

Figure 6.7. Making Communication Skills Interactive in the Virtual Classroom.

With permission from Jocelyn Dotolo and Becky Nutt.

call best practices, and—as demonstrated here—an assessment question. In these interactions, they use a combination of visuals accompanied by text or audio dialog to illustrate communication techniques. These are made interactive with follow-up questions such as the one shown here using polling. When converting existing classroom materials to a virtual classroom format, they realized the need to create more visual, interactive demonstrations, as opposed to talking about the concepts.

Chapter 1
Meet the New
Virtual Classroom

Introduction

Chapter 2
Learning
in the New VC

Chapter 3
Features to Exploit
in the New VC

Chapter 4
Teaching Content Types
in the New VC

Part 1: Learning and the New Virtual Classroom

Chapter 5
Visualize Your
Message

Chapter 6
Make It Active – Part 1

Chapter 7
Make It Active – Part 2

Part 2: Engaging Participants in the New Virtual Classroom

Chapter 8
Managing Mental Load
in the New VC

Chapter 9
Make a Good
First Impression

Chapter 10
Packaging Your
VC Session

Chapter 11
Problem-Based Learning
in the New VC

Part 3: Optimizing Your Virtual Events

Chapter 12
Getting Started

Part 4: Creating Effective Learning Events in the New Virtual Classroom

7

Make It Active

MAXIMIZING ENGAGEMENT IN
THE NEW VIRTUAL CLASSROOM

BECAUSE INTERACTIONS ARE SO CRITICAL to successful virtual classroom sessions, you will want to use them to maximize opportunities for engagement. In this chapter we review techniques for getting more of your participants engaged more of the time. These include the use of inductive interactions, lead-in questions, inclusive response features, closed-ended questions, breakout rooms, and paired chat activities. Since frequent interactions will absorb limited virtual classroom time, you can stretch your learning opportunities with pre-session, interim session, or post-session assignments.

Replace Meaning Taking with Meaning Making

You may have heard the expression that instructors should be "a guide on the side rather than the sage on the stage." This is another way to say that effective instruction offers frequent opportunities for learners to construct their knowledge through active engagement with the content. Courses that emphasize instructor lectures assume that learners are able to **take meaning** from the information provided. We call this the "*sponge approach*" to learning. The

sponge approach—whereby the instruction pours out content and the learner (hopefully) absorbs it—is risky. Environments that put the learner at the center of the experience offer greater opportunities for **meaning making** through active building of new knowledge and skills.

One way you can increase the amount of time students are engaged is to convert traditional didactic teaching sequences into *inductive learning* events.

What Are Inductive Events?

In a traditional training presentation, the instructor presents some content, provides examples, and then asks questions to promote understanding and address misconceptions. For example, in an Excel lesson, the instructor explains the format for a spreadsheet formula, shows some sample formulas, and assigns exercises in which participants identify or construct valid formulas. Note that in this typical scenario the instructor is active for two-thirds of the event (explanations and examples) and the participants are active for one-third (practice questions). In an inductive design, you reverse the ratios to two-thirds participant activity and one-third instructor facilitation, as shown in Figure 7.1.

How to Design Inductive Events   Begin an inductive sequence with some carefully selected examples and/or non-examples that illustrate the main lesson concepts or guidelines. Ask participants to study these examples and **derive** the definitions, rules, or guidelines. In Figure 7.2 you see one screen from a short inductive interaction taken from our Excel demonstration lesson on

Figure 7.1. Reverse the Activity Ratio in Inductive Learning.

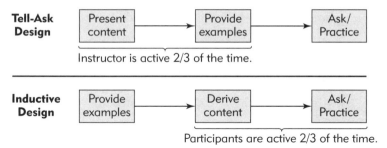

Figure 7.2. Participants Induce the Format Rules from Excel Formula
Examples.

From the Excel lesson on *The New Virtual Classroom* CD.

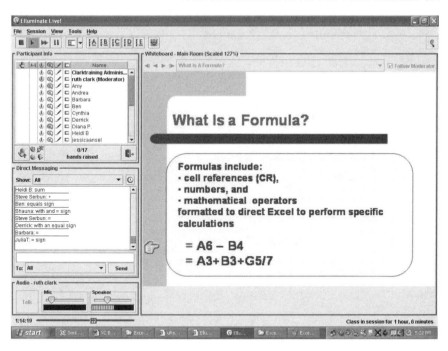

the CD. After introducing the concept of a formula, the instructor displays
two formula examples. Participants are asked two questions. First, they type
into the chat box what they notice about how all formulas start. The initial
equal sign that begins all Excel formulas is a critical feature, since it is the

opposite of the well-learned rule of placing an equal sign *between* two mathematical statements. Second, they identify the formula operators—the symbols and what they mean. To guide accurate inferences, the equal sign and the operator symbols in the examples are displayed in red. After identifying the format conventions, participants type into chat the correct formula to accomplish a specific calculation. This practice exercise confirms that participants have made correct inferences about Excel formula formats and can apply them.

In our CD demonstration lesson on defining business goals during needs assessments, the instructor shows some valid and invalid business goals, followed by an interaction in which participants type the main features of business goals into chat. The instructor acknowledges their responses and integrates them into a formal definition. The instructor types this definition on the white board while participants enter it into their handouts. She then follows with a confirmation exercise, asking participants to identify valid business goals from a list of valid and invalid examples.

Evidence for Inductive Learning   An experiment reported by Beishuizen, Asscher, Prinsen, and Elshout-Mohr (2003) compared learning from a lesson in which a main idea was followed by five examples to a second version in which the five examples were followed by a main idea. They found significantly better learning in versions that started with examples followed by the main idea. The authors conclude, "An advance organizer should consist of a concrete set of examples, which enable the reader to construct the concept by induction. Offering the main idea afterwards serves as a check on the correctness of the concept constructed by the reader" (p. 311).

When to Use Inductive Interactions   Inductive presentations are best for teaching of concepts or principle-based tasks that can be illustrated with multiple examples. Avoid inductive presentations for facts and procedures that are best communicated directly. The amount of effort to construct an inductive lesson is no different from a traditional lesson. Rather than a presentation followed by examples and practice, you start with examples, ask learners to derive the content, and then assign practice. Inductive teaching encourages your learners to **make meaning** by active processing rather than passive absorption.

However, you will need more time to facilitate an inductive event than to present a traditional "show-and-tell" lesson. Participants will need time to review the examples, reflect, and abstract the common features of the examples. In general, the higher participation required by an inductive event will take two or three times longer than a traditional approach. The payoff will be higher participation ratios, leading to greater satisfaction with the lesson and increased ownership of the content. You will need to decide which topics in your lesson are most important and should be taught inductively.

You can buy back some lost time by assigning review and analysis of more complex samples as an offline activity. We discuss time-saving strategies at the end of this chapter.

We are not advocating a complete abandonment of show-and-tell instruction. However, one way to minimize the sponge approach to learning is to identify important content in your lesson for inductive learning events. If you want to try an inductive approach on steroids, consider a guided-discovery lesson architecture. In Chapter 11 you can read how to adapt a guided-discovery design to the virtual classroom environment.

Use Topic Lead-In Questions

Start each lesson or lesson topic with one or two *lead-in questions*. A lead-in question is designed to stimulate interest in the topic, activate prior knowledge, and help focus attention to the lesson objectives. For example, in Chapter 6 (Figure 6.3) we showed a polling lead-in question from a lesson on graphics. Participants select the visual they think is most effective for learning. The instructor notes the selection ratios and, if time permits, may ask some participants to explain their rationale. No answer is given at this point. At the end of the session, the same question is presented to allow participants to apply the research findings discussed.

Lead-ins can also take the form of short discussions. Show a visual or pose a problem relevant to the lesson topic and ask participants to analyze the scenario, discuss the visual or problem in a breakout room, and summarize their discussion in the main room. For example, an instructor might ask participants to discuss a cartoon that illustrates an issue related to the session.

Increase Your Ratio of Closed to Open-Ended Questions

Experienced instructors are familiar with open and closed-ended questions. Many instructors overly rely on open-ended questions because they are easy and fast to construct. The drawback to open-ended questions is that responses consume more time than closed-ended formats. Participants need time to consider their answers and then articulate their ideas, either in text or audio. In the amount of time it takes to pose and process responses to one open-ended question, three or four closed-ended questions could be presented and discussed.

Of course, there are times when open-ended questions are most appropriate. For example, when an issue arises that is likely to have a variety of potential responses that cannot be readily predetermined, use an open-ended format. Questions such as: "Who can describe an experience he had that is similar to the one given?" or "What reasons do you have for your response?" are better suited to open-ended formats. It is often useful to start with a closed-ended question, such as a polling question, and follow it with an open-ended discussion of reasons for selection choices learners made.

In the virtual classroom, brief responses to open-ended questions can be typed into the direct message window or onto the white board. Longer responses are best handled via audio. In contrast, the polling feature or response icons are best suited for closed-ended questions, which can be framed as "yes-no" or multiple-choice options. We recommend that you include frequent closed-ended questions that require learners to process your content in meaningful ways throughout your lessons.

Remember that all knowledge questions, whether closed or open-ended, should be at the application level, not at the recall or "regurgitate" level!

Rely on Inclusive Versus Individual Response Options

In Chapter 6, we distinguished between response options that allow everyone to respond simultaneously versus those that are more suited to either a small group or a single individual. For the most part, favor those facilities that permit everyone to respond over those that only allow an individual response. For example, polling and chat open participation to everyone, in contrast to audio or application sharing, which only permit one individual to respond at a time. If your class is small, the white board also offers a forum for multiple responses of typing, drawing, or otherwise marking up a displayed image. The occasional use of audio is recommended for responses to open-ended questions and elaboration on closed-ended responses. This will maintain social presence and keep participants alert, because they could be called on at any time.

Make Appropriate Use of Breakout Rooms

Breakout rooms offer an excellent way to increase participant engagement. In small groups of three to five, there are more frequent opportunities to use the microphone and white board. A number of research studies have shown that, when effectively structured, learning in a small group can be better than learning individually (Clark & Mayer, 2003; Jonassen, Lee, Yang, & Laffey, 2005). Apply the four guidelines in Figure 7.3 to maximize success in your breakout rooms.

Keep Groups Small and Diverse. Typically, an activity involving three to five participants is about right. You want a group small enough to promote

Figure 7.3. Four Guidelines for Using Breakout Rooms.

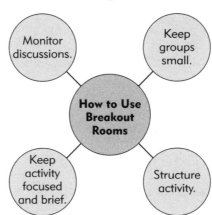

everyone's involvement and large enough to yield different perspectives and sufficient resources to a discussion or project. There is some evidence that heterogeneous groups are better for learning than groups with participants of similar background knowledge, industry, or department. For efficient assignment of larger groups into breakout rooms, use a random distribution tool such as the one shown in Figure 7.4.

Structure the Breakout Room Activity. Rather than give an open-ended assignment such as: "Discuss how you might use different media in a blended training solution," provide a more focused scenario and set up a template on the white board. For example, Figure 7.5 from our CD demonstration lesson on defining business goals shows the template that each small breakout group used during a three-to-four-minute discussion period. The white board data from each breakout room can be copied back into the main room as

Figure 7.4. A Dialog Box for Random Distribution into Breakout Rooms.
From Elluminate Version 7.0.

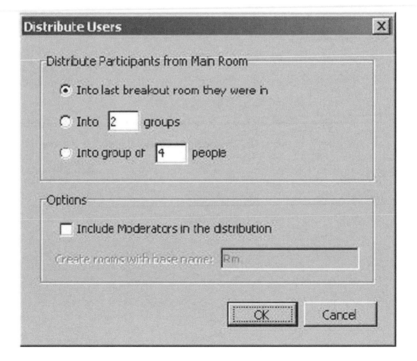

Figure 7.5. A Template Guides Participants Working in a Breakout Room.
From Business Goals Lesson on *The New Virtual Classroom* CD.

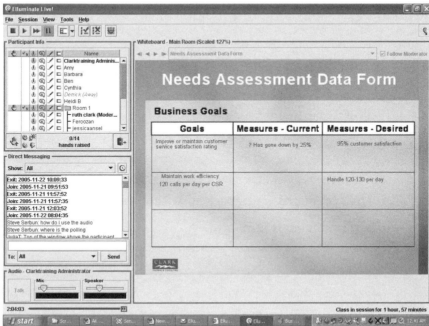

each group debriefs its discussion. As part of your structure, assign each group a facilitator to start the activity, to ensure equal participation, and to serve as a spokesperson during the whole class debriefing in the main room.

Keep the Activity or Discussion Focused and Brief. If you have lengthy activities that require considerable collaboration and reflection, these are better completed outside of the virtual classroom environment. For example, participants in our "Leveraging the Virtual Classroom" course complete a project in which they prepare and eventually deliver a virtual classroom session. These projects are completed in between virtual sessions and posted for everyone to review.

Monitor Small Group Activities. Just as in the face-to-face classroom, move in and out of the breakout rooms to monitor the discussions and provide coaching as needed.

Extend the Virtual Classroom with Assignments

As you shift to a more learner-centered format, you will need more delivery time, compared to a receptive session during which content is covered rather than processed. To regain some time, make assignments to be completed outside of the virtual classroom. If you think participants will not complete assignments on their own, include a worksheet with the assignment and ask participants to email it to the instructor by a given deadline. Or announce your virtual classroom session to be four hours (for example) rather than two hours. The first two hours includes the synchronous event and the second two hours is for independent or group work in or external to the virtual classroom session. Two popular alternatives for asynchronous work are reading and research assignments and application projects.

Reading and Research Assignments

If you have a large amount of content, why not let participants read materials—either in a document or on an Internet site? To ensure that the assignment is completed, attach a worksheet or other deliverable that must be emailed to the instructor or brought to the virtual classroom. Be sure to make use of that assignment in the virtual classroom session. For example, if you are teaching a class on hiring interviews, participants will need to know legal and organizational hiring guidelines. Rather than presenting this information in a lecture, provide links or documents containing the information, along with a short exercise in which participants identify hiring questions that meet legal and organizational specifications.

Project Assignments

Transfer of learning is promoted when participants apply new knowledge and skills to a work-related problem or task. Often, project work requires considerable time and reflection and is best undertaken outside the virtual classroom. For group projects, provide facilities for teams to work asynchronously and synchronously. A project room on a website can offer a space for participants to post their work and research findings. Discussion boards can facilitate ongoing communication about a project. If the assignment is more suited to individual work, provide a place for students to post their results, which can be reviewed by others prior to the virtual classroom session and then discussed by a review team during the virtual classroom session.

Assign Paired Chat Exercises

In the physical classroom, we typically ask pairs of participants to work together—for example, to compare answers to an exercise and discuss any differences. Most virtual classroom chat facilities allow participants to send private messages to others in the session. These are seen by the recipient, and usually by the instructor as well. Pair up class members and ask them to work together through private chat on an exercise or discussion assignment.

If you know your participants' backgrounds, you might pair them up yourself by writing names on the white board. For example, you might want to match a more experienced with a less experienced participant. Or you may want to bring together individuals from a similar industry or from different divisions in your organization. In our demonstration lesson on defining business goals on *The New Virtual Classroom* CD, the instructor posts an exercise asking pairs to work in the chat facility to identify questions they would ask in an interview.

Group Management Tips

If you are teaching a skill-building class in which you need to closely monitor and give feedback to individual participant responses, keep the class size small— somewhere in the range of twelve to fifteen participants. If you are conducting a large group session, such as a briefing, you may want to limit the number of people who can respond at one time. For example, if you want participants to respond via chat or on the white board, you could assign numbers to individuals and ask odd numbers, for example, to respond. Some virtual classroom tools automatically assign numbers to participants when they click on the "raise-your-hand" button. This technique gives you a quick and easy way to number off!

The Bottom Line

We commonly refer to virtual classroom attendees as participants. The focus of this chapter is on making them just that—**participants!** This goal requires instructional professionals to construct and conduct virtual classroom sessions that maximize learner engagement. Some approaches for doing so include:

- Converting rule-example-practice presentations to inductive activities in which learners make meaning rather than take meaning
- Using lead-in questions to introduce lessons and new topics
- Making heavy use of closed-ended questions using response options that are inclusive rather than individual
- Using breakout rooms in ways that promote learning
- Using private chat for paired participant assignments

Because greater interactivity will require more instructional time, consider buying back some of that time with pre-session, interim-session, or post-session assignments during which learners review important content and/or apply new knowledge and skills to small group or solo project assignments.

COMING NEXT: MANAGE MENTAL LOAD IN THE NEW VIRTUAL CLASSROOM

As an instructor-paced medium, the virtual classroom imposes greater mental load on participants than will self-paced media such as books or asynchronous e-learning. Furthermore, instructors new to the virtual classroom will experience overload themselves as they learn to manage all of the features available to them. In Chapter 8 we offer guidelines to minimize cognitive overload among your participants, as well as among new instructors.

On *The New Virtual Classroom* CD

You can see examples of the techniques discussed in this chapter, as follows:

- *Inductive Events*—all three lessons make use of inductive strategies to teach concepts or, in the case of the interviewing lesson, to teach most of the content in a guided-discovery format.
- *Topic Lead-Ins*—in the How to Construct a Formula in Excel lesson, we used cell reference review questions to lead into the main topic of

formulas; in the Defining Business Goals and How to Plan an Interview lessons, we asked participants to define needs assessment or list solutions they have found during needs assessments during the introduction to the class.

- *Closed and Open Inclusive Questions*—we made use of open and closed questions with emphasis on high-inclusion response options of polling, chat, and white board marking.

- *Breakout Rooms*—we used breakout rooms in both the Defining Business Goals and the How to Plan an Interview lessons. In both lessons, the discussions and activities were structured with white board directions posted in the rooms.

- *Session Extensions*—the How to Construct a Formula in Excel lesson assigns a spreadsheet project after the class to be emailed to the instructor. The How to Plan an Interview lesson provides several resources and asks participants to study these resources as the basis for an interim-session project assignment.

For More Information

Clark, R. C. (2003). *Building expertise.* Silver Spring: MD: International Society for Performance and Instruction.

Hofmann, J. (2004). *Live and online: Tips, techniques, and ready-to-use activities for the virtual classroom.* San Francisco: Pfeiffer.

E X P E R T S ' F O R U M

COMPETITION FOR INTERACTION AND RELATIONSHIP

Mark Yeager, Vice President of Marketing, iLinc Communications

I have been very active in the fields of corporate training and e-learning for more than sixteen years. Often, the students participating in a virtual classroom session will be required to apply their newly learned skills in a vacuum in which there may be no others performing the same work or tasks. Students in this circumstance will benefit greatly if they are able to build interpersonal relationships with fellow students in their virtual classroom that will continue after the session is over.

We find it very important to create opportunities within virtual classroom sessions that will drive interaction between students, increasing the propensity of these students to stay in contact with each other after the class as they apply what they have learned.

One of the most effective stimulators that we have found for sustaining these relationships is including competitions as part of the learning program. Students can be broken down into teams of two or three with a common challenge. After being presented with a specific scenario, the teams are tasked with deriving a solution that best addresses the problem. The "winner" can be decided by the instructor or by a majority vote of the students, for which no student can vote for his or her own team.

The competition builds closer relationships among those on the same team and facilitates the exchange of contact information. The competition needs to have an element of fun attached to it. When we perform competitions in our virtual classroom sessions, instructors will commonly tie the competition to a reality television show and mimic the rules of the program. They often will have a white board image that appears to be similar to the reality television show, and the students will be separated into teams with names that match the nomenclature used on the show.

USING INTERACTIONS TO OVERCOME DISTRACTIONS

Kathy Fallow, Director, Teletraining and Synchronous Learning,
Vertex Solutions

As director of teletraining and synchronous learning for a Washington, D.C., consulting firm, I work with federal clients to design synchronous learning events, including classroom, broadcast, and the virtual classroom. Federal agencies, like many large corporations, want to design training events in the virtual classroom that engage the learner and provide effective results. While the traditional classroom captured their attention by physically capturing their presence, today's virtual classroom participants must try to concentrate on presented material in a work environment filled with distractions such as cell phones, emails, instant messages, and meeting requests. Technology-savvy, they learn to multitask in order to accomplish their daily activities. If we are to capture their attention, sustain interest, and ensure learning, we cannot present content in a manner that allows them to disengage, for they will surely return to the many other items demanding their attention. In this chapter, Clark and Kwinn offered several methods to capture the attention of learners by maximizing engagement.

One such technique is the use of inductive interactions. A project I recently completed involved using WebEx to train help desk staffers on the proper way to respond to callers' questions about an online application. Rather than teach the solutions for the most common technical problems, I presented my class with a scenario that replicated an actual conversation with help desk staff. Students were asked to study the caller's statements to pick up clues about what might be causing the problem. Students were then paired up to discuss (using private chat) how they might respond to the caller. Did they need to ask the caller to supply additional information before trying to identify and solve the problem? Was there more than one solution to this problem? What steps would they take to ensure that the problem was resolved and that the caller understood how to avoid a reoccurrence? I then asked each team to identify its approach and to take control of the shared application, if necessary, to demonstrate their solutions. What could have been taught as lecture and demonstration became a lively "pair and share" activity that caused students to examine the details of the scenario, reflect on their findings, discuss alternatives, and validate the best solutions for the problem.

Chapter 1
Meet the New
Virtual Classroom

Introduction

Chapter 2
Learning
in the New VC

Chapter 3
Features to Exploit
in the New VC

Chapter 4
Teaching Content Types
in the New VC

Part 1: Learning and the New Virtual Classroom

Chapter 5
Visualize Your
Message

Chapter 6
Make It Active – Part 1

Chapter 7
Make It Active – Part 2

Part 2: Engaging Participants in the New Virtual Classroom

Chapter 8
Managing Mental Load
in the New VC

Chapter 9
Make a Good
First Impression

Chapter 10
Packaging Your
VC Session

Chapter 11
Problem-Based Learning
in the New VC

Part 3: Optimizing Your Virtual Events

Chapter 12
Getting Started

Part 4: Creating Effective Learning Events in the New Virtual Classroom

PART THREE

Optimizing Your Virtual Events

FROM INTRODUCTIONS TO ENDINGS, attention to key components of the virtual classroom event is essential to success. Here's what we'll cover in this part of the book.

Chapter 8: How to manage participant and new instructor mental load during virtual classroom events.

Chapter 9: Planning and facilitating effective introductions.

Chapter 10: Planning and preparing supporting elements for virtual classroom events, including pre-work, handouts, and adjunct media.

Chapter 11: The what, when, why, and how of problem-based learning in virtual classroom settings.

Chapter 1
Meet the New
Virtual Classroom

Introduction

Chapter 2
Learning
in the New VC

Chapter 3
Features to Exploit
in the New VC

Chapter 4
Teaching Content Types
in the New VC

Part 1: Learning and the New Virtual Classroom

Chapter 5
Visualize Your
Message

Chapter 6
Make It Active – Part 1

Chapter 7
Make It Active – Part 2

Part 2: Engaging Participants in the New Virtual Classroom

Chapter 8
Managing Mental Load
in the New VC

Chapter 9
Make a Good
First Impression

Chapter 10
Packaging Your
VC Session

Chapter 11
Problem-Based Learning
in the New VC

Part 3: Optimizing Your Virtual Events

Chapter 12
Getting Started

Part 4: Creating Effective Learning Events in the New Virtual Classroom

8

Manage Mental Load in the New Virtual Classroom

INSTRUCTOR-PACED LEARNING ENVIRONMENTS like the virtual classroom are especially prone to learner overload because participants cannot control the rate of information flow. From the instructor's perspective, managing and monitoring the various virtual classroom facilities imposes cognitive overload on new facilitators. Because humans have a very limited working memory, instructional professionals must diligently conserve students' memory capacity for learning purposes. In this chapter we summarize a number of proven guidelines for avoiding student and new instructor cognitive overload by:

- Minimizing extraneous content in your lessons
- Minimizing extraneous mental processes that do not lead to learning
- Helping new instructors manage their mental load in virtual classroom sessions

Overload in the Virtual Classroom

As an instructor-paced learning environment, the virtual classroom imposes a greater mental workload than self-paced media such as this book or asynchronous e-learning. In self-paced media, each participant can view information at his or her own rate and usually can review a topic or repeat an exercise as often as he or she wishes. Learning from a dynamic environment—one that presents new knowledge and skills at a rate outside the individuals' control—adds considerable mental overhead.

Behind the scenes, new virtual classroom instructors are faced with the multitasking challenge of managing an array of tool features, monitoring learner responses in chat and audio, presenting new content effectively, and keeping the overall instructional process flowing in a timely manner. As one instructor put it: "You have to be hyper-vigilant during the session, as you are multitasking and handling a lot of things simultaneously." Another concurs, observing: "It requires a lot of practice to manage synchronous delivery in a way that makes the user experience enjoyable. The facilitator has to be good at multitasking" (Pulichino, 2005, p. 16).

The virtual classroom has a high overload potential for learners and for the new instructor. Fortunately, we have a number of proven techniques to manage learner overload. And we can draw on the experience of those who have learned to multitask effectively in the virtual classroom. We begin with a brief discussion of mental load caused by our limited working memory capacity. Then we summarize two main approaches to managing participant load in the virtual classroom: (1) minimize the amount of content included and (2) minimize instructional elements that lead to extraneous mental processing—processing that does not lead to learning. Last, we turn our attention to the instructors, with suggestions for managing overload as they are getting started in the virtual classroom.

What Is Cognitive Load?

In Chapter 2 we saw that learning is constrained by our two memory systems: working memory and long-term memory. As a limited capacity processor, working memory can hold only a few chunks of information. And when required to hold information, working memory has fewer resources available for processing. During instruction, it's important to allocate its limited capacity to processing that leads to learning.

Because instructor-led learning environments already put more stress on working memory than self-paced environments, we need to be especially diligent to manage student cognitive load in the virtual classroom. In the face-to-face classroom, the instructor uses body language cues to detect signs of learner overload. In the virtual classroom, the instructor must learn new techniques to monitor and manage mental load.

Less Is More: Weed Out Extraneous Content

To reduce the amount of content imposed on working memory, consider eliminating some content or distributing it over time, over diverse media, or both. The techniques for managing cognitive load are summarized in Figure 8.1.

Figure 8.1. Reduce Content in Virtual Classroom Sessions.

Identify Need-to-Know Content

One good way to reduce cognitive load is to eliminate extra mental baggage by focusing on need-to-know content and identifying which topics among the need-to-know are best handled in the virtual classroom. To define your essential content, begin with a job analysis that first identifies the major tasks linked to organizational performance goals. Next, define the steps or guidelines associated with those tasks and then any key concepts or processes linked to those steps and guidelines. A focus on critical job competencies should reduce your content inventory to the essential knowledge and skills to be included in training.

Identify Content Appropriate for the Virtual Classroom

Next, consider which topics are best addressed via the virtual classroom and which are best reserved for asynchronous or face-to-face learning activities or reference resources. Use the virtual classroom for topics that can leverage its unique visualization and interaction capabilities. Avoid lengthy information transmission sessions that put learners in a sponge role. For straight information delivery, consider other venues such as documents and Internet sites.

One of our clients divided course content among virtual classroom, asynchronous e-learning, and online reference. The training outcome was to use proprietary statistical analysis software to analyze manufacturing data and to guide manufacturing processes. They chose to teach the more conceptual or far-transfer topics in the virtual classroom. These included selecting the appropriate types of statistical tests, representing data visually, and interpreting data. Software procedures were introduced in the virtual classroom but left for asynchronous events, including self-study animated e-learning demonstrations of basic tool procedures and performance support embedded in the application software, as well as independent project work.

Keep Virtual Classroom Sessions Brief

While some organizations are offering multi-day multi-hour virtual classroom sessions, many learners find lengthy online sessions to be more tiring than in-person sessions of similar duration. For example, NIL, a Cisco training partner, converted a technical classroom course into a virtual classroom offering consisting of two three-week sessions of virtual classroom training. Each daily class included three to four hours of virtual classroom, followed by asynchronous work using the NIL virtual labs. Although NIL found that learning outcomes in the virtual class did not differ greatly from their ILT training, most participants commented that they found the virtual classroom sessions too long (Clark, 2005). We recommend, in general, that virtual classroom sessions not exceed two hours, and any sessions over ninety minutes should incorporate a break.

USERS SPEAK

What our advisory team says about virtual classroom session lengths:

- Webinars to large audiences (50+) are a maximum of 60 minutes

- Brainstorming sessions are 90 to 120 minutes

- Sales presentations are up to 2 hours

- Most training offerings are 75 to 90 minutes. Occasionally, we conduct 4-hour sessions (with 2 or 3 breaks)

- Working meetings run from 60 to 120 minutes
  Amy Finn, VP, Education and Chief Learning Officer, Centra Software

- Our sessions are anywhere from 30 minutes (e.g., sales demos) to 4 hours (customer product training). Our average length is 1 hour
  Marcus McNeill, Director, Product Strategy, Surgient

- Our training sessions for external customers range from 8 hours to 20 hours, with 16 hours an average
  Steven Serbun, e-Learning Technical Manager, Bentley Systems Inc.

Avoid Redundant Information and Modalities

As you plan your virtual classroom sessions, weed out redundant expressions of content. For years, we thought we helped learners by giving them more information. For example, we thought it beneficial to provide content in both text and audio. Recently, however, instructional psychologists have discovered that learning is better when you stick to the essentials. For example, if you are explaining a visual, don't use both on-screen text AND narration. Instead, explain the visual with audio narration only. If your slide contains mostly text, such as a statement of the lesson objectives, don't read the text to participants. Pause and let them read it themselves. Then add any additional clarifications you feel are helpful. Providing your learners with just enough content for them to build new knowledge is the most efficient path to learning (Clark, Nguyen, & Sweller, 2006).

Eliminate Extraneous Themes and Games

Another common misconception is that it's a good idea to inject themes and games to hold participant interest. For example, in Figure 8.2 we show a slide from a virtual classroom course using a baseball theme to add pizzazz and motivate participants. Participants "up to bat" advance to a base with a correct answer

Figure 8.2. Irrelevant Themes Can Depress Learning.

or strike out with an incorrect answer. Correct answers to bonus questions lead to a home run. Sounds like fun? Be careful. A well-intentioned attempt such as this one to make training more engaging may in fact depress learning!

Research has shown that any additions not directly relevant to the instructional goal risk interfering with learning. Mayer (2005b) calls this the *Coherence Principle*. He and his colleagues found that adding what psychologists call *seductive details*—visuals or words related to the lesson theme but not relevant to the learning objective—depresses learning. For example, Harp and Mayer (1997, 1998) spiced up a lesson on lightning formation with pictures and stories about people struck by lightning, how airplanes are affected by lightning strikes, and so forth. Individuals who studied the spiced-up lessons rated their lessons as more interesting than those who studied the "just the facts" lessons did. But they also learned less. By clogging working memory with add-ons that might be entertaining but do not lead to learning, you reduce the mental capacity available for learning. In short, avoid a *Las Vegas* approach to instruction.

Use Care with the Web-Cam

As of the writing of this book, we don't have much controlled research on how and when to make best use of the web-cam facility. We are making an educated guess that using the web-cam to project video images of the instructor or participants at the same time the instructor is explaining white board visuals adds an extraneous visual load to your instruction. The virtual classroom interface is already quite complex. When you add an additional visual, be sure that it contributes to learning. When the instructor is explaining visuals on the white board and asking for frequent participant responses, as we have recommended, adding an additional visual such as a video image of the instructor or participants is likely to distract limited cognitive resources from the main instructional events.

In making this recommendation, we draw on research on learning agents tested in asynchronous e-learning. This research has shown that **it is the voice of the agent**—not the image—that is most important to improving learning. In a review of this research, Mayer (2005c) concludes: "People do not necessarily learn more deeply from a multimedia lesson when the speaker's image is added to the screen" (p. 209). We look forward to future research to confirm or to refute this recommendation in synchronous learning environments.

Segment and Sequence Content

Suppose you had to teach a course on Excel. Would it be better to explain the concept and structure of formulas first and then show how to use formulas in spreadsheets? Or would it be better to integrate all of the information so that concepts are learned in the context of a new procedure? Recent experiments that compared learning from *segmented* versus *integrated content* found that outcomes were best when content was segmented. When teaching processes or procedures, present and practice related concepts first, followed by the stages of the process or steps of the procedure.

You can see this technique demonstrated in our virtual classroom lessons on *The New Virtual Classroom* CD. In the Excel lesson, we first teach about formulas, including their formatting rules. Then we teach the steps for using formulas in spreadsheets. In the business goals lesson, we present the concept of business goals prior to guidelines for eliciting and clarifying those goals during management interviews. By segmenting your content into discrete topics and sequencing major concepts and related facts first, you ease the burden on working memory by spreading out the content.

The various facilities available to participants in the virtual classroom software may be a source of cognitive load to those new to this delivery medium. Help participants become familiar with the virtual classroom software by assigning them to a pre-class tool-orientation session. Alternatively, use the first few minutes of your first session to engage everyone with the various response options. In this way, you can reduce the amount of mental effort devoted to tool mechanics so it can be allocated to learning.

Set Ground Rules to Minimize Distractions

In a face-to-face classroom, instructional professionals sometimes have to pause or intervene to ensure one speaker at a time during presentations and discussions. The chat window can offer a seductive venue for off-topic private discussions among participants. Participants may not realize that the instructor can see all chat text—public and private. Nip this temptation in the bud by setting ground rules during your introduction that permit use of the chat facility only as directed by the instructor or when participants have a relevant question or comment. While establishing ground rules, ask participants to turn off cell phones, email, and other potential distracters in order to focus full attention to the instructional event. Let them know when breaks will allow them an opportunity to check messages, etc. Instructors should not hesitate to provide participant guidelines that will promote learning, just as they do in any synchronous learning setting.

Minimize Extraneous Mental Work

Just as we should weed out extraneous content, so should we eliminate mental activities that do not lead to learning. These include unproductive working memory processing that results when participants have to: (1) learn context prior to its application, (2) connect related but physically separated information, (3) recall factual information to complete a task, and/or (4) solve multiple practice problem assignments.

Sequence Content Just in Time

Extra mental load can occur when content is presented out of sync with the task that requires the use of that content. For example, in a software application class, the instructor might begin with an overview of the tool bar by explaining all of the functionalities with associated commands or icons. This factual information is needed when the participant will make use of those features. It is not useful when presented out of context of need. Instead, provide only a very high-level overview of functionalities as an introduction. The overview should be followed by separate lessons on software tasks, at which point the "just-in-time" factual information on tool bars is most relevant.

Minimize Split Attention

Learning psychologists refer to related content that is physically or temporally separated as a *split attention effect*. A common example of physical split attention is reading some technical information that refers to a table or diagram located on the back of the page you are reading. Understanding the content requires the reader to flip the pages back and forth and to invest

Figure 8.3. Integrated Text and Visual.
Adapted from *Training* magazine, December 2005.

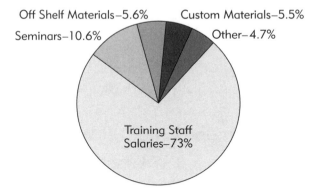

2005 Budgets: 51.1 Billion!

Off Shelf Materials–5.6%   Custom Materials–5.5%

Seminars–10.6%   Other–4.7%

Training Staff
Salaries–73%

Figure 8.4. Separated Text and Visual Make Processing Difficult.
Adapted from *Training* magazine, December 2005.

2005 Budgets: 51.1 Billion!

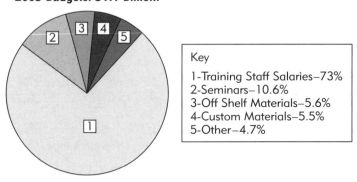

Key

1-Training Staff Salaries–73%
2-Seminars–10.6%
3-Off Shelf Materials–5.6%
4-Custom Materials–5.5%
5-Other–4.7%

mental work to integrate the two separated information sources. The frustration felt in these situations is our working memory complaining about the overload! Split attention can occur on pages or screens where, for example, text describing a visual is positioned away from the diagram.

Compare the data in Figures 8.3 and 8.4. You can interpret Figure 8.3 much more efficiently because the labels are integrated into the chart.

Incorporate Visual Memory Support

Avoid asking learners to recall factual information in order to complete a task. For example, when giving an assignment to use a spreadsheet formula to solve a problem, the learner must recall and coordinate quite a few items. First, she must recall the formula formatting rules and operators. Second, she must translate the requirements of the scenario into a mathematical statement and then convert that statement to an appropriate formula. Third, she must activate the correct spreadsheet cell, input the formula, and strike the enter key. When first learning this task, it will demand a great deal of working memory capacity.

To avoid mental fatigue, offer memory support—at least in the initial stages of learning. In Figure 8.5 you can see an example from our demonstration Excel lesson on *The New Virtual Classroom* CD. On the spreadsheet,

Figure 8.5. The Left Box Is Placed on the Application for Memory Support During Practice.
From the Excel Lesson on *The New Virtual Classroom* CD.

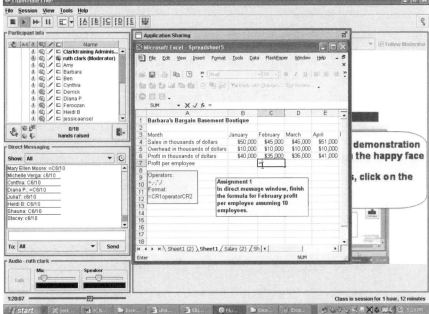

Assignment 1 is written in text. To the left of the assignment is a memory-support box with a summary of the formatting rules associated with formula construction. To minimize split attention, position memory support close to where the activity will take place. Ideally, this will be on your assignment slides or application screens. In some cases, you will need to include memory support in a separate handout that learners can access during exercises.

Ease into Practice Problems

When learning a new skill that involves multiple steps, cognitive load will be high at first. Asking learners to perform a number of practice problems imposes a double burden on working memory. First, working memory invests effort in trying to solve the problems. Second, it also attempts to build new mental models. Learning from problem-solving activities alone has proven to be very inefficient. Recent research shows that learning is more efficient when the instructor eases into practice problems gradually through faded examples (Clark, Nguyen, & Sweller, 2006).

To implement a fading process, begin with a step-by-step demonstration that illustrates how to perform the new task or solve a problem. Next, provide a second example in which you work several of the steps as a demonstration but leave the last few steps for your learners to complete. Continue with additional examples in which learners complete more and more of the steps and you do fewer. End with practice assignments in which the learners will perform all of the steps. This fading procedure frees working memory to learn by initially studying examples. Then working memory capacity is gradually allocated to solving problems.

In the Excel demonstration lesson on the CD, the instructor initially uses application sharing to show how to select the correct spreadsheet cell, input the formula, and press the enter key to get an answer. This demonstration is followed by two additional demonstrations in which the instructor starts the procedure and participants complete it.

Build Fluency Via Asynchronous Drill and Practice

We are able to perform complex tasks such as reading or driving effectively because we have automated the many underlying subtasks such as decoding individual letters, sounds, and words or steering and slowing the car. Automated tasks free up working memory capacity for different tasks completed in parallel. As a result of having automated your word decoding skills, you can derive meaning by scanning phrases and paragraphs.

Automaticity is achieved by hundreds of practice sessions. You may recall using flash cards—manual or automated—to make your reading or math skills automatic. This type of repetitive practice is called drill and practice and is best conducted in individual asynchronous settings. If your overall instructional goal would benefit from automation of subskills, assign drill-and-practice via asynchronous e-learning before or after virtual classroom sessions.

Managing Instructor Overload

Cognitive overload is a common experience among instructors who are new to the virtual classroom environment. Tasks such as setting up breakout rooms, clearing polling answers, changing the polling options, and advancing slides must be performed while the instructor monitors participant chat questions, provides explanations, and manages the overall session flow. In this section we offer some tips to help new instructors manage their own mental load in the classroom.

Set Up Features and Functions Ahead

Set up as many of the virtual tool functions as possible *prior to the start* of your session. For example, set up or construct your polling options, pre-load any multimedia files you plan to use, and have your applications ready to deploy via application sharing. Anything that can be prepared ahead will make the event that much smoother for the event facilitator.

Team Teach

New instructors should work with co-instructors or with *producers*. A producer is a professional who is tool-savvy and can help the instructor manage the interface. Usually, the producer is not a content expert, so labor is divided between the instructor—who is primarily responsible for delivering content and responding to participant interactions and questions—and the producer—who

---

USERS SPEAK

What our advisory team says about new instructor challenges:

One of the biggest challenges faced by our facilitators is multi-tasking—especially watching the direct messaging area while still speaking seamlessly. They want to react to questions and comments without interrupting the flow. Facilitators can learn to ignore text comments until an appropriate break in the flow of their comments, however.

Roger Hanley, VP, Academic Strategies, Elluminate

Recognizing that instructors need time to develop and master the virtual classroom skills is very much a critical success factor in moving to this delivery method. Think about it—instructors have developed their "teaching styles" over many years and many courses. In addition to knowing the material, they instinctively know how to draw out questions, scribe answers, deal with "problem students," etc. They know how to look in someone's eyes to see if they're "getting it."

Now an equivalent for most of these can be done in the virtual classroom, but it involves using technology and changing the teaching style. That takes an instructor out of his or her comfort zone and often interrupts the flow. They get distracted, they lose their places in the content, etc. Project stakeholders have to allow time in the schedule for instructors to deliver pilot classes to get comfortable with the technology and to develop their "virtual classroom" style.

Marcus McNeill, Director, Product Strategy, Surgient Corp.

---

helps with activities such as clearing polling answers, setting up breakout rooms, launching multimedia, and other tasks. To promote smooth teamwork, provide the producer with an annotated script to guide his or her support activities. Producers can help new instructors become more familiar with and take advantage of all of the features available to them in the virtual classroom. Alternative teaching teams could include two subject-matter experts who trade off the presentation duties with tool duties or a subject-matter expert paired with an instructional specialist who keeps the session moving and interactive.

Introduce Features Gradually

When we were new virtual classroom instructors, we tended to stick with the more straightforward tool functions. For example, in the tool we used, polling and text chat were very easy to manage. In contrast, we did not tackle breakout rooms and application sharing until we were comfortable with the basics. Depending on the tool being used, new instructors might start by using a limited number of straightforward functions and adding features gradually as they gain comfort with the software.

Manage Learner Responses

New instructors may want to set ground rules that will help them manage the learning experience. For example, they may want to ask participants to hold questions—either chat or audio—until the instructor reaches a convenient time to pause and take questions. As they gain more comfort with multitasking, the more experienced instructors may change their ground rules. When we first started facilitating, we asked learners not to use the chat feature until directed. After several sessions, we modified that guideline by asking participants to use the chat feature whenever they wanted, but only for on-task comments or questions. As our comfort increased, we gained confidence in our ability to monitor the chat window while presenting our content.

Practice, Review, and Reflect

As with any new skill, the more virtual classroom sessions the new instructor conducts, the easier they become. One great tool to improve your skills is the recording feature. Record your early sessions to review and critique later. Note your progress from your first session to your tenth and one hundredth session! Meet with other virtual classroom instructors and display a recorded segment to illustrate new techniques or obtain feedback.

The Bottom Line

Cognitive overload is a common experience for participants and for facilitators who are new to virtual classroom environments. To manage participant load, you should (1) eliminate extraneous content and distribute relevant content over time and media and (2) reduce extraneous mental work by avoiding split attention, using just-in-time learning sequences, offering visual memory support, and transitioning from examples to practice exercises gradually. To manage new instructor load, we recommend advance preparation, team teaching, gradual use of virtual classroom features, and setting ground rules.

COMING NEXT:
MAKE A GOOD FIRST IMPRESSION

The first few minutes of any learning event set the tone for that event! In Chapter 9 you will read about how to launch your virtual classroom session effectively. An effective class start is never an accident in any delivery environment. In the virtual classroom, good first impressions are the result of prework and a careful orchestration of the first few minutes of your event.

On *The New Virtual Classroom* CD

In our How to Construct a Formula in Excel lesson, we applied the following techniques to manage cognitive load of the learners:

- Teach the concept and rules about formulas before the procedure of entering a formula.

- Keep the lesson brief.

- Explain visuals with instructor narration and use text only when learners need to reference it over time.

- Avoid extraneous themes or the web-cam.

- Provide visual memory support of formula rules during formula practice on spreadsheets.

- Use a fading technique to transition from examples to practice.

For More Information

Clark, R. C., & Mayer, R. E. (2003). *e-Learning and the science of instruction.* San Francisco: Pfeiffer.

Clark, R. C., Nguyen, F., & Sweller, J. (2006). *Efficiency in learning.* San Francisco: Pfeiffer.

EXPERTS' FORUM

THE CHALLENGES OF CUSTOMER STUDENTS

Trudie Folsom, User Education, Intuit® Construction Business Solutions

I am a senior instructional designer for Intuit Construction Business Solutions. We develop and deliver virtual classroom training to customers who purchase Intuit Master Builder, which is robust construction management software. Our trainers are third-party contractors who are Master Builder experts. We have discovered that there are a number of challenges in trying to manage cognitive load when participants are software customers who pay to attend class and trainers are subject-matter experts (SMEs).

Less Is More   Those of us who develop these training materials experience a continual tug-of-war with the SMEs who teach our online classes. We try to keep the content to "need to know" and "best practices" to avoid cognitive overload. However, to our trainers, less isn't more; more is more and less isn't enough! Generous by nature, they want to share all that they know, right away. This includes each button on the toolbar, every shortcut, and the various ways participants can perform a single task. Participants seem to value having their cognitive capacities overloaded, too. At the present time, we only conduct level 1 evaluations; even if they can't retain it all, participants tend to rate very highly the SMEs who offer the most information. So customers seem to think that more is more, too.

Prework   Another challenge is requiring that participants take asynchronous web-based prework to help manage the cognitive load in the virtual classroom. Prework could eliminate the need for the trainers to cover basic tasks (such as navigation and data entry) and give trainers more time to do what they do best—share their real-world software experience with participants. The problem is that refusing to allow in class participants who haven't done the prework frequently translates into customer complaints.

I also discovered something that seems obvious in hindsight: When prework isn't enforced, it has the potential to create a greater divide between levels of knowledge of participants. Those who take the prework are now much further along than those who didn't. Trying to manage a classroom made up of those who completed the prework and those who didn't increases the cognitive load on trainers. And the participants who "follow the rules" and take the time to complete the prework are understandably resentful of those who don't. One solution may be moving to a learning management system that enforces prerequisites and does not permit enrollment until prework is completed.

Managing Learners   When participants are employees, training departments have the ability to evaluate them to understand what performance gaps they may be bringing to class and address those gaps prior to class. The nature of customer training is different. Due to privacy concerns and the sheer numbers of customers who attend our classes every month, we cannot gather much information about participants ahead of time. Participants come to the classroom with various levels of interest, motivation, software knowledge, computer skills, and comfort with the virtual classroom. Having such a wide range of participants in the same class greatly increases the cognitive load of our trainers.

Trying to manage cognitive load in participants and trainers is challenging when the participants are paying customers. When participants are employees, companies have more control over who attends. In addition, it is in a company's best interest to manage cognitive load when the result of the training, improved performance, has a direct impact on the company. The benefits to managing cognitive load in customers aren't so clear.

SHARING THE LOAD BETWEEN TEACHERS AND STUDENTS

Dr. Paul Sparks, Director of Online Master's Program in Educational Technology,
Pepperdine University

At Pepperdine we use online applications in very learner-centered (not teacher-centered) ways. For example, we ask students to discuss and discover together in small groups. Social constructivism suggests the best way to learn is to discover yourself with the support of others. Also, we tell stories back and forth. Stories are a great way to learn. At Pepperdine we use TappedIn for synchronous e-learning sessions.

The New Virtual Classroom certainly presents many challenges on instructor and student mental load. The additional cognitive load of online applications requires significant time to master. Luckily for instructors, these tools offer many possibilities as well. Interestingly, the younger the students, the more comfortable they tend to be with Internet communication tools and the attendant multiprocessing. In fact, at Pepperdine we find that incoming college students have an amazing ability to multiprocess. They also have a real distrust of traditional training models.

Team-teaching reduces load by splitting the presentation responsibility in half. Involving students in presentations can extend the load benefits even further. Real-time group sharing and collaboration are wonderful solutions to problem solving and content coverage. Asynchronous student-to-student interactions can also increase the amount of feedback for learners, while not impacting the instructor. Most applications capture interactions in a transcript, eliminating the need to take notes or remember key ideas.

Chapter 1
Meet the New
Virtual Classroom

Introduction

Chapter 2
Learning
in the New VC

Chapter 3
Features to Exploit
in the New VC

Chapter 4
Teaching Content Types
in the New VC

Part 1: Learning and the New Virtual Classroom

Chapter 5
Visualize Your
Message

Chapter 6
Make It Active – Part 1

Chapter 7
Make It Active – Part 2

Part 2: Engaging Participants in the New Virtual Classroom

Chapter 8
Managing Mental Load
in the New VC

Chapter 9
Make a Good
First Impression

Chapter 10
Packaging Your
VC Session

Chapter 11
Problem-Based Learning
in the New VC

Part 3: Optimizing Your Virtual Events

Chapter 12
Getting Started

Part 4: Creating Effective Learning Events in the New Virtual Classroom

9

Make a Good
First Impression

WE'VE ALL HEARD THE EXPRESSION: "You don't get a second chance to make a good first impression." Given the time constraints and physical separation between you and your participants, making them feel welcome and oriented from the start of your session will ward off a potential feeling of isolation and make students more open to their learning experience. In this chapter we describe four features of good introductions and how to implement them. Good introductions are:

- Interactive to establish social presence and engage participants
- Informative to set expectations and orient participants
- Visual to engage participants
- Efficient to use limited time effectively

Make a Good First Impression!

The first ten to fifteen minutes of any instructor-led event sets the tone for the learning to follow. It can be an uphill battle to recover from a poor introduction that fails to engage and motivate your participants or to set appropriate expectations. Often rushed for time, instructional professionals may concentrate on the "meat" of their lessons or presentations and leave the introduction to "on-the-fly" inspiration. We recommend that you make a priority of planning and developing a powerful introduction!

Introductions in the virtual classroom serve several purposes, including establishing social presence, setting participant expectations, assessing participant backgrounds, building participant comfort with the technology and the instructor, and motivating commitment to the event. To accomplish these goals, we recommend that your introduction be interactive, informative, visual, and concise, as outlined in Figure 9.1.

Make Your Session Interactive from the Start

As we stressed in Chapters 6 and 7, session interactivity is the single most important priority for success in the virtual classroom. Interactions in the introductory minutes of your event should (1) establish social presence, (2) build participant familiarity with the software mechanics, (3) assess participant background information, and (4) activate relevant prior knowledge.

Figure 9.1. Features of an Effective Introduction.

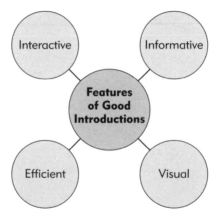

Establish Social Presence

The concept of *social presence* is not new. It was first described in the 1970s and is defined as the degree to which a communication medium allows participants to feel connected to others. Face-to-face classrooms offer the most opportunities for social presence, although the instructor may not take advantage of them. In the physical classroom, individuals can see, hear, and dialog with one another. In contrast, asynchronous e-learning courses or self-study books offer few opportunities for social presence. For the most part, these media are designed for individual self-study and consequently offer limited opportunities for social interactions.

High social presence leads to greater learner satisfaction in computer-mediated communication settings (Gunarwardena & Zittle, 1997). In addition, well-structured online learning activities in small group settings can yield greater achievement than solo learning (Lou, Abrami, & d'Apollonia, 2001; Wang & Newlin, 2002). Given the potential benefits of group dynamics, we recommend you leverage the features of the virtual classroom that build social presence.

In the face-to-face classroom, good instructors make contact with participants before the event starts. As participants enter the room, they greet participants, introduce themselves, and orient them to the learning space. Follow a similar protocol virtually: as participants enter the session, use the microphone to greet them by name and to welcome them. Ask them to test their microphones with an audio greeting to you and the other participants. As time permits, engage participants in light banter about their locations, the weather, the class, and so forth. Avoid dead air during

those pre-session minutes. Use the emoticons to respond during pre-class discussions. By using the emoticons yourself, you encourage your participants to make spontaneous use of them to express their feelings during class. The frequent use of emoticons can compensate for the lack of participant body language.

Build Familiarity with the Interactive Facilities

As you plan your introductory interactions, make a special effort to engage everyone in all of the major response features available in your virtual classroom environment. For example, include some introductory questions that use polling, white board drawing or text, hand raising, direct messaging, and the microphone. Your goal is to quickly build high comfort levels with the technology to transfer a potential learning barrier into a learning tool. An introductory white board map activity (shown in Figure 9.2) is a popular start-up activity. This activity integrates physical with virtual presence and

Figure 9.2. A Map Activity Introduces Participants to Each Other and the White Board Tools.

With Permission of Sandra Johnsen Sahleen—Univar USA Inc.

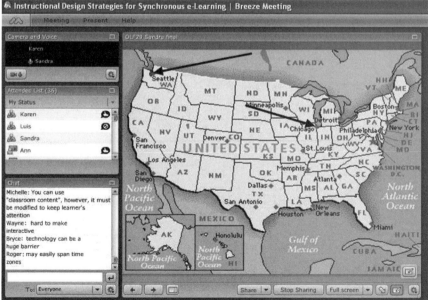

builds comfort using the white board in a relaxed setting. Following a map activity, in a small class, each participant can be invited to use the microphone to give a brief weather report for his or her location. Since audio is especially powerful to promote social presence, find ways to encourage everyone to use the microphone early in the virtual classroom session.

Assess Participant Backgrounds

Good instructors get a pulse on their learners right away. They typically elicit the following participant background information: experience related to the instructional objectives, job and work assignments, reasons for taking the class, and any topic-specific information such as which version of a particular software package participants are using. Demographic and behavioral questions are especially useful for learning about your participants. For example, in Figure 9.3 you can see an introductory polling question from our "Leveraging the Virtual Classroom" course to assess participants' virtual

Figure 9.3. A Polling Question to Identify Participant Background Experience.

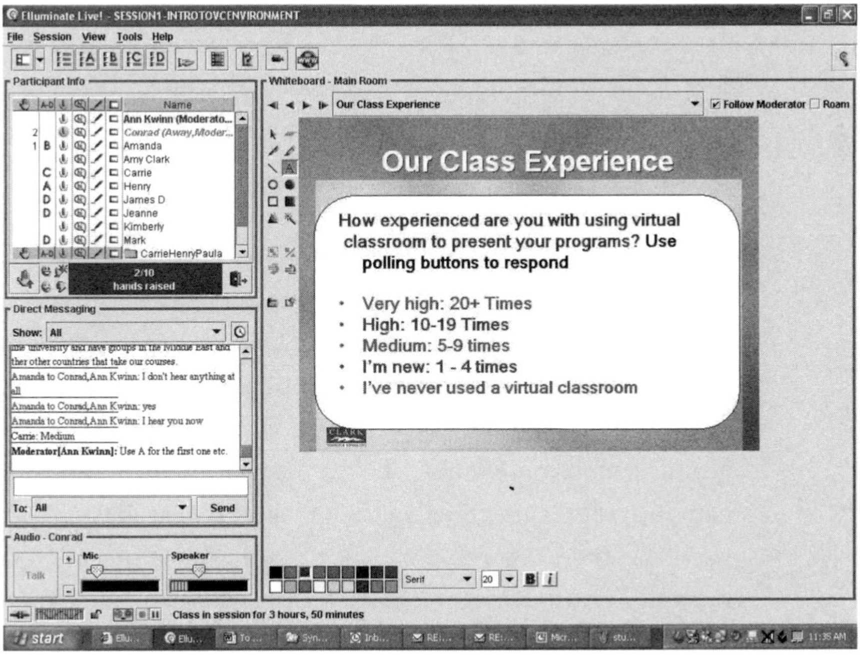

classroom teaching experience. This behavioral question gives the instructor a more accurate index of participant experience than a subjective self-assessment question such as asking participants to rate their experience levels as high, medium, or low.

It's always good in any learning setting to assess participant goals and expectations for the class. If your class size is small enough, ask participants to type their expectations on the white board. If your class size is larger than twelve to fourteen, create a polling question that includes the most common goals and expectations. Make your last response option: OTHER. Ask those selecting "other" to type their expectations into chat and/or to elaborate verbally.

Activate Relevant Prior Knowledge

Remember that new knowledge is generated by linking information presented in the learning environment with prior knowledge in long-term memory. Since the integration takes place in working memory, you promote learning when you awaken the relevant prior knowledge in long-term memory with some kind of activity. If your session is a continuation of a class, begin with an interactive review.

For example, in our Excel class on formulas on the CD, a review consists of a few quick interactions asking participants to identify cell references taught in a prior lesson. If your session is the first (and perhaps only) class, use something familiar to the audience—either a common prior experience or a metaphor relevant to the new topic. If introducing new software, activate prior experiences with similar software or with manual tasks that the software will be automating. For example, when teaching software editing functionalities, you can relate them to manual editing processes of using an eraser to delete text, scissors to cut and paste text, and so on. If focusing on a communication or management topic, ask participants to identify a problem they have encountered related to the session skill. Alternatively, begin with a brief video clip or story that illustrates the types of work situations that could benefit from the communication or management skills of the lesson. Engage learners with an activity based on the video or story.

Make Your Introductions Informative and Motivational

During the first few minutes, communicate session times and lengths, names and locations of handouts or class texts, session objectives, outcomes or agenda, class expectations, and ground rules. Most of this information should have been disseminated prior to the session in a welcome letter or on your learning management system. However, since sometimes participants don't receive or read notifications or they may have questions, a quick review often proactively circumvents logistical questions.

Regarding ground rules, you may want to ask participants not to send private chat messages to other participants once the session starts, since these can be distracting. Likewise, you may request that attendees turn off email, pagers, cell phones, and any other potential distracters in their environment.

Finally, incorporate a short story, statistics, video, final class project, or demonstration to dramatize the benefits and relevance of the class knowledge and skills. Make your opener interactive. For example, in our session on defining business objectives as part of a needs assessment, we start with a question about the dollar investment made in training in the prior year. Most individuals guess way below the actual amount of fifty billion dollars! This financial grabber gives us a good lead-in to our discussion of defining and supporting operational objectives. In our class on constructing effective e-learning, we start by showing some examples and asking participants to grade each example and discuss reasons for their grades.

Introduce Yourself

Even when instructional environments are learner-centered, the instructor is on center stage. Participants want to know about your background, qualifications, and experience with the workshop topics and skills. Don't be too modest. Participants need to feel confident that their time is well spent with you as their guide.

In addition, communicate your personal commitment to the knowledge and skills you are about to impart. When shopping for a new home, Ruth learned a good lesson from an excellent real estate salesperson. As the agent showed each property, she pointed out three to five nice features—even features that hadn't been previously discussed. She was skilled at making the benefits of each product salient to a potential buyer. In the same way, no matter what your personal feelings might be for your topic, take a minute to put on your sales hat by expressing your enthusiasm for the benefits participants will gain.

Your introduction is also a good time to discuss ways you will work with participants individually outside of the session, for example, to help them with projects or to give feedback on their work. If you will have virtual office hours, post them on the white board during your introduction.

Make Your Introduction Visual

Second to interactions, visuals are your best tool to engage learners. As participants are logging in, have one to three slides set to cycle on the white board. You can create this effect with an automatic slide rotation in PowerPoint. These slides should include a topically relevant visual with the session title and session start time, a photo of the presenters with their names, and a reminder, with a relevant screen capture, for participants to test their audio and check their settings. We show an example in Figure 9.4.

As you kick off your session, incorporate relevant visuals in your introductory slides. The map exercise displayed in Figure 9.2 is a good example. Instead of the typical text agenda, display an organizational visual such as a road map showing qualitative relationships among session topics.

Make Introductions Concise

While writing this chapter, we attended a one-hour webinar on the features of a new virtual classroom software release. As regular users, we were very interested in the presentation. So were a number of others, as the session

Figure 9.4. Pre-Session Virtual Classroom Slide.
From the Excel lesson on *The New Virtual Classroom* CD

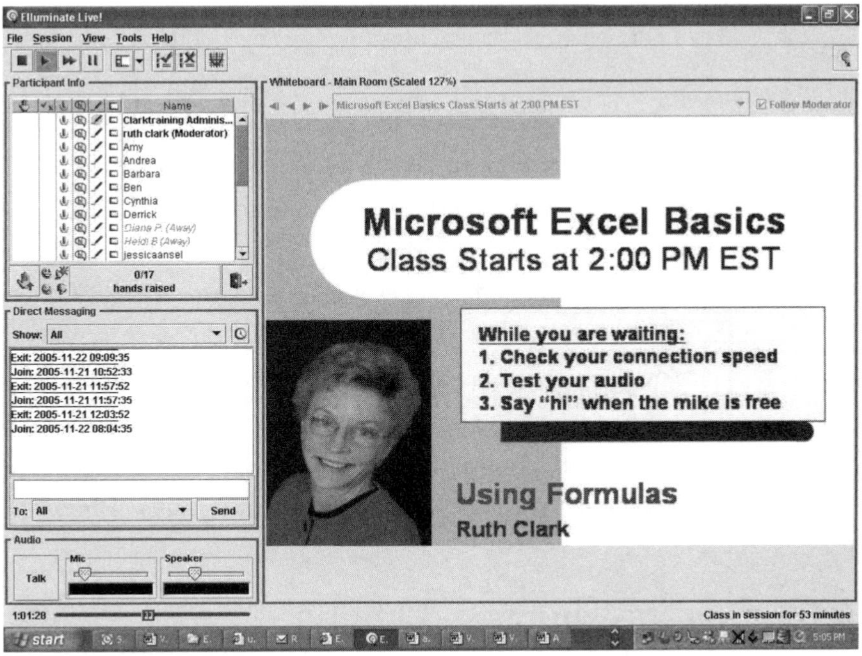

included forty-nine participants. After a map activity, each person was invited to introduce him- or herself via audio. The introductions consisted of each person stating his or her name and organization. These audio introductions took twenty minutes of the one-hour session. We felt cheated! Although audio is nice to establish social presence, we felt this was not an appropriate use of time for a one-hour event attended by a large number of people.

Our point is—make your introductions concise! An introduction to a one-hour event should not exceed five to seven minutes. If you are introducing a multi-session class attended by ten to twenty people, then it's appropriate to devote more time to individual introductions. In fact, your introduction may well consume fifteen to twenty minutes of your first session. Keep in mind that participants are primarily there to learn new information or acquire new skills. Your introductions should set the stage and then move into the content. An overly long introduction will result in mental (and maybe physical) dropout.

To accomplish the goals of an introduction and keep it concise, use the more efficient response facilities, including polling, direct messaging, and white boards. You might also use a breakout room to allow participants to do more extensive introductions in a small group and report back with some summary information, such as the expectations of participants. If you use a breakout room, post a short list of the information you would like exchanged or summarized on the white board in each room. Alternatively, pair up individuals and ask them to interview their partners using private chat. Post on the white board the information you would like them to obtain from their partners. Typical topics are company or division, job title and responsibilities, reason for attending the class, anticipated project topics, and so forth. After the private chats, each person could fill out some salient information about his or her partner on a white board grid prepared ahead of time.

A Sample Introductory Outline

Depending on the size of your audience, the length of your event, the number of sessions involved, and the instructional goals, incorporate several of the following into your session introduction:

1. *Sign-on slide:* Course title, event time, instructor photo, set-up tips

2. *Introductory title slide:* Course title, instructor photo and name

   Instructor welcomes and gives brief personal introduction

3. *Virtual classroom facilities overview slide:* labeled screen capture of interface

   Instructor overviews tool use and invites participants to try out features

4. *Map activity:* Participants identify themselves on map

   Instructor gives clear directions. When complete, instructor may invite participants to give weather reports from their areas via audio

5. *Ground rules slides:* Instructor sets expectations for session

- Use of chat

- Turn off cell phones, etc.

- Use of the "stepped away" icon, etc.

6. *Class objectives and agenda:* Instructor elaborates as appropriate, stressing value of skills

7. *Participant background information:* Interactive exercises to find out about prior knowledge, expectations, job applications, etc.

8. *Session lead-in activity* to activate prior knowledge, motivate, etc.: Instructor facilitates discussion around the lead-in

The Bottom Line

The time invested in a well-designed introduction will pay off in an event in which learners are familiar with the virtual classroom tools, each other, class expectations, and the instructor. We have described a number of techniques to establish social presence, get participants engaged from the start, and conduct an efficient introduction. Adapt our guidelines based on the amount of time your event(s) will consume and on the size of your audience.

COMING NEXT:
PACKAGING YOUR VIRTUAL CLASSROOM SESSION

In Chapter 10 we look at the virtual classroom in the context of a full learning system. We elaborate on the virtual classroom as part of a blended learning environment, as introduced in Chapter 1. We also make recommendations for the surrounding support elements you will need for a successful virtual session, including pre-session events, handouts, and facilitator support.

On *The New Virtual Classroom* CD

You can review the introductions we provide in our three demonstration classes.

How to Construct a Formula in Excel

This lesson includes the most extensive introduction. The first sixteen slides make up the introductory phase of the class and include "while you wait" slides, agenda and objectives, ground rules, tool orientation, participant introductions, including a map activity, a poll on their Excel experience, and a white board activity as a short interactive review of the prior lesson on cell references.

How to Define Business Goals

In addition to the standard elements mentioned above, you will see an orientation to the handouts that participants should have received and two introductory activities. One asks participants to type on the white board how much was spent on workforce learning in the previous year. The second asks participants to type in their definitions of a needs assessment.

How to Plan an Interview

The introduction includes a polling question to assess experience with needs assessments and a white board assignment asking participants to type in solutions—other than training—they have found when conducting needs assessments. This introduction is designed to activate prior knowledge and help the instructor assess participant experience.

EXPERTS' FORUM

HOW TO STRUCTURE AN INTRODUCTION

Brian Mulliner, eLearning and Development Consultant,
Wells Fargo

At Wells Fargo I have used the Centra Virtual Classroom to facilitate virtual application and soft-skill training, software and website/application demonstration, business group/staff meetings, and large conferences (more than two hundred people). During the opening segments of any virtual classroom session, we have found the following events set the stage for a successful event:

1. *Introducing leaders:* Introducing yourself and/or any co-presenters using photographs helps to personalize a virtual classroom training experience.

2. *Introducing participants:* Allowing participants to introduce themselves in a creative way, using the chat area, white board, voice, and/or a combination helps participants connect with the leader/facilitator, other students within the class, and the virtual feedback tools. Several examples follow:

   - Place a map of the United States of America (or map of a geographic area in which you are training) within the training window, grant your participants the ability to use the mark-up tools, and then instruct them to place stars on the map where they are located. Point out the farthest star, closest star, etc., from where the event is being virtually hosted and ask each individual to introduce him- or herself.

   - Ask participants to open up the text chat area, activate the public text chat, and then enter their favorite food, sport, color, etc. Once every participant has responded, then quickly tally the response totals (for example, three people said they loved pizza) and display the results for the class. It is also effective to simply have your participants enter their job titles/functions, how long they have been with the company, and their reasons for joining the event within the public text chat area. After every participant has responded, then pick several to highlight, as appropriate.

3. *Reviewing virtual interaction tools:* Explaining to the participants how to use the virtual classroom feedback tools, including how to raise their hands, use text chat, and respond to yes/no questions, is vital to a successful virtual classroom.

4. *Implementing virtual ground rules:* Establishing good ground rules is critical to the success of any virtual learning experience. Asking your participants to turn off their telephone ringers, pagers, cell phones, email, and instant message alerts will help them to focus and keep them from multitasking.

THE IMPORTANCE OF THE FIRST IMPRESSION

Heidi Bazilian, Online Classroom Teacher/Facilitator, PA Virtual Charter School and University of Phoenix Online

All the world's a stage and all the public speakers merely players. One of the most important items in any presentation, live or virtual, is the first impression. No matter what the goal or purpose of the presentation, the presenter is the one who sets a tone for the remainder of the presentation that will be the primary feeling the audience takes away from that presentation. Therefore, the presenter must carefully consider the introduction.

My experience in virtual teaching has been in the asynchronous environment in the high school and university settings. Now, though, I also have the opportunity to present to colleagues in a live online venue. One of the things normally stressed in public speaking is the preparation of the presenter. Since I am not seen by my audience, my first impression lies in the look of my first slides or white boards and the sound of my voice. In preparing for my presentations, I always take my audience into account. According to suggestions from the Advanced Public Speaking Institute, you should know from your audience and purpose what to wear: "Always dress one step more formally than your audience. It is better to err on the side of formality than to look sloppy" (see www.public-speaking.org/public-speaking-articles.htm). Likewise, you should know from your virtual audience and purpose what to say and how to say it.

When presenting to colleagues, I take a more conversational tone. I can bank on common experiences, attitudes, and knowledge. My openings can include humor, shared anecdotes, and connection polls. The opening minutes also offer an opportunity to make your participants comfortable with the tools of the classroom. I like to do it in a participatory activity, rather than in an instructional manner. It is also a way to lighten the tension and nervousness participants sometimes feel as they sit alone in their homes in your virtual classroom.

When presenting to students, I find I am more successful in building a rapport with them by sharing personal stories and information with them. In this way I become a human at the other end of the cable, and that makes the whole virtual experience more personal. The enthusiasm I show in my voice and my enjoyment of the process are contagious. I want them to catch that bug!

Chapter 1
Meet the New
Virtual Classroom

Introduction

Chapter 2
Learning
in the New VC

Chapter 3
Features to Exploit
in the New VC

Chapter 4
Teaching Content Types
in the New VC

Part 1: Learning and the New Virtual Classroom

Chapter 5
Visualize Your
Message

Chapter 6
Make It Active – Part 1

Chapter 7
Make It Active – Part 2

Part 2: Engaging Participants in the New Virtual Classroom

Chapter 8
Managing Mental Load
in the New VC

Chapter 9
Make a Good
First Impression

Chapter 10
Packaging Your
VC Session

Chapter 11
Problem-Based Learning
in the New VC

Part 3: Optimizing Your Virtual Events

Chapter 12
Getting Started

Part 4: Creating Effective Learning Events in the New Virtual Classroom

10

Packaging Your Virtual Classroom Session

THROUGHOUT THE BOOK WE HAVE FOCUSED ON the virtual classroom event itself—suggesting the kind of visuals and interactions that will promote learning and engagement during your session. However, a number of elements external to the event will shape the overall effectiveness of your virtual classroom sessions. We refer to these surrounding elements as *"packaging."* Our guidelines for packaging include the following recommendations:

- Integrate your virtual classroom sessions with other instructional media.
- Provide pre-session support that will enhance results from your virtual classroom event.
- Design handouts to accompany your virtual classroom sessions.
- Build facilitator comfort with the virtual classroom.

Blended Solutions

In Chapter 3 we mentioned that delivery media are not equivalent, since different instructional media can accommodate diverse instructional components. Moving images can be delivered on computers and video, but not in books. Learning activities that benefit from time and reflection are better allocated to asynchronous media, whereas instructional goals that benefit from social presence and synergy are better achieved in synchronous settings. The job of the instructional professional is to analyze the learning goal in order to define what important instructional components (modes, methods, and architectures) are needed to achieve it and then select the best mix of media available to realize those goals. Using two or more delivery media to accomplish a learning objective is called a *blended solution.*

Instructor-Paced vs. Learner-Paced Media

There are various ways to categorize instructional delivery media. As summarized in Figure 10.1, we divide media options into two main categories: (1) instructor-paced synchronous environments, which include face-to-face and virtual classrooms, and (2) learner-paced asynchronous media that are primarily designed for self-study and/or reference. Asynchronous self-study media include web-based lessons, books, websites, and various forms of electronic performance support systems (EPSS). Both synchronous and

Figure 10.1. A Taxonomy of Instructional Delivery Media.

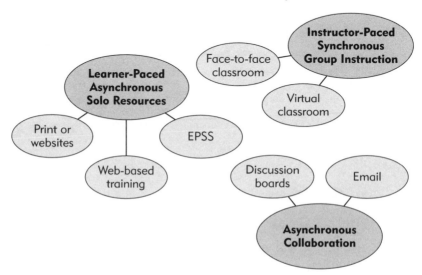

asynchronous environments can incorporate asynchronous collaborative options such as discussion boards and email for virtual team work.

The main differences between instructor-paced and learner-paced environments revolve around cognitive load and social presence. Instructor-paced environments tend to impose more mental load on participants because they proceed at the instructor's pace—not the learner's. At the same time, they offer opportunities for social exchanges between participants and instructor and among participants. To use these environments effectively, you should minimize cognitive load, as discussed in Chapter 8, and promote collaborative learning.

In contrast, self-study environments allow for consumption of information at a rate controlled by the learner. Typically, the content can be reviewed and revisited as desired. Therefore, they impose less cognitive load. Use these environments for reading or reviewing information and for project work that requires time and reflection. Asynchronous e-learning is also a good choice for extensive drill and practice of skills that must be learned to high degrees of accuracy or speed, plus content that can benefit from the use of video, animation, or simulations. As you can see, synchronous and asynchronous media complement each other, and an appropriate mix can give you the best of both worlds.

As you review your instructional goals, decide how to achieve them most effectively by considering which goals are best served by:

1. Time to review and reflect at the individual's own rate—asynchronous media

2. High social presence—face-to-face or virtual classrooms, coaching, etc.

3. Hands-on access to equipment—classrooms with laboratory facilities

4. Drill and practice to achieve automatic performance—asynchronous e-learning media

5. Use of rich media such as video, audio, or animation that provide important visual or auditory cues

6. Immersion in a highly interactive simulation in which students can receive feedback on the results of their actions

You can then plan ways to extend your virtual classroom sessions with pre-session or interim-session work that is more effectively or efficiently accomplished asynchronously. Helping participants acquire information and skills through readings—articles, books, or websites—and through asynchronous project work—either alone or with a group—can dovetail nicely with virtual classroom sessions. During the virtual classroom, discussions and interactions can expand on readings, engage participants in exercises and questions about prework, or review and refine projects completed outside of the virtual classroom. In the same

---

USERS SPEAK

Our advisory team members discuss blended solutions:

• Groups at Wells Fargo are using blended learning solutions quite regularly. Individuals may start out with a WBT course (typically Flash/Breeze launched and tracked via an LMS) for pre-work, attend a live classroom training event, and then use the virtual classroom for wrap-up/final or follow-up training. Blended learning solutions typically cut travel budgets and time out of the office, a real win-win for managers who need to cut their budgets and for participants required to maintain their sales goals.

Brian Mulliner, e-Learning and Development Consultant, Wells Fargo

• At Surgient we offer the *Virtual Training Management System* (VTMS), which enables organizations to provide live, hands-on labs in conjunction with instructor-led and self-paced software training. Students can reliably and securely access their own labs from anywhere in the world using a web browser (e.g., home, office, hotel). For example, one of our customers has a course that starts in the virtual classroom (e.g., introduction, key concepts) . . . then it moves on-site (e.g., instructor-led training at the customer's location) . . . then the remainder of the course is concluded online back in the virtual classroom. The entire course is delivered over three weeks and involves the use of hands-on labs in each phase.

Marcus McNeill, Director, Product Strategy, Surgient

way, you may want to mix face-to-face classroom events with a combination of any of the above. That way, you don't waste expensive face-to-face time on instructional processes that are more efficiently and effectively achieved in other venues.

For example, in our "Leveraging the Virtual Classroom" course, we ask participants to review two short recordings of virtual classrooms and note the differences before attending the first session. During the first virtual session, participants collaborate in breakout rooms to discuss the two sessions and to list the features they feel make up a good virtual classroom event. After each virtual classroom session, participants complete a project asynchronously in which they apply the skills taught in the class. They post their projects prior to the next virtual session, allowing the instructor and other participants to review and critique their work.

In some classes, the type of content drives the blend. More conceptual or complex content is scheduled in the virtual classroom, where the instructor can offer explanations and guidance, and answer questions. More procedural content is scheduled for self-study using e-learning demonstrations combined with performance support.

The number of ways to blend media is only limited by your imagination and resources.

Virtual Classroom Pre-Session Communication

Orienting participants prior to the first virtual classroom event will make your event smoother and more efficient and will increase learner satisfaction with the virtual classroom format. Some commonly used pre-session techniques include (1) a tool orientation prior to the first virtual class session, (2) a pre-session telephone conference with the instructor, and (3) a welcome notification that summarizes all critical information.

Tool Orientation

Technology problems are a common source of session disruptions. Technology problems may be technical in nature or may stem from lack of user experience with the tool. You can reduce these disruptions with a brief pre-event warm-up session in the virtual environment. The warm-up event helps new users verify and optimize their connectivity to the virtual classroom and check their headsets and microphones. In addition, it may include a brief orientation to the tool response facilities. Be sure to have technical support staff available during the orientation sessions. Depending on the size of your organization, standard orientation sessions for new users could be scheduled on a regular basis, such as weekly or monthly. Alternatively, a pre-session special meeting for new virtual classroom participants could be scheduled prior to the first session.

Instructor-Participant Telephone Introductions

If you are teaching a multi-session class to a relatively small group of twenty or fewer, you can get a lot of mileage out of a brief pre-session telephone introduction. By speaking with each attendee individually for even just a few minutes, you build a personal relationship before the session starts. We recommend telephone rather than email contact for a more personal introduction. The call also gives you the opportunity to identify relevant information regarding participant background knowledge, expectations, job applications of new skills, and so forth.

Pre-Session Notifications

Send a welcome letter or email to all participants that includes the following information:

- Program logistics: Dates, times, links, log-on information, plus all relevant technical information such as reminders to get headsets, links for pre-session technology tests, and so on
- Program information: Session benefits, objectives, prerequisites, number of sessions, assignments, time estimate for sessions and outside session work, policies, and administrative procedures
- Speaker or instructor qualifications
- Prework assignments with links to adjunct materials as needed
- Contact information

You will find a sample welcome letter on the CD, which you can adapt to your own needs. Many organizations automate the course welcome information in their learning management systems.

Planning Effective Handouts

It's common practice in virtual classroom sessions to hand out printed or electronic versions of the slides that are used during the virtual classroom session. **We recommend against this common practice!** Handing out copies of the slides will add cognitive load to the virtual classroom that, because it's instructor-paced, is already overloaded. Providing slides as handouts results in two potential sources of irrelevant cognitive load. First, slides as handouts are visually redundant of what participants are seeing on the screen. Research has shown that learning is depressed when redundant sources of information are provided during instruction (Clark, Nguyen, & Sweller, 2006). For example, Cerpa, Chandler, and Sweller (1996) found that participants who studied a computer lesson on spreadsheets and had handouts that duplicated the screens learned less than participants who relied on the computer lesson only. The researchers conclude that, for more complex content, "an integrated computer-based training package was superior to an integrated computer-based training format plus hard-copy format" (p. 364).

In addition to redundancy, overload occurs because the slides represent only part of the instruction—with the instructor narration carrying the rest of the message. Participants will instinctively take notes on their slide handout pages to capture the instructor's words. However, note-taking during an instructor-led event adds irrelevant cognitive load. Rather than attending to and processing new information, learners divide their limited mental capacity among listening, watching the slides, responding to questions, and writing notes. The result is mental overload and less learning.

Several recent reviews of research on note-taking during lectures show that (1) students record incomplete notes—usually fewer than 40 percent of the important lecture ideas, (2) note-taking provides no significant learning benefits for adult learners with higher-order learning goals, and (3) note-taking demands more mental effort than reading or other learning assignments (Kobayashi, 2005; Piolat, Olive, & Kellogg; Titsworth & Kiewra, 2004).

If you are not handing out slides, what should you provide? We recommend that you create working aids that package the key instructional content in a form that can be readily used back on the job. The most common formats for working aids include step-by-step procedure guides, checklists, templates, or summary tables. Figure 10.2 shows an instructor guiding the participants through a strategy template handout. The box under the slide text directs participants to an activity to complete in the handout. Providing working aids reduces cognitive load by minimizing note-taking during the class and promotes transfer of learning to the job by leaving participants with a reference guide. It's a good idea to make use of the job aids during the class

Figure 10.2. Instructor Gives Direction on How to Use Handout During the Session.

With Permission of Tony Karrer, TechEmpower

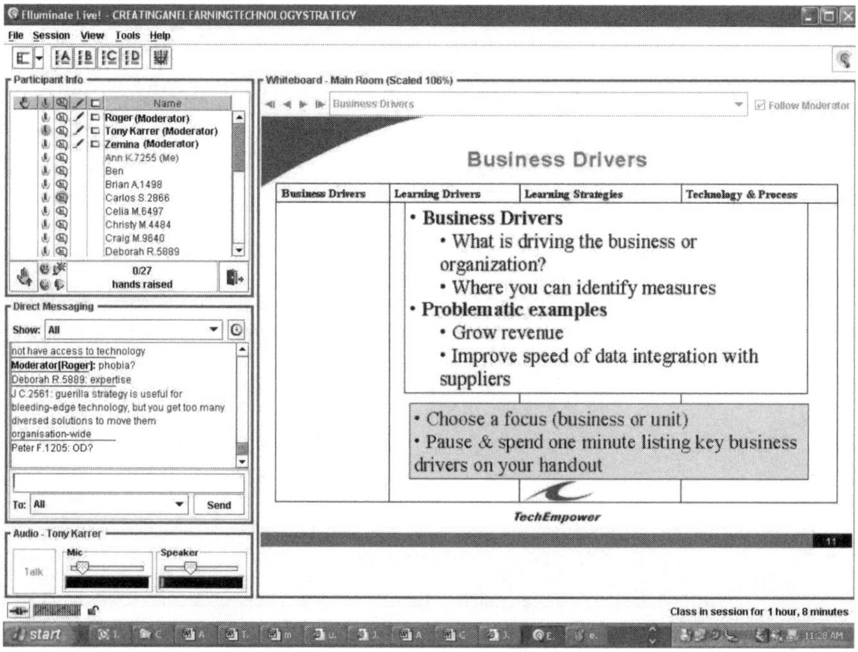

to increase the chances that they will be used again later on the job. For example, when assigning a practice exercise involving use of new technology, ask participants to refer to their procedure reference guide.

Facilitator Preparation

Recent adopters of virtual classroom technology cite instructor training and preparation as one of the most critical steps for successful virtual sessions. According to Marjan Bradesko, senior advisor of learning solutions for NIL, a Cisco Learning Solutions Partner, "Getting used to the virtual classroom was a challenge for both high and low experienced ILT instructors." As a result, students rated new and senior instructors the same in the NIL virtual classroom—unlike in the classroom setting, where rating differences are highly noticeable. Because all instructors were uncomfortable initially in the virtual setting, the differences between novice and experienced instructors were masked (Clark, 2005).

Many experienced traditional classroom facilitators are thrown off by the lack of body language feedback when teaching to an unseen audience. Gone are signals such as eye contact and facial expressions showing boredom, confusion, or interest. Gone also are the opportunities to move around the room and adjust position, pacing, or topics in response to participant body signals. Many of the physical classroom facilitators' techniques are predicated on body language, much of which is lost in the virtual classroom. Teaching in the virtual classroom requires a different skill set, not only to use the technology but also to learn new ways to "read" your audience.

In addition, managing features such as polling, multimedia, and breakout rooms while conducting the class and monitoring participant chat questions imposes multitasking challenges for new instructors. In Chapter 8, we offered a number of techniques to manage cognitive load of new instructors.

In this section we offer additional techniques for facilitators who are new to the virtual classroom, including facilitators with a great deal of face-to-face classroom experience.

A. Build Technology Comfort

In our first virtual classroom sessions, we relied on the easier response facilities, mostly polling and chat. We initially avoided the breakout rooms and application sharing because they took more tool finesse. As a result, our first sessions failed to fully utilize the technology. However, as we gained experience we gradually incorporated more of these techniques.

The sooner the technology fades into the background of the instructor's psyche, the better. Devoting cognitive effort to manipulating the tools drains mental energy from the main facilitator tasks. If presenters are wrestling with breakout rooms or setting up application sharing windows, they are less able to be with and respond to their participants. Consider one or more of the following tips to build comfort with the technology:

- Begin by attending several virtual classroom sessions given by experienced facilitators. Go beyond normal participation by noticing the instructional strategies the facilitator uses. Make note of how he engages participants. Consider how he uses audio, breakout rooms, and chat. Observe the pacing and the types of visuals he uses.

- Attend a basic "How to use the virtual classroom" course that focuses on tool mechanics and follow it with practice sessions using your own slides and a couple of student volunteers. Most virtual classroom software vendors offer tool training free of charge.

- Attend a "How to leverage the virtual classroom for learning" course, a class that goes beyond the tool mechanics to illustrate how to use the features of the virtual classroom in ways that lead to learning.

- Work with a producer who will help you with the virtual classroom tools. Producers can help you plan your event as well as provide assistance during the event by clearing polling, setting up application sharing, setting up breakout rooms, and so forth.

- Team teach. Pair up with another instructor—ideally someone experienced with the virtual classroom tool you will use. But even if you are both new, two heads and four hands are better than one head and two hands, and you will find useful ways to back each other up.

B. Plan Sessions That Leverage the Virtual Classroom

- If you are adapting an existing classroom course, look at your content and determine which topics are best suited for the virtual classroom and which elements might be assigned to other learning environments, as discussed at the start of this chapter.

- As you select your topics and objectives for the virtual classroom, remember that in this environment you must rely heavily on the images shown on the white board. Consider how to visualize your message as we described in Chapter 5. Use large graphics and text. When you do use text on slides, include only a few words. Explain your visuals with narration. Don't write out a complete audio script. You want to be conversational in your presentation—not reading previously prepared words.

- As you assemble your program, integrate the interactions discussed in Chapters 6 and 7, using diverse response options. More than anything else, frequent, meaningful, and varied interactions will engage your learners and guarantee participant satisfaction. But these interactions need to be prepared ahead and built into your slides and instructor notes. Don't rely on "on-the-spot" interactions. While your participants are responding to your interactions, you can be looking ahead in your notes, setting up breakout rooms, or just catching your breath.

- Prepare instructor guides. Whether you are preparing virtual classroom training for yourself or for others who will serve as instructors, prepare useful instructor guides. For example, you might develop a three-column page that includes content summary of the main instructional points, activity instructions, and the slide to be projected. Or you can print out the slides three to a page and write content and activity notes in the space to the right of each slide. You can view a sample instructor guide prepared by Karen Hyder in her commentary at the end of this chapter, as well as on the CD.

USERS SPEAK

Our advisory team members discuss instructor training for the virtual classroom

• At Wells Fargo, all virtual classroom facilitators are required to go through a two-hour leader training course. Topics within the two-hour class include joining virtual classroom and eMeeting events as a leader, uploading content/slides, advancing slides, using markup tools, etc. Within the training, we model positive virtual classroom facilitation skills.

Brian Mulliner, e-Learning and Development Consultant, Wells Fargo

• We train leaders online, in the physical classroom, asynchronously, and through blended learning. We offer over sixty online virtual classroom courses defined by role/pathway, physical classroom training that goes beyond just delivery techniques and best practices, and many other methods to train new leaders and existing leaders.

Amy Finn, VP Education and Chief Learning Officer, Centra Software

---

C. Show Time: Be Prepared

• Arrange for as quiet and distraction-free a working area as possible. Turn off cell phones, desk phones, email, and any other background distractions prior to your event.

• Remember to prepare yourself physically. Have water at your side and use the bathroom ahead of time. Have a prominent clock near your computer. Some instructors also log onto a second computer as a student. This helps them see the environment as the participants see it.

- Be online thirty to forty-five minutes ahead of time. You should allow plenty of time to load your slides and multimedia, test your audio, and be ready to greet those who enter the room first—just as in a physical classroom.

- Use audio to meet and greet participants as they enter the room. Have everyone try out their audio with some introductory comments. This establishes social presence and participant comfort with audio, and helps head off technology problems from the start.

- Launch your event on time, following the guidelines for getting off to a good start in Chapter 9

To conclude, the four main elements related to packaging your virtual events are summarized in Figure 10.3.

The Bottom Line

Your virtual classroom sessions are only one component of a successful learning event. Supporting elements that complement your virtual classroom sessions include use of diverse media to extend learning, effective handouts, and

Figure 10.3. Components of the Virtual Classroom Package.

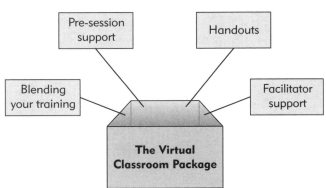

information provided to participants prior to the first session. Finally, if you are a new virtual classroom facilitator, apply several of the tips we described in the chapter to get off to a confident start.

COMING NEXT: PROBLEM-BASED LEARNING IN THE VIRTUAL CLASSROOM

In Chapter 2 we introduced four lesson design architectures: receptive, directive, guided discovery, and exploratory. Throughout the book, we have assumed a directive design in which short lessons present content, explain examples, and ask participants questions to reinforce learning. However, in some situations you may want to use a more inductive learning approach. In Chapter 11 we overview a form of guided discovery called problem-based learning and offer guidelines and examples of ways to adapt problem-based learning to the virtual classroom.

EXPERTS' FORUM

HOW TO LAY OUT A LESSON INVENTORY AND SCRIPT

Karen Hyder, Trainer of Trainers, Kaleidoscope Training and Consulting;
Speaker Coach/Online Event Host,
The eLearning Guild

Working as an online training skills coach, I've seen hundreds of trainers manage the unwieldy array of preparation and technical steps, learning objectives, and interactions by using an inventory and script to structure all the elements of the session into a flexible, visual, and linear format. Table 10.1 (which is also on the CD accompanying this book) is a sample lesson inventory and script. Use it as a session checklist. *A few notes:* In this table, the "tech check" confirms that the next step is prepared. Plan B may not be necessary for each step. When the instructional designer relies on a visual through application sharing or an activity using a software simulation, technology failure is a showstopper. An effective Plan B can refocus on the learning and keep the session flowing.

Table 10.1. Sample Inventory and Script for Online Session.

Inventory and Script for Advanced PowerPoint Session

Learning Content	Method	Graphic	Tech Check	Talk Track	Interaction	Intended Response	Response Method	Plan B
Using a PPT slide master	PPT slide intro	Sample slides to mark up	Ensure PPT file is loaded into session Tell how to mark up white board	In this lesson, we'll talk about a shortcut that expert PPT users rely on to make a change that affects each slide in the file.	What types of things would you want to globally change about this file?	1. Logo; 2. Fonts; 3. Bullet shapes; 4. Position of text	White board	Chat or verbal responses from participants
	App share changing the master		Open PPT file. Size Window. Test app share of PPT.	Note the current design template. Fonts sizes, colors, logo, background. We want something more streamlined. New logo.				Screen shots of master template. Point to objects on screen.

(Continued)

Table 10.1. Sample Inventory and Script for Online Session. (Continued)

Inventory and Script for Advanced PowerPoint Session

Learning Content	Method	Graphic	Tech Check	Talk Track	Interaction	Intended Response	Response Method	Plan B
	Demo inserting new graphic onto master slide		Open PPT file to be changed	Click on the logo and delete it. Insert new logo.	(For intense review of inserting graphics, prompt for steps.)	Insert picture from file. . .	Verbal	Chat (would be slow)
	Demo font change	Sample fonts Times, Tahoma		Let's make another change. Font. Smaller, sans serif.	Which would you choose?	Arial, Tahoma, Franklin Gothic		Screen shots of master template. Also, create updated master screen shot to reflect sample changes.

Activity	Ask participants to open practice file and instructions.	Make changes as instructed on slide.		Post instructions on slide. Review before they break for practice time.
Discussion			How will you use master templates?	Change background elements I don't like. Make text fit on one line.	Chat, verbal
Quiz			Quiz: 1. When to use? 2. What can be changed? 3. Be careful of?		Bonus poll: What shortcut will get you to the slide master from the normal view?

Notice the emphasis on interactions and responses. In a virtual classroom, the only way to find out what a learner is thinking is to ask. I find that when I ask clear, relevant questions and tell participants how to respond, they respond. When they respond correctly, I know they are learning.

This sample script can help a trainer plan and visualize each step in the session. It serves as an inventory for learning content, a checklist for technical preparation, and lists tasks and interactions planned for the session. The talk track is a script for the trainer. Suggested questions for the trainer are also scripted.

The notion of "scripting" might seem extreme to seasoned trainers. Consider the benefits of using carefully selected language and establishing use of new language as part of your preparation. It's not enough to ask, "Were you able to complete the assignment?" Instead, be ready to direct participants to respond. "If you were able to complete the assignment, click the Smiley button. If not, click Thumbs Down. Type your reactions and questions in Chat." This language might not be instinctive to face-to-face communicators. The use of accurate language and clear instruction will increase participants' ability and willingness to contribute to the learning session. Scripting the session might also cast a new light on topics that don't require a virtual classroom session, but instead, lend themselves to asynchronous work.

PARTICIPANT AND FACILITATOR PREPARATION

Rhea Fix, President, Red Pepper Consulting

I very much appreciate the methodology offered for choosing how to use the various online learning approaches to greatest advantage. Many organizations offer instructor-led sessions when they have instructors available, and self-paced when they do not. While instructor resources are necessary to having the instructor-led choice available, we easily forget to approach the decision based on the requirements for the learning processes taking place.

I'm a big believer in not only pre-session communication, but in communication throughout the process. The standard email messages generated by an LMS can be quite cryptic, long, and filled with information so generic that students do not take the special conditions for various blended solutions into account. I think an advance organizer message might be sent in addition to the one automatically generated. This message can be more conversational, set the context for the class with regard to the complete program, and answer a lot of the "why" questions a participant might ask about attending.

Tool orientations are a wonderful resource, along with reference job aids that participants can print out for use before or during the session. In addition, participants need a help desk number they can call for technical support. When you fail to include a technical support solution, your facilitators become virtual classroom help desks. Anxious for success, facilitators give out their contact information to students who may need help, only to be inundated by calls and emails requesting support down the line. Use an internal resource or the vendor-supplied support desk as part of an overall strategy.

On offering a copy of the PowerPoint slides for participants, as a contingency plan, I've sent the slides to participants to use in case the virtual class somehow went down during the session, and I've used them as such more than once!

The suggestions for preparing facilitators are right on target. Two colleagues from other companies use team teaching and facilitator shadowing to great advantage. One of them tells the story of working with a company that uses producers and team teaching often. She relates that one of their three-person teams once prepared for an online class session when a construction crew near the office knocked out the power to their building. The team members grabbed their laptops and ran to a facilitator's home nearby to facilitate the session from there. Each of them connected to a different telephone and cable connection in different rooms and conducted the class successfully, although the producer handled all the technical issues and chat questions from his connection in the bathroom. That's comfort with technology!

GUIDELINES FOR PARTICIPANT AND INSTRUCTOR SUPPORT

Brian Mulliner, e-Learning and Development Consultant, Wells Fargo

We apply the following guidelines for providing participant and instructor support for virtual events:

1. *Prework and participant instructions:* Make sure your participants have all the necessary materials/information for class. Materials may include participant

workbook(s), virtual classroom job aids, reading materials, exercises, and course URLs. Event information may include date, time, and prework requirements. Remember to include a technical support number.

2. *Leader/facilitator's guide:* A leader/facilitator's guide may capture the choreography of the program. The leader, participants, and virtual tools may be required to complete different tasks at the same time, so you may want to include a detailed plan that explains the overall course design, including time guidelines, transitions, leader scripting and facilitation tasks, slide screen shots, extra notes and tips, and production tasks.

3. *Check with participants:* You may want to send an email to participants several days prior to a scheduled class to remind them of the start time (including time zone), instructions for attending class, software to be downloaded and prework requirements, and technical support numbers.

4. *Have participants complete a "system check":* Have participants complete the "system check" one week prior to the virtual event. If they are unable to pass the "system check," this will allow adequate time for troubleshooting. You may also ask participants to log into the event ten minutes early to ensure that they are able to get into the course prior to start time.

5. *Review the course content/have a dress rehearsal:* Make sure that you are comfortable with the course content. If you did not design the course yourself, you might want to contact the instructional designer with questions. You also may want to schedule a practice event to rehearse your course delivery prior to the live event.

6. *Offer structured instructor training:* All our virtual classroom facilitators are required to go through a two-hour leader training course. Topics within the two-hour class include joining VC and eMeeting events as a leader, uploading content/slides, advancing slides, using markup tools, managing participant feedback, creating and launching surveys, facilitating Centra evaluations, sharing applications/screens, conducting Web Safaris, inserting URLs/launching web

pages, and responding to basic technical difficulties. Within the training, we model positive virtual classroom facilitation skills, highlighting various skills periodically. After training, each participant is provided with resources, including a virtual classroom leader quick reference guide, facilitation tips guide, planning and scheduling templates and tools, and technical information and help resources.

Chapter 1
Meet the New
Virtual Classroom

Introduction

Chapter 2
Learning
in the New VC

Chapter 3
Features to Exploit
in the New VC

Chapter 4
Teaching Content Types
in the New VC

Part 1: Learning and the New Virtual Classroom

Chapter 5
Visualize Your
Message

Chapter 6
Make It Active – Part 1

Chapter 7
Make It Active – Part 2

Part 2: Engaging Participants in the New Virtual Classroom

Chapter 8
Managing Mental Load
in the New VC

Chapter 9
Make a Good
First Impression

Chapter 10
Packaging Your
VC Session

Chapter 11
Problem-Based Learning
in the New VC

Part 3: Optimizing Your Virtual Events

Chapter 12
Getting Started

Part 4: Creating Effective Learning Events in the New Virtual Classroom

11

Problem-Based Learning in the New Virtual Classroom

FOR LEARNERS WITH RELEVANT CONTENT EXPERIENCE who need to build skills involving problem solving and judgment, consider a blended instructional approach that incorporates a guided-discovery architecture. In this chapter we define and illustrate a type of guided-discovery course design called problem-based learning (PBL). We discuss the conditions under which problem-based learning is likely to succeed and summarize a design plan for adapting problem-based learning to a virtual classroom environment.

Instructive vs. Inductive Learning Environments

In Chapter 2 we introduced three components of effective instruction: communication modes, instructional methods, and design architectures. Throughout this book we have focused primarily on *directive architectures* in the virtual classroom. Directive architectures are *instructive*. By that we mean they are heavily guided. Directive architectures are characterized by a series of short lessons that give explanations and show examples, followed by practice and feedback. These instructional methods help learners gradually build new job-relevant knowledge and skills. Directive architectures are most effective during the beginning stages of learning.

In some situations, however, a guided-discovery architecture might offer a more appropriate design for your learners and instructional goals. In this chapter we offer guidelines and examples for creating an *inductive learning* environment using a blend of delivery media that includes the virtual classroom. Specifically, we will describe how to adapt a type of guided discovery known as *problem-based learning* to the virtual classroom.

What Is Problem-Based Learning (PBL)?

PBL is a type of guided-discovery course design in which learners work collaboratively to solve a problem or complete an assignment and learn new concepts and skills in the process. PBL was first introduced in medical education over thirty years ago and has since diffused to multiple domains, including medical education, MBA programs, higher education, chemical engineering, and economics, to name but a few (Savery, 2006). PBL is characterized by the following features:

1. *Problem-centered.* Learning is **initiated and driven** by actual or realistic work assignments. These may be case problems or design tasks. A medical diagnosis case starts off with a patient interview. A course on loan analysis begins with a loan application. A course on design of websites starts with a client request for a website to support a small business.

2. *Solo and collaborative.* Problem solution or task completion is usually accomplished by a combination of solo and collaborative teamwork. For example, after reviewing a medical case individually, the learning team works together to list the learning issues and define the resources they will use to resolve the case. In a website design task, the team meets initially to discuss and agree on a work process. The team discussion is followed by individual work to post alternate solutions to a common online space.

3. *Product and process goals.* The learning goal is often not only the problem solution, but also the process used to arrive at the solution. For example, it's important in a website design task to follow a structured process that includes requirements definition and prototype building. A loan analysis should follow a specified business process to collect and analyze relevant data.

4. *Instructional resources provided.* Instructional resources can include traditional lesson tutorials, annotated examples of solutions, process worksheets, references, and expert consultations, to name a few. For example, for a web design task, lessons, readings, sample annotated websites, and expert advice are available on various topics, including graphic art, online usability, design processes, and e-commerce.

5. *Traditional and naturalistic feedback.* Feedback is available throughout and at the end of the lesson or course. Traditional forms of feedback involve review of project processes and products by instructors and peers. This type of feedback is guided by a checklist or rubric of required solution features or project events. Feedback can also include more naturalistic consequences in which learners receive real-world reactions to the quality of their solutions. For example, in our classroom workshop "How to Plan, Design, and Evaluate e-Learning," teams test their prototype lessons with a group unfamiliar with their topic. The simulated "learners" take the lesson designed by the project team, followed by a criterion test created by the instructor and matched to the objectives of the case. A successful project lesson yields high average test scores with low standard deviations. This type of feedback provides an approximation to real-world evidence of the effectiveness of the instruction.

6. *Reflection.* Reflection on what is learned as a result of problem solution is a critical ingredient promoted by the PBL instructor. Often participants become very immersed in the problem and its solution. It is up to the facilitator to incorporate activities

that will lead to reflection and analysis of what new concepts and skills were learned from the problem. Some common reflection techniques include small team debriefings of lessons learned, keeping a journal, or preparing a "If we had to do it over" synopsis.

PBL in the Virtual Classroom

Because virtual classroom technology is still relatively new, there are few examples of PBL in this environment. Therefore, we created a short demonstration virtual classroom lesson as part of a PBL course on conducting performance assessments. You can see the entire lesson on *The New Virtual Classroom* CD. This lesson focuses on interviewing skills. The lesson outcome goal is to create an effective interview guide to be used during a senior manager interview as part of a performance assessment.

We begin the lesson with an introductory interaction in which participants write on the white board performance solutions other than training they have uncovered when doing needs assessments. The goal of this activity is to activate prior knowledge about performance assessments as well as to determine the background experience of the participants.

Following this exercise, we show a video of the beginning moments of a senior manager interview. Figure 11.1 is a screen shot from this portion of the session. Following the video, teams work in breakout rooms to answer several questions about what they learned from the opening minutes of the interview and to identify what questions they would want to ask in the next portion of the interview.

After debriefing the team discussions in the main room, the participants are assigned to write an interview guide and are asked to list on the white board what they need to learn in order to construct that guide. The instructor then posts a list of resources they can use after the virtual session as they write up their interview guides. Resources include text readings, sample interview guides, and links to experienced consultants. Teams will work asynchronously to write an interview guide and post it to the class website prior to the next virtual session.

Figure 11.1. The Beginning of an Interview Sets the Stage for the Problem.
From the Interviewing Skills Lesson on *The New Virtual Classroom* CD.

Problem-based learning (PBL) designs initiate lessons or courses with a problem or assignment and use the problem or assignment to drive the learning. The instructor offers resources and gives learners time and flexibility to review resources as desired and to complete assignments. PBL allows learners greater freedom to achieve learning goals as they solve the presented problem, compared to a more structured directive architecture, in which the instructor provides the content, asks questions about it, and may assign an application case study.

The PBL format assumes that learners can solve a problem or complete an assignment while they are learning. To complete these two goals simultaneously imposes more mental load than directive learning environments. Therefore, PBL is risky for novice learners with no background related to the course objectives (Clark, Nguyen, & Sweller, 2006). Use guided-discovery designs such as PBL only when they are appropriate to your learners and instructional objectives.

When to Use PBL

PBL is not for all learners and all instructional goals. Figure 11.2 summarizes the main situations that point to PBL as a good course design candidate.

Use PBL for More Experienced Learners

Most guided-discovery learning architectures, including problem-based learning, impose too much cognitive load for learners who are unfamiliar with the content (Clark, Nguyen, & Sweller, 2006). Asking beginners to learn at the same time that they are solving a problem is usually asking too much. You can still use case studies in lessons designed for novices. However, it's better to assign cases or tasks to beginners **only after** a series of traditional directive lessons. This approach allows novices to build basic mental models **before** they apply them to a case study. Remember that, in PBL, the lesson **begins** with a case, and the case problem is the **driver** for learning. Reserve PBL for more advanced classes.

Figure 11.2. When to Use Problem-Based Learning.

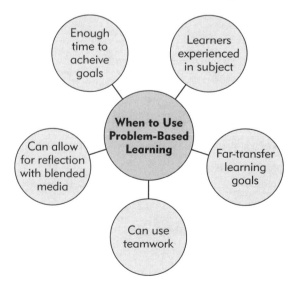

Use PBL for Far-Transfer Tasks

Guided discovery is best suited for tasks that are far-transfer in nature. By that we mean tasks for which there is not a single correct solution and that involve considerable judgment and problem solving. Design and develop assignments or case problems that have multiple potential solutions such as designing a care plan for a patient, creating a small business website, or applying ethics guidelines when faced with a controversial decision.

Use PBL When Groups Can Work Together Synchronously and Asynchronously

Because there are usually multiple perspectives to far-transfer problems or tasks, PBL lends itself well to collaborative learning. Therefore, consider PBL when you have a group of learners who can work in both synchronous and asynchronous modes. Assign teams ranging from three to five members to work on case problems together. The diverse ideas and resources of the team enrich the learning context.

Balance opportunities for individual study and project work with synchronous team sessions that generate synergy and leverage diverse viewpoints and expertise. PBL is ideal for blended-delivery designs that combine the virtual classroom with asynchronous modes of learning, including self-study and asynchronous team work mediated with discussion boards or project rooms for posting and reviewing work in progress.

For example, after an initial orientation meeting in the virtual classroom, individual class members may work alone to review a case introduced during the synchronous session, along with its supporting resources. Each team member can post the learning issues and/or proposed project work process. The second virtual classroom meeting may use breakout rooms to discuss team processes, define learning resources, and develop a project plan. The third virtual session may incorporate an instructor-led lesson that overviews best-known processes for resolving these types of problems and/or offers basic instruction in the underlying related knowledge and skills.

Be sure to assign teams frequent and specific project milestones to be presented and discussed in virtual sessions. Frequent specific assignments with regular deadlines will keep the course on track and ensure completion of interim asynchronous work.

Use PBL When You Have Ample Instructional and Development Time

Problem-based learning takes more time. First, to design and develop an effective PBL course will generally require more time than designing and developing a traditional directive class. For instance, often cases and case resources designed for PBL make use of realistic media such as video interviews and realistic case artifacts such as credit reports or patient histories. Second, the learning time will typically be longer than traditional lessons in order to incorporate opportunities for team discussions, individual review of resources, and individual and group reflection on case products. Therefore, consider PBL when you will have enough time for design and development as well as delivery of the various synchronous and asynchronous components.

Does PBL Work?

We do not yet have extensive evidence of the effectiveness of PBL compared to more traditional directive instruction. Hmelo-Silver (2004) concluded that, while there is no clear evidence that PBL offers significant learning advantages over traditional instructional approaches, PBL medical students report more positive attitudes than students engaged in traditional courses. Learning while working on a realistic problem seems more relevant than training that presents knowledge and skills outside of an application context. Therefore, PBL lessons have great motivational potential. At the same time, learning while simultaneously solving a problem runs the risk of creating mental overload. Clark, Nguyen, and Sweller (2006) caution: "For now, we suggest that you consider whole task course designs [e.g., PBL] only for learners with considerable relevant prior experience because these learners are likely to have already learned many of the components" (p. 180).

Projects vs. Cases in PBL

You may want to use projects and/or case problems as the basis for your PBL class.

What Is Project-Based Learning?

A project is a real-world problem or requirement for which a team will plan, implement, and evaluate a solution. *Project-based learning* is similar to the reality TV show "The Apprentice." Teams are assigned an actual task to perform and are evaluated by real-world outcomes. Solving real-world problems or cases can be highly motivating! However, real-world tasks are less controlled than constructed cases and thus may not offer opportunities to learn and practice a specified range of skills. Learning will be driven by the variables and constraints inherent in the real-world situation. In addition, in domains in which errors have high-risk consequences, real-world projects, if used at all, must be closely supervised by an instructor or mentor.

In a project-based approach, participants (or sometimes the instructor) bring to class a real-world problem that meets specified criteria relevant to the instructional goal. Each participant can "present" his or her project and lobby for its adoption. The instructor or a combination of instructor and participants select several of these projects. Then students select or are assigned to project teams.

A colleague of ours uses a project-based approach in her university course on conducting training needs assessments. She solicits local companies to provide a real-life problem or issue they are facing and assigns teams to each project. A typical class will be working on four to six different projects throughout a semester. Regular face-to-face class meetings provide opportunities to discuss project challenges, and the combination of all of the projects offers a variety of learning opportunities.

What Is Case-Based Learning?

A case is a constructed scenario or task that offers prepared supporting data, along with resources and guidance tailored to the case. Constructed cases offer more control over variables linked to acquisition of specific knowledge and skills. They also offer an opportunity to see and discuss multiple different approaches and solutions to the same case. Like projects, constructed cases should reflect realistic work environments. In fact, often cases are adaptations of real-world situations simplified or altered to achieve the learning objectives.

Valaitis, Sword, Jones, and Hodges (2005) evaluated an online PBL course that used a case to teach nursing students about fetal alcohol spectrum disorder (FASD). The case was initiated with patient background history and a video interview of the patient by a health care professional. Figure 11.3 shows a screen capture from the video interview. The nursing students were positive about the videos, commenting that "the interviews were a little bit more helpful to me than actually reading through some of the forms, just because it seemed like you were there and doing that observation. . . ." (Valaitis, Sword, Jones, & Hodges, 2005 p. 241).

Kamin, O'Sullivan, Deterding, and Younger (2003) found richer team discussions followed a medical case presented with video, compared to a group that reviewed the same case in print. In a medical case, video can provide data on patient appearance and sounds that cannot be conveyed as realistically in print.

Figure 11.3. A Medical Case Is Initiated with a Patient Interview.
With permission from Ruta Valaitis. Accessed December 7, 2005, from www.fhs.mcmaster.ca/pblonline/scenarios.htm.

Additionally, the realism of video may engage learners more than a text case. A training design team at Microsoft converted a case presented in text to a multimedia environment that included video interviews, a case company website, and case-relevant documents such as network diagrams. The design team reported that class participants treated the video case as though it were a real client much more than when the case was presented in print.

In sum, consider video delivery of your case when visual and auditory realism are important elements of the case or when your audience is likely to be more engaged with greater degrees of realism.

Planning a PBL Course

Figure 11.4 summarizes our design model for creating PBL classes. We draw on our interviewing skills sample lesson from the CD as well as the fetal alcohol spectrum disorder (FASD) lesson to illustrate each phase of the model.

Define the Process and Product Deliverables

The center box—the *task deliverable*—is the driving element for your design. Start by defining the product and process deliverables as part of your job analysis process. Sample product deliverables include a patient care plan, a

Figure 11.4. A Design Model for PBL Lessons.

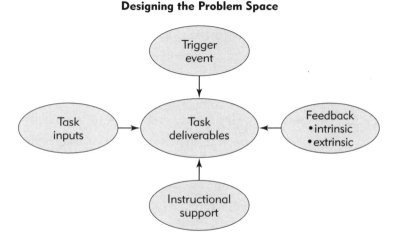

Designing the Problem Space

loan funding decision, an interview guide, or a website design. Process specifications include best practices to follow while creating the product or solving the problem. The process may include a systematic approach to assessing patient or client needs, creating product prototypes, gathering various types of data, and so on. During the job analysis, identify the products and processes linked to organizational strategic goals. Create a checklist or rubric that lists the key features required of an acceptable product and solution process. The checklist will be used to guide learners as well as serve as an evaluation tool for instructors.

In our interviewing demonstration lesson, the final deliverable is an interview guide. Some of the criteria for an acceptable guide include questions to elicit: (1) management's business goals and goal indicators, (2) management's beliefs about the source of the problem, and (3) constraints that will shape the final intervention. In the FASD medical class, the final deliverable is a project in which students apply what they have learned in a practical way, such as creating a patient teaching plan or developing a long-term plan of care.

Identify Case Supporting Data (Task Inputs)

In order to work on a case problem or create a product, the learning teams will need relevant case data, also called _task inputs_. To define needed data for your case problem, during the job analysis, make a list of all the inputs that good performers use to create the deliverables. For a task deliverable of a loan decision, some inputs include applicant credit report, applicant work history including salary data, business statements, and so forth. If the task deliverable is a small-business website, some inputs include information on the specific business, such as the type of products or services offered, a profile of the customer's functionality requirements such as e-commerce, and an existing logo and other branding data.

In our interviewing lesson, our case resources include a fact sheet on the client, an organizational chart, an introduction to the interview, and sample customer complaint data. For the FASD medical case, supporting data included the patient history shown in Figure 11.5. Supporting data can be made available via documents, audio or video interviews, website, graphs, and tables, and other means.

Figure 11.5. A Patient Record Adds Context to a Medical Case.

With permission from Ruta Valaitis. Accessed December 7, 2005, from www.fhs.mcmaster.ca/pblonline/scenarios.htm.

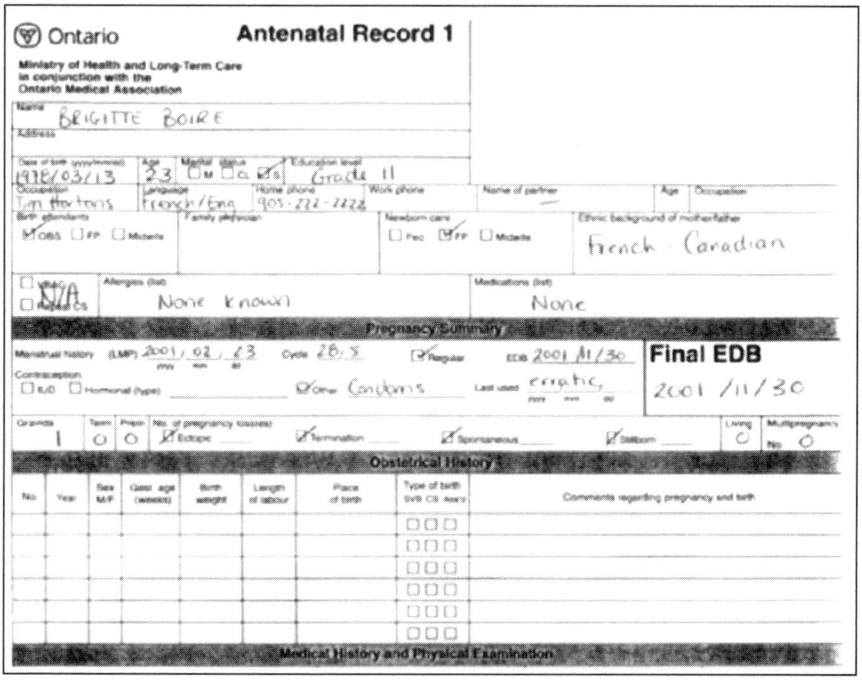
Ontario
Antenatal Record 1
Ministry of Health and Long-Term Care
in conjunction with the
Ontario Medical Association
Name: BRIGITTE BOIRE
Address
Date of birth: 1978/03/13 Age: 23 Education level: Grade 11
Occupation: Tim Hortons Language: French/Eng Home phone: 905-222-2222
Ethnic background of mother/father: French - Canadian
Allergies (list): None known
Medications (list): None
Pregnancy Summary
Menstrual history (LMP) 2001/02/23 Cycle 28/5 Regular EDB 2001/11/30
Final EDB 2001/11/30
Contraception: Other Condoms Last used erratic
Gravida 1 Term 0 Prem 0 Living 0 Multipregnancy No 0
Obstetrical History
No. Year Sex M/F Gest. age (weeks) Birth weight Length of labour Place of birth Type of birth SVB CS Ass'd Comments regarding pregnancy and birth
Medical History and Physical Examination

Design Resources for Instructional Support

Since the goal of PBL is learning, various types of instructional resources must provide the knowledge and skills needed to help learners achieve the final deliverable product and process. These can include traditional tutorial lessons, textbooks, process worksheets or project planners, expert mentor guidance in the form of real or virtual experts, and sample annotated task deliverables from other projects, to name a few.

Our interviewing lesson includes textbook readings, sample interview guides, and email links to experienced professionals. The FASD course provided an informational video on FASD, an animation of embryological facial development, and email contacts to real-life experts, including a public health nurse, a nurse practitioner, and a legal guardian of two children with FASD. Figure 11.6 shows the interface for accessing the medical experts. "Anna Guardian," an

Figure 11.6. Experts Can Be Accessed by Email in a Medical Case.
With permission from Ruta Valaitis. Accessed December 7, 2005,
from www.fhs.mcmaster.ca/pblonline/scenarios.htm.

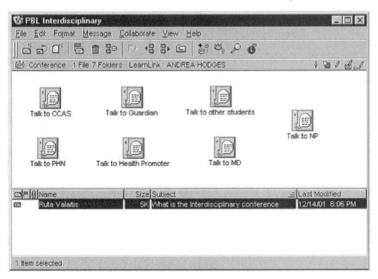

individual who actually served as a guardian for children with FASD, was an especially popular resource. One participant commented, "Having a real person with real experience, that was really good," noting that Anna Guardian was more genuine than the characters in the PBL case videos (Valaitis, Sword, Jones, & Hodges, 2005, p. 242). Another participant commented: "That public health nurse posted a huge response . . . very, very detailed. And it was really good to have those resources" (p. 242).

Plan Feedback and Evaluation

Your task deliverable and process checklists will summarize the criteria of an effective end product and process. The instructor, other class members, or external customers could all be sources of feedback on the deliverables. We call this type of instructional feedback *extrinsic*. In addition, your project might lend itself to real-world feedback—what we call *intrinsic feedback*. For example, small business website prototypes could be presented to customers (actual or volunteers), who would rate them for usability and design. In a pharmaceutical company, sales teams created a sales "script" for a new product and practiced it in a class role play, with medical doctors serving as consultants critiquing each plan.

Feedback and evaluation should be used to promote reflection on lessons learned from the problem—both the specific domain content and processes—as well as strategic skills such as research techniques, collaborative skills, and learning processes. Reflection on lessons learned from the case or project is one of the most important elements of a PBL program. Imagine the increased learning potential of the TV show "The Apprentice" if at the end, teams explicitly compared their approaches and articulated lessons learned! Hung (2006) suggests that participants be assigned to keep a journal during the learning process to promote reflection.

Our interview class requires each participant to develop an interview guide. A team that includes the instructor and two class participants rates the guides using a checklist. At a subsequent virtual classroom session, participants are able to see how the introductory video "plays out" and compare the actual interview with their own plans.

Plan the Trigger Event

Case studies begin with some form of kickoff, or what we call a *trigger event*. The trigger event should reflect real-world initiators and be delivered in as realistic a manner as possible. Some sample trigger events include a video or email assignment from a supervisor, a schedule of patients to be seen by a health care professional, or a telephoned client request. The trigger event should give some case background, expectations, and directions for accessing related case data and instructional support.

In our interview course, the trigger event is a video of the initial stages of an interview with the client manager. Based on the trigger event, participants define their learning issues and what questions they would ask the manager being interviewed. In the medical case, the written and video case information serves as the trigger event.

Plan Your Delivery Media Blend

As you define the various elements of your case, consider how each can best be delivered. Which elements should be incorporated in virtual classroom sessions and which elements are best made available for asynchronous work? In general, case events that involve study or reflection or require time to complete are best assigned to asynchronous environments. In contrast, events that benefit from the synergy of social exchanges are best handled in the virtual classroom. Consider an alternating series of events in which synchronous sessions are complemented by interim session work.

We planned our interview lesson class to include two virtual classroom sessions with interim asynchronous assignments. The class is kicked off in the virtual classroom with the video showing the initial stages of the interview. Teams meet in breakout rooms to summarize what they learned from the video and consider what additional data they will need. In between virtual sessions, teams access and analyze data, consult instructional resources, and post a draft interview guide. The second virtual class session reviews the draft interview guides and shows the full video interview. Figure 11.7 summarizes the main elements of the interview guide PBL learning environment.

Figure 11.7. A Summary of PBL Case Elements for Interview Lesson.
From *The New Virtual Classroom* CD

I. Deliverables
NA interview guide that includes questions that will:
    1. Define operational goals and metrics
    2. Identify solution constraints
    3. Identify manager's view of problem's causes
    4. Identify organizational contacts

II. Trigger Event
1. Introduction to the interview via video

III. Case-Task Inputs
1. Organizational chart
2. Complaint data
3. Job standards

IV. Instructional Support
1. Expert advice
2. Interview guide samples and templates
3. Text book readings

V. Feedback
1. Review of guides by instructor and class peers

The medical case was primarily delivered via asynchronous online resources, supplemented with chat sessions. Participants reported that online chats were the most effective method for making decisions, although they also commented that chat sessions were overwhelming and frustrating (Valaitis, Sword, Jones, & Hodges, 2005). In the virtual classroom, you can use the breakout rooms for outcomes that lend themselves to group decisions and discussions.

The Bottom Line

Learners with background experience in the course content will find an inductive learning environment such as PBL more motivating than a traditional instructive approach. Use guided-discovery architectures such as PBL for learners who are relatively more advanced, for far-transfer instructional goals that involve problem solving, and for longer courses in which you can interweave asynchronous learning opportunities.

The design and deployment of effective PBL is a complex topic, and we have only introduced the main concepts here. For additional information, consult the references listed on the next page. No doubt in the next few years we will learn more about implementing effective PBL sessions in virtual classroom environments.

COMING NEXT: GETTING STARTED IN THE NEW VIRTUAL CLASSROOM

In our final chapter, we describe seven principles that underpin the approach we recommend for best success with virtual classroom technology. Included are tips for how to tackle a conversion from a face-to-face classroom course to a virtual classroom course, in addition to how to plan a virtual classroom course from scratch.

On *The New Virtual Classroom* CD

You can review the virtual classroom lesson that uses a PBL approach in our lesson on How to Plan an Interview.

For More Information

Hmelo-Slver, C. E. (2004). Problem-based learning: What and how do students learn? *Educational Psychology Review, 16*(3), 235–266.

Hung, W. (2006). The 3C3R model: A conceptual framework for designing problems in PBL. *The Interdisciplinary Journal of Problem-Based Learning, 1*(1), 55–77.

Jonassen, D. H. (2004). *Learning to solve problems.* San Francisco: Pfeiffer.

Savery, J. R. (2006). Overview of problem-based learning: Definitions and distinctions. *The Interdisciplinary Journal of Problem-Based Learning, 1*(1), 9–20.

Valaitis, R. K., Sword, W. A., Jones, B., & Hodges, A. (2005). Problem-based learning online: Perceptions of health science students. *Advances in Health Sciences Education, 10,* 231–252.

EXPERTS' FORUM

A PROBLEM-BASED LEARNING MODEL APPLIED THREE WAYS

Julie Marsh, President, InterWorks

As the president of InterWorks, a small training and communications company located in San Francisco, I have been involved in creating PBL projects for many years. My partner (and husband) Paul Drexler and I started off in a rather unique way, by developing a consumer game for Grolier Publishing called SFPD Homicide. Our game used a point-of-view design and a unique database structure to simulate a homicide detective's job, from discovering the body to gathering sufficient evidence to convict. We realized that we had developed an effective simulation when SFPD Homicide was used to teach police procedures and accident investigation. Figure 11.8 shows the interface for questioning a suspect.

 InterWorks decided to apply this design approach for corporate training and was selected by Bank of America to develop a simulation for loan officers and underwriters called Fair Lending Challenge. We used many of the same techniques for

Figure 11.8. SFPD Homicide Game.

With permission from InterWorks.

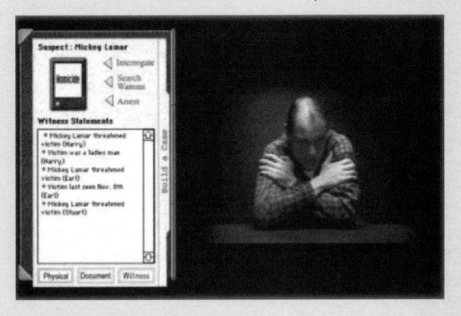

this product that we had used for our murder mystery. As Paul said, "The only real difference between approving a loan and solving a murder is the dead body." Both tasks require interviewing, research, inductive and deductive reasoning, thoroughness, and following a set of proscribed steps within defined perimeters. Figure 11.9 shows the interface for interviewing an applicant. You can see the similarities to SFPD Homicide!

Fast forward a few years. Paul and I were working at Bechtel Corporation, the world's largest engineering and construction company. At Bechtel, where safety is the top corporate value, we received support from some strategic managers to develop an innovative approach to safety training using PBL. The subjects were chosen on the basis of safety issues that were of greatest concern to the company. These ranged from fall protection (most fatalities are caused by falls), ergonomics and office safety (construction incidents were falling, but office incidents were on the rise), driving safety (a common cause of accidents), to people-based safety (a behavior-based approach to reducing at-risk behaviors adopted by the company as a standard). Figure 11.10 capture shows the interface from the Office Safety PBL program.

Figure 11.9. Fair Lending Challenge.

With permission from InterWorks.

Figure 11.10. Office Safety.

With permission from InterWorks.

While the subjects (and budgets) varied, all projects involved:

- Practice opportunities based on realistic scenarios in which the learners make decisions that they would actually face on the job
- Specific feedback based on the learner's actions
- Rich use of media
- High degree of interactivity and game play
- Believable and engaging characters
- When appropriate, humor

Some key lessons learned:

- Simple is better.
- A low budget does not necessarily produce an inferior product; it forces the team to hone in on the "have to haves" and eliminate the "nice to haves."
- Navigation cannot be too obvious or easy.
- Programs need to reflect the real world to be effective.
- Learners love games!

Please note that these three programs are all designed as asynchronous, self-paced learning solutions and would need to be adapted for use in the virtual classroom.

Our PBL safety training projects have proved successful and popular. Our pretests and post-tests demonstrate significant knowledge gain. In addition, these programs are some of the most frequently used by learners at Bechtel. Finally, our PBL programs have contributed to the safest year in Bechtel's history (2005)!

AN EXAMPLE OF BLENDED PROBLEM-BASED LEARNING

Dr. Marty Rosenheck, VP of Design and Development,
Cedar Interactive, Inc.

My company designs and develops blended learning solutions and curricula for large and medium-sized organizations. I have found that the virtual classroom can be a critical element in a blended curriculum when the participants are in different locations. In this context, the virtual classroom is best used to discuss, solidify, and clarify content learned through asynchronous means. It also serves to build a virtual community of learners and to provide time-bound punctuation points in a largely self-paced curriculum.

For example, we designed a case-based curriculum for a large organization to train new hire customer service representatives, whose complex job combines computer system usage, customer service skills, and policy knowledge. The curriculum incorporates case-based learning design principles—learning by doing, scaffolding, progression from simple to complex cases, and spiral design, all in a community of learners. The virtual classroom is designed to be the linchpin of this virtual learning community.

The curriculum includes a number of segments that contain a sequence of synchronous and asynchronous learning events that are tied together by the virtual classroom. (See Table 11.1.) Each segment begins with an overview and demonstration that includes a brief introductory video and a paper-based self-study module that sets the conceptual foundation for that segment. The virtual learning community then meets in a virtual classroom to discuss the video and text. The facilitator does almost no presentation; instead, she asks questions and spurs discussion about the asynchronously presented information. This virtual classroom session

Table 11.1. Blended Problem-Based Learning Curriculum.

Learning Events	Methods
Overview and Demonstration	Video, Self-Study Text, Virtual Class
Guided Simulations	Web-Based Multimedia Simulations (Prototypical Cases), IM and Discussion Board
Facilitated Practice Cases	Live Systems with Training Data (Variations of Prototypical Cases), IM and Discussion Board
Summary and Review	Virtual Class
Evaluation Cases	Online Case-Based Tests
Structured OJT	Work an Actual Cases with Mentor Support; Case Presentations to Virtual Class

serves to solidify a mental model of the content and clear up any misconceptions. This sets the foundation for the guided simulations, facilitated practice cases, and structured OJT to follow.

At the next stage, learners engage in guided simulations that consist of asynchronous web-based simulations of prototypical cases. These multimedia simulations challenge the learner to handle video-based customer interactions, system usage, and policy decisions. Each choice point provides a *teachable moment*, at which learners can access just-in-time online information and guidance. Following the guided simulation, they begin a facilitated practice set in which they work cases with real systems in a controlled environment, using dummy data. As they work through these simulated and practice cases, learners have access to the virtual learning community and the facilitator for support via instant messaging and a discussion board.

Following this set of simulated and live practice cases, a summary and review session is held in the virtual classroom. At this time, learners reflect on their experiences with the cases and solidify and reinforce the principles that emerged inductively. After completing a set of online evaluation cases, the next event is structured OJT. Here they try simple cases with real customers with the help of a mentor. As they engage in structured OJT, the virtual classroom serves as a "roundtable" in which participants present cases they have worked for discussion and feedback.

The virtual classroom provides an opportunity for human interaction with distant members of the virtual learning community and the facilitator that would not otherwise be feasible. In this case-based curriculum, the virtual classroom provides motivation through peer interaction and connection, reflection and consolidation of learning, and a synchronous time-bound structure for a largely self-paced curriculum. Most of all, it adds a human dimension to what might otherwise be an isolating experience.

Chapter 1
Meet the New
Virtual Classroom

Introduction

Chapter 2
Learning
in the New VC

Chapter 3
Features to Exploit
in the New VC

Chapter 4
Teaching Content Types
in the New VC

Part 1: Learning and the New Virtual Classroom

Chapter 5
Visualize Your
Message

Chapter 6
Make It Active – Part 1

Chapter 7
Make It Active – Part 2

Part 2: Engaging Participants in the New Virtual Classroom

Chapter 8
Managing Mental Load
in the New VC

Chapter 9
Make a Good
First Impression

Chapter 10
Packaging Your
VC Session

Chapter 11
Problem-Based Learning
in the New VC

Part 3: Optimizing Your Virtual Events

Chapter 12
Getting Started

Part 4: Creating Effective Learning Events in the New Virtual Classroom

Creating Effective Learning Events in the New Virtual Classroom

FROM PRINCIPLES TO PRACTICE, leverage the powerful features of the virtual classroom wisely to maximize your return on investment. In this part of the book, we will cover the following.

Chapter 12: Pulling it all together with seven basic principles of effective virtual classroom events. Tips for planning virtual classrooms that are conversions from face-to-face events as well as starting from scratch.

Chapter 1
Meet the New
Virtual Classroom

Introduction

Chapter 2
Learning
in the New VC

Chapter 3
Features to Exploit
in the New VC

Chapter 4
Teaching Content Types
in the New VC

Part 1: Learning and the New Virtual Classroom

Chapter 5
Visualize Your
Message

Chapter 6
Make It Active – Part 1

Chapter 7
Make It Active – Part 2

Part 2: Engaging Participants in the New Virtual Classroom

Chapter 8
Managing Mental Load
in the New VC

Chapter 9
Make a Good
First Impression

Chapter 10
Packaging Your
VC Session

Chapter 11
Problem-Based Learning
in the New VC

Part 3: Optimizing Your Virtual Events

Chapter 12
Getting Started

Part 4: Creating Effective Learning Events in the New Virtual Classroom

12

Getting Started in the New Virtual Classroom

APPLY THE SEVEN BASIC PRINCIPLES in this chapter to harness the many features available in the virtual classroom in ways that promote learning. In this chapter we summarize our guidelines for new developers and facilitators of virtual classroom events. We include suggestions for converting face-to-face lessons into a virtual classroom format as well as for creating synchronous sessions "from scratch."

Basic Principles for Harnessing the Virtual Classroom

To get newcomers off to a successful start with the new virtual classroom, we lead with seven principles that serve as the foundation for the planning and creation of effective virtual classroom events, shown in Figure 12.1.

Figure 12.1. Seven Basic Principles for Virtual Classroom Success.

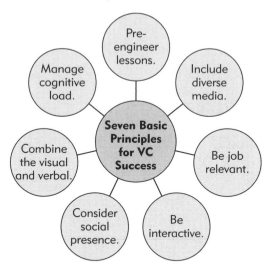

Principle 1. Pre-Engineering Virtual Classroom Events Is the Surest Path to Success

Whether the virtual classroom session will be built and delivered by one individual or by a team, and whether it is designed primarily for teaching new skills or for briefing purposes, we recommend pre-engineering. By pre-engineering, we mean advance planning and preparation of all the major elements of the event, including content and interaction slides, an outline or summary of the narration to accompany the slides, participant handouts, and adjunct materials such as reference resources, pre-letters, facilitator guides, and so forth.

Although pre-engineering will require developers' and facilitators' time, keep in mind that the greatest investment an organization makes in the virtual classroom is the salaried time of those attending, as well as productivity lost while in training. A pre-engineered event gives the greatest return on investment because the quality will be less dependent on instructor or participant variables. Through pre-engineering, all of the key instructional strategies will be incorporated into the instructional materials, including slides, video clips, application sharing materials, handouts, and facilitator guides.

Principle 2. Diverse Delivery Media Complement One Another

Since various training media offer different opportunities for instruction, more often than not, learning goals are best served by a blended approach. Consider supplementing the virtual classroom with asynchronous events, which impose less cognitive load by allowing learners to review and reflect at their own pace (Figure 12.2). Readings, website research, labs, project application work, and drill and practice to build automaticity are but a few activities that are often best accomplished asynchronously. By offloading content delivery to alternative media such as print or websites, you buy time to use the virtual classroom for interactive sessions rather than lectures. If you need more human contact or hands-on equipment practice, supplement the virtual classroom with face-to-face sessions.

Principle 3. Good Virtual Events Are Explicitly Job Relevant

Adult workers rated the job relevance of their virtual classroom sessions as a major factor contributing to their overall satisfaction (Stonebraker & Hazeltine, 2004). As a developer or facilitator of the virtual classroom, keep your focus on the participants' work at all times. If your course is built on a job analysis, which we recommend, your sessions should be teaching job tasks and associated knowledge to support those tasks. Ensure that your

---

Figure 12.2. Uses of Asynchronous Learning Events.

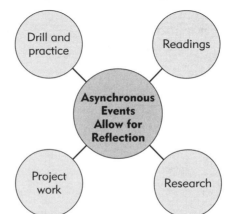

examples, demonstrations, and practice exercises incorporate a job-realistic context. In your session introductions, establish each participant's job and how he or she intends to apply the skills to be taught. Plan an application project that requires all participants to apply the course skills to their job tasks. If you do include a project requirement, ask participants to offer their initial ideas about their own projects as an introductory activity.

Principle 4. Learning Is Interactive

Learning only occurs when new content is actively processed in memory. First, frequent relevant interactions counteract the tendency of participants to become side-tracked by other tasks or distractions in their environment. Second, responses to interactions help the instructor compensate for the lack of body language that face-to-face instructors rely on to judge participant reactions and understanding. Third, overt interactions are essential for learning new knowledge and skills. Fourth, the virtual classroom environment offers many facilities for participant interactivity. Suppress any temptation you may have to "dump" content in lieu of allowing students to interact with the content. In short, make interactivity a top priority!

Principle 5. Social Presence Promotes Learning

How often have you left a face-to-face event not knowing anything about the others who attended? When properly structured, engagement with others results in greater learning than does solo work. Activities such as discussions, project work, and small group assignments, when well-managed, increase everyone's opportunity to interact in ways that increase learning. For skill-building events, we recommend frequent use of breakout rooms, paired chat, and participant audio to foster social presence. You can extend social presence into asynchronous events by asking participants to post project assignments and review the work of others, as shown here.

Figure 12.3. Social Presence Increases When Participants Interact with One Another.

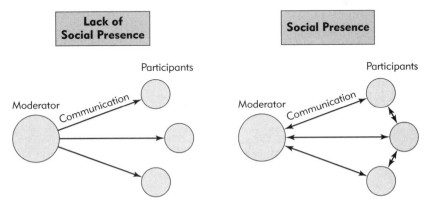

Principle 6. Appropriate Visual and Verbal Modalities Accelerate Learning

An appropriate visual that is explained effectively can improve learning by over 80 percent compared to relying on a text explanation alone. All forms of e-learning rely heavily on computer screens to convey content. Screens lend themselves well to visualizations, including still graphics, photographs, video, and animated demonstrations. After interactivity, we believe effective visuals are the next most important element to pre-engineer into your virtual classroom session. Effective visuals engage learners, promote learning, and help to reduce mental load. To reduce load and sustain attention, use the various pointer tools available in the white board and explain graphics with brief audio narration. To maximize the potential of visuals, overtly engage your participants with them. For example, learners can discuss a visual via audio, mark up a visual on the white board, or respond to questions about visuals using polling or chat.

Principle 7. Cognitive Load Must Be Managed in All Instructor-Led Events

Because the rate of the presentation is outside of the participants' control, all instructor-led events, including the virtual classroom, are especially prone to cognitive overload. To manage cognitive load in the virtual classroom, keep sessions relatively brief, heavily interactive, and reliant on visuals explained by instructor narration to deliver content. In addition, use worked examples to lead into practice exercises, as described in Chapter 8. To supplement virtual classroom events, be sure that participants have access to working aids to guide task completion during and after the virtual event.

Engineering Your Virtual Classroom Session

After receiving your virtual classroom assignment or determining that the virtual classroom is the most effective delivery medium to achieve your goals, proceed based on your starting point. Here we address guidelines for the two most common situations facing virtual classroom developers or facilitators: (1) converting an existing face-to-face course and (2) starting from scratch.

Conversions from Face-to-Face Classrooms

When the audience is geographically dispersed, many organizations are converting traditional instructor-led training into virtual classroom sessions. When faced with such conversions, begin by assessing the quality of the existing course. Often conversions to e-learning offer opportunities to improve classroom courses by making them more job relevant, more visual, and more interactive. Even if your classroom course is in excellent shape, you will still have to make some adjustments to convert it to synchronous e-learning. In this section, we show you how.

Upgrading the Existing Course

Begin with an inventory and assessment of the current course. Examine the student handouts, instructor guides, and slides for evidence of the basic elements of instructional effectiveness. Answer the following questions:

1. Is the course overall logically sequenced and segmented into lessons?

2. Does each lesson include one to three learning objectives that use verbs that mirror job activities? For example for a salesperson, rather than "List the key benefits of Product X," a more effective objective is: "Explain how product X benefits clients with profiles A, B, or C."

3. Do the content, examples, demonstrations, and exercises incorporate job-realistic context?

4. Are there frequent exercises and assignments that require learners to respond in job-realistic ways?

5. Is 50 percent or more of the class time spent on learner-centered activities such as discussions, exercises, projects, case studies, and so forth?

6. Are visuals used in the course, and are there additional opportunities to add relevant visuals?

7. Is the content documented in ways that provide learners with reference aids for skills and knowledge they need to apply to the job after the class?

If any of the above is missing or inadequate, use your conversion project to improve the basic course structure by reorganizing, rewriting, or adding missing elements such as visuals or interactions. If your existing materials are highly inadequate and the course is high-profile, make a case to start a course development effort from scratch and follow the guidelines listed later in this chapter.

Converting the Existing Course

Even if the existing classroom course meets all or most standards for an instructionally effective event, you will need to adjust that course in ways that allow facilitators to take advantage of the features unique to the virtual classroom that are different from the face-to-face classroom. Here are some guidelines:

1. Reorganize content as follows:

   • Re-distribute some content to alternative media (Figure 12.4). For example, build in readings, websites, or asynchronous e-learning programs to off-load some of the content-heavy segments of the class. Allocate much of the virtual classroom time to events in which participants engage deeply with the content, the facilitator, and each other.

Figure 12.4. Distribute Some Content to Asynchronous Media.

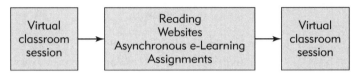

   • Re-segment remaining content into interactive virtual classroom sessions of approximately one to two hours each. In general, e-learning is better received in several smaller doses, rather than all at once. Learning outcomes are also better when the virtual sessions are interspersed with asynchronous assignments that require participants to apply the skills conveyed in each session.

2. Visualize content (See Chapter 5 for details.)

   • Inventory and re-purpose existing visuals for the converted course (Figure 12.5). Arrange for any technical adjustments needed to project video clips, such as editing or converting to different file formats. Redesign existing visuals that are too detailed or too small for virtual classroom delivery. Highly complex visuals can sometimes be broken down to multiple simpler visuals that build across several slides.

   • Work with a graphic artist to add more visuals where indicated. Most classroom sessions will have too high a ratio of words to visuals to convert directly into a virtual classroom session. You

Figure 12.5. Converting Visuals for the Virtual Classroom.

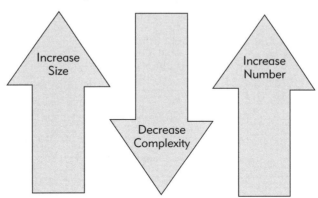

will need to identify or create additional visuals. In addition to representational visuals, add explanatory visuals such as organizational, relational, transformational, and interpretive.

- Consider ways to make visuals interactive. Ask yourself how best to promote engagement, such as marking on visuals, responding to visuals via audio or chat, or constructing polling questions with visual alternatives.

3. Add interactions (See Chapters 6 and 7 for details.)

- Inventory and re-purpose all existing interactions. You may need to video or audio record a classroom session to capture interactions or demonstrations delivered by the instructor that are not documented. Think of ways to convert lengthy open-ended classroom assignments into shorter close-ended interactions. For example, how could a series of short-answer questions be converted into polling questions? Consider how group activities run in the physical classroom can be converted into breakout sessions in the virtual classroom. Alternatively, some classroom assignments such as project work should be moved in whole or in part to asynchronous settings.

- Add new interactions. A lesson designed for a physical classroom will usually lack sufficient interactivity to sustain attention and learning in the virtual classroom. Adding new interactions will improve the instructional quality of the event. Apply the guidelines in Chapters 6 and 7 to create frequent, varied, inclusive, and job-related interactions.

4. Rework the introduction

- Inventory and recycle existing introductory content. Some of the classroom introductory materials may be used "as is." Learning objectives, agendas, and instructor and participant introductions are a few examples. You may need to make some adjustments to the existing introductory materials, such as breaking up the content, putting it on slides, and adding relevant visuals such as instructor photos.

- Add introductory material to accommodate the virtual classroom. Augment existing materials in ways that establish social presence of all participants as well as engage participants with the response facilities of the virtual classroom right from the start. Create some introductory exercises that allow participants to use the various response facilities to learn something about each other. (See Chapter 9 for more details.)

5. Inventory and convert supporting materials

- Review student handouts. If you're lucky, you may be able to recycle many of the existing student handouts. If you have reorganized the lessons for your conversion, you may have to do some editing, including resequencing of content.

- Revise handouts as needed. In many cases, traditional classroom sessions over-rely on student note-taking. Because of the amount of cognitive load already imposed by instructor-led events, we recommend that you prepare class handouts that use tables, checklists, and examples and can serve as job aids. If you can gather some of the notes taken by students attending the traditional classroom event, you may be able to re-purpose their content. If you anticipate using the recorded virtual classroom event in an asynchronous format, adapt the handout to supplement the recorded sessions.

- Revise orientation letters. Much of the welcome letter material for the physical classroom will need to be rewritten to reflect the new logistics and technical requirements of the converted class. Follow the guidelines in Chapter 9 as the basis for your introductory information.

- Revise instructor guides. Instructors, especially instructors new to the virtual classroom, will need different types of information than is typically included in the traditional classroom instructor guide. Review the sample virtual classroom instructor script included on the CD and described in our Experts' Forum discussion at the end of Chapter 9.

Starting from Scratch

You may be developing a new class that will make extensive use of virtual classroom technology. Before the decision to use the virtual classroom is carved in stone, consider whether, in fact, an e-learning solution is appropriate to meet the goals of the training and can be effectively supported by your organization. On our CD we include a Virtual Classroom Readiness Checklist that asks the many questions that should be considered before embarking on a virtual classroom design and development project.

Once the decision has been made to use the virtual classroom as part of your media blend, follow the initial stages of course design and development, just as you would for any training, by conducting a job analysis, defining learning objectives, and constructing course and lesson outlines. The main differences in your activities are:

- Plan for visuals from the start. As you do your job analysis, use digital cameras or get screen captures to start a repository of images you can draw on during development. If subject-matter experts make sketches on wall charts or paper, take pictures. The more visual representations you can gather during the analysis phases, the easier your visualization efforts during development.

- Plan for fine-grained interactions from the start. As you write your lesson outlines, define a detailed sequence of content, along with ideas for interactions to accompany the content. Remember to vary the response formats and to make use of inductive and lead-in questions, breakout rooms, and response formats that maximize participant engagement, including polling, chat, and white board interactions.

- Consider alternative media to deliver content and for student project work adjunct to the virtual classroom sessions. Divide your content among the delivery media available to you, taking advantage of the strengths of your alternatives.

- Storyboard your session flow. Use PowerPoint slides to draft initial lessons, adding placeholders for additional needed art, interactions, content, etc., that will be filled in as the storyboards are completed. Use the notes section to summarize the main content points and add any additional directions to the instructor. If you have access to a graphic artist, he or she may have many good ideas to help you visualize your content. Storyboards offer a natural interface to work with the graphic artist.

The Bottom Line

From pre-engineering to management of cognitive load, by applying the basic principles summarized in this chapter you will develop virtual classroom sessions that are valued by the participants and offer a return on investment to the organization. In conversions of existing face-to-face courseware to the virtual classroom, take advantage of the opportunity to upgrade the legacy elements of the class as well as to make adaptations. When developing virtual classroom sessions from scratch, adapt your normal course development process in ways that effectively leverage virtual classroom features.

You best serve your clients by taking advantage of the features of new virtual classroom technology in ways that support human learning. As with all new technology, the instructional community will evolve unique strategies that best exploit the nascent learning opportunities in today's virtual classroom. We hope this book will serve as a helpful resource on that evolutionary path.

Ruth Colvin Clark, Ruth@Clarktraining.com

Ann Kwinn, Ann@Clarktraining.com

On *The New Virtual Classroom* CD

A Virtual Classroom Readiness Checklist offers a number of questions for you to consider when determining when and where to make use of synchronous e-learning technology for your instructional goals.

EXPERTS' FORUM

TEACHING JOB-RELEVANT SALES TASKS

Rhea Fix, Red Pepper Consulting

I have been involved in the design/development, facilitation, and blending of training programs to employees nationwide using web-meeting tools such as Breeze, Placeware/Live Meeting, WebEx, Learncentrix, and others. I have also used audio-only and voice over IP solutions as an element of long-term course interactions. I work with organizations to design and implement classroom, online, and blended solutions.

Principle 3 in this chapter recommends virtual classroom sessions that are job-relevant. I designed a course that needed to refresh business salespeople on an existing product and teach about a new product enhancement with an end goal to increase the number of new bids that salespeople wrote for existing clients based on the enhanced product. We offered online prework that refreshed the existing product and included a quiz for experienced salespeople to "test out" of the prework. A second prework module overviewed the enhanced product. The virtual classroom session (facilitated with Learncentrix LCMS) demonstrated how to apply the knowledge by creating a client bid using the enhanced product. Homework for the course required each participant to create a bid for the enhanced product for any existing client. Participants "turned in" their homework online for review by facilitators. The facilitator offered corrective feedback. The salespeople were then free to propose the enhanced product in a bid to their clients. Several participants turned in their homework bids to clients. Several achieved their entire first quarter quota for the product by just turning in the homework.

In other well-designed courses, I have seen utilization of email communications with embedded scenario information or scripts from voice messages that provide information on projects to reinforce, give corrective feedback, or act as potential distracters to learners. I especially appreciated the courses in which all learners role played different parts on a fictitious project for a fictitious company. All of the application exercises were disguised as deliverables for the project.

Principle 5 recommends effective use of social presence. One of my favorite virtual class experiences was in attending a semester-long class facilitated by Allison Rossett. She kept us socially engaged during the entire session. Articles were often sent during the week before online sessions to give added context to the regular reading and assignments. She asked us about the examples in the articles and did not do much summarizing of content. We spent class time discussing concepts and applying knowledge. I found this more effective than courses that relied mainly on lecture and demonstrations. When engagement was expected, as a rule, participants tended to come to class more prepared and ready to discuss the material.

RECOMMENDATIONS FOR A RICH EXPERIENCE

Peter C. Ryce, Breeze Evangelist, Adobe Systems, Incorporated

The challenges of working with a virtual classroom range from adapting existing instructional behaviors to competing for students' attention in an uncontrolled environment. However, the benefits combine to offer an even richer experience than possible in a physical classroom.

Leverage the Capabilities of PowerPoint   Despite what some educators may think of PowerPoint, it remains one of the most widely used content development and training tools available. PowerPoint is a robust, mature presentation application that includes many things designed to engage an audience—make the most of it.

PowerPoint has a plethora of animation options, flexible navigation, and support for additional functionality that can include interactive content. With over ninety million users and over a decade of legacy content, PowerPoint is the most popular content development tool for training and is a great place to start for most trainers.

Preparing for Ad-Hoc   Not all learning is done in the structure of the class session—virtual or otherwise. In the physical world, the time spent asking questions after class, or visiting a TA during open hours, or critiquing fellow students' work are all important adjuncts to standard classroom instruction. Virtual classrooms can be used after school, too. The key to being successful here is availability and immediacy. The benefit of a classroom is often in the wealth of materials that are readily at hand to effectively respond to whatever question is raised. Well-stocked, persistent virtual classrooms offer much of the same benefit. The immediate retrieval of course materials and results, access to additional information, and anytime, anywhere access all ensure the same, if not greater, benefits as for the real classroom.

Old Dogs and New Tricks—Adapting Physical Media   More and more, physical actions that are common in a classroom (such as an instructor drawing on a white board) are able to be computerized and shared across a virtual classroom too; just as a real marker writes on a white board, its position is sent to a sensor attached to a computer and the computer simply re-creates the same pattern of motion in a drawing application to give an identical version on screen. Similarly, overhead projectors and foils or transparencies can be replaced by "document cameras" that capture a video of what is placed below it—making virtually any physical document instantly shareable.

Recordings—Worse Than Home Movies?   Inevitably, there will be some students who just cannot make it to the "synchronous" learning event and will need to review the recording. So how valuable is the recording? How much of the critical interaction can be represented? Perhaps more than you think. There are products that can record more than just a "video" of what was seen on screen. Recordings can now provide interactive search, allowing viewers to find key words or topics that were on a slide or a note, or discussed in chat. Also, much of the interactive content can be presented as interactive again right from the archive. And distributed materials associated with the session can even be downloaded or printed directly from the recording itself.

Beyond Polling   For most applications, polling is restricted to multiple-choice or multiple-answer questions. But some applications go beyond simple polling, offering fill-in-the-blank-style quizzing, column matching, and more. These can often be used to stimulate conversations and capture subjective data.

Simulations   Much of what we are asked to learn today is software-based. Many tools can be used to turn a live software demonstration into a repeatable capture, and then further into an interactive simulation that allows participants to truly test their knowledge. This content is ideally delivered in the synchronous classroom and then leveraged for asynchronous follow-up.

Game Play   Preventing cognitive overload and engaging learners is extremely hard to do. The attention span of most students is low, even in real-world classrooms where external stimuli have been consciously restricted. The virtual classroom is even more difficult to control. The possible distraction of email, phone calls, television, co-workers, family members, and so forth all make keeping your audience engaged a challenge. One of the best ways to gain whole-scale engagement is through interactive competition. The connected nature of online learning offers the unique opportunity to involve everybody through multi-player games. And gaming does not have to be unrelated (any game can initiate the key social interactions or re-energize an audience), but gaming can be related to the material being presented.

Applications   Many interactive applications can be easily created for online use or re-purposed from existing content. For example, you can quickly build online applications without any programming, using nothing more than a spreadsheet and some readily available software. This is ideal for creating targeted applications such as a mortgage calculator or financial or scientific scenario modeling visualizers. Also, being online offers the unique capability of interacting with "live" data and real applications, where appropriate. As illustrated, actual job-related materials go a long way toward engaging learners.

Consensus Applications The potential for this has yet to be tapped. There are a number of common group decision-making tools that are visual, subjective, and not easily represented by any other method of data capture, such as polling. An example of this would be a SWOT evaluation. Many people use this tool, which has individuals place a dot somewhere in a quadrant of four that represents a two-axis continuum of strengths to weakness and opportunity to threat. The distribution of placed dots spread across the two-dimensional chart quickly reveals consensus or disagreement in not one but two related issues.

Through all of these mechanisms, our virtual classrooms can go beyond simply re-creating traditional classrooms and can truly take us to a better way of instructing and learning.

GLOSSARY

Application sharing A virtual classroom facility that allows the instructor to show all participants a software application running on his or her computer. Often used to demonstrate computer applications in software training. Applications can be turned over to participants, allowing them to practice using the application.

Architecture A course or lesson design plan that specifies the organization and placement of course content, the amount and placement of learner interactions, and the degree of learner control over sequencing. Two examples include directive (also called instructive) and guided discovery.

Asynchronous e-learning Instructional programs delivered on a computer that are designed primarily for self-study. These programs can be taken at any time by anyone at his or her own pace. May or may not include options for synchronous or asynchronous communication with others. Common examples include web-based training courses.

Attitude interactions   Questions that solicit information about how participants feel. End-of session evaluations and reactions to a new tool or policy are examples.

Automaticity   A skill that is encoded into long-term memory and can be deployed without using working memory resources. Automated skills can be completed quickly and error-free without conscious processing. Automaticity builds only after hundreds of practice trials.

Behavioral interactions   Questions that solicit information about things participants have done, are doing, or will do in the future. Experience with a specific software tool is an example.

Blended learning   The use of multiple instructional delivery media that may allow for a combination of instructional methods, for example, in self-paced self-study modes and in group collaborative modes.

Breakout room   A virtual classroom facility that allows small groups of participants to work together independently with access to all of the facilities available in the main room. Commonly used for small group work or discussions.

Case-based learning   Instructional environments that require participants to solve constructed problems or assignments (case studies) that incorporate elements that will lead to achievment of the learning goals. Compare to project-based learning.

Chat   A virtual classroom facility that allows all participants to type comments into the interface. Depending on the options selected, messages can be seen by all or can be sent to selected individuals. Like polling, chat allows responses by all participants at the same time. It is a good option for structured questions with multiple options or brief open-ended questions. Also called direct messaging.

Close-ended questions Items that have specific and defined responses such as multiple-choice or short-answer questions with specific answers. Contrast to open-ended questions.

Cognitive load The amount of mental work imposed on working memory. Cognitive load can come from the difficulty of the instructional content, the manner in which instructional materials are organized and displayed, and the mental processes required to achieve the learning goal.

Coherence principle Learning is better when extraneous visuals, text, or audio are omitted from instruction rather than included. See also Las Vegas instruction.

Collaborative learning A structured instructional interaction among two or more learners to achieve a learning goal or complete an assignment.

Communication function The purpose of a graphic to help learners build the correct mental model. For example, a procedure is conveyed by a transformational graphic that shows a series of steps either with arrows and text in a line drawing or with an animated demonstration.

Concepts Lesson content that involves a group of objects, events, or symbols called by the same name. Some examples are chair, spreadsheet, and virtual classroom.

Decorative visual A graphic used to add aesthetic appeal or humor.

Demographic interactions Questions that solicit relatively permanent information about participants, such as geographic location, work organization, and job role.

Direct messaging A facility in new virtual classroom technologies that allows participants to type comments into a box and send to everyone or to selected individuals. Also called chat.

Directive architectures   Lessons or courses that are highly structured and typically incorporate short learning episodes that include brief explanations, examples, and practice with feedback. See also instructive events.

Effect size   A statistic indicating the number of standard deviations a test group differs from a control group. Effect sizes equal to or less than .20 are considered small and are of little practical importance. Effect sizes around .50 are medium and are of moderate practical importance. Effect sizes greater than .80 are large and are of crucial practical importance.

e-Learning   Learning environments mediated by a computer. These include (1) asynchronous self-paced courses (formally called computer-based training), (2) synchronous real-time instructor-led courses, as well as (3) blends such as a recorded synchronous course reviewed asynchronously.

Emoticons   Icons included in virtual classroom interfaces that participants can use to express feelings. Some examples include happy face, confused face, applause hands. See also icons.

Evidence-based practice   The incorporation of valid research evidence into decisions about selection or design of instructional programs. Such research is usually based on controlled group experiments.

Explanatory visuals   A graphic that illustrates relationships among content and helps learners build deeper understanding. Some examples include graphic expressions of quantitative data such as bar charts, relationships among qualitative data such as concept maps, and interpretive visuals such as schematic diagrams.

Extrinsic feedback   Feedback on a project deliverable from instructors or peers that is instructional in nature. For example, your tennis coach directs you to change your racket position. Contrast to intrinsic feedback.

Exploratory architecture   A learning environment in which learners are allowed high degrees of learner control, such as selecting which lessons to review, which exercises to complete, or which instructional methods to access. The Internet is an example of a large exploratory environment.

Facts   Lesson content that refers to unique, specific, one-of-a-kind objects, events, or symbols. Some examples include specific application screens, codes, and forms.

Faded worked examples   A demonstration in which some steps are worked by the instruction and the remaining steps are worked by the learner.

Far transfer   Knowledge and skills that must be applied in diverse contexts. Some examples include making a sales presentation or designing training. To perform far-transfer tasks, the worker must use judgment to adapt guidelines to diverse situations. See also principle-based tasks.

Guided discovery architectures   Course or lesson design plans in which participants derive knowledge and skills from study of multiple examples, problem or task assignments, or other experiential activities. These courses rely on an inductive model of learning. See also problem-based learning.

Icons   Small graphics available in virtual classrooms that participants use to express feelings or reactions. Typical examples include smiley faces, puzzled faces, and clapping hands. See also emoticons.

Inclusive response options   Interactive opportunities in the virtual classroom that allow all or most participants to respond. Polling and chat interactions are two examples.

Individual response features   Interactive opportunities that allow participants to respond. Examples include polling, audio button, and chat.

Inductive events   Opportunities for participants to derive guidelines, features, or rules from viewing examples or engaging in experiences. For example, asking participants to list the features of a good website after viewing samples of well-designed and poorly designed websites.

Instructional components   The psychologically active ingredients of any learning environment that determine the instructional effectiveness of that environment. Includes instructional modes, methods, and architectures.

Instructional method   See methods.

Instructional mode   See modes.

Instructive events   Opportunities for participants to learn though highly guided instructional environments that typically provide explanations, examples, practice, and feedback. See directive architecture.

Integrated content   Organization of lessons in which supporting concepts are presented at the same time as lesson tasks or process stages. Contrast with segmented content.

Interface   The design of an application screen that offers end users various functionalities such as buttons, icons, and windows. Effective interfaces are intuitive, simple, and user-friendly.

Interpretive visual   A graphic used to illustrate an invisible theory, principle, or cause-and-effect relationship. An equipment schematic and a molecular model are two examples. Also called interpretive graphic.

Intrinsic feedback   Feedback that comes from real-life consequences of a project deliverable or process. For example, when hitting a tennis ball, the sound and movement of the ball provide intrinsic feedback. Contrast to extrinsic feedback.

Jig saw   A form of structured collaborative learning in which several small groups each complete a portion of an assignment, which is then assembled in a full group setting to complete the assignment.

Knowledge interactions A question with a correct or incorrect answer designed as a practice exercise or test. The goal is to help participants learn new information or skills.

Las Vegas instruction Lessons that incorporate irrelevant graphics, visual and audio effects such as gratuitous animations or sounds, and games added for entertainment value. Also called "edutainment." Las Vegas approaches to learning run the risk of depressing instructional outcomes.

Lead-in interactions Questions used in the beginning of a lesson or lesson topic to activate prior knowledge in working memory and/or to motivate interest in the content to follow.

Learning agent An on-screen character used often in asynchronous e-learning courses that offers various forms of explanations, advice, or feedback to support the learning process.

Live remote training A synonym for virtual classroom instruction.

Long-term memory A relatively permanent mental repository of knowledge and skills in the form of mental models that are the basis for expertise. The mental models in long-term memory interact directly with working memory to influence the virtual capacity of working memory.

Media The delivery technology used to provide instructional materials to learners. Includes items such as books, video, and computers.

Mental model A knowledge structure stored in long-term memory that is the basis of expertise.

Meta-analysis A statistical technique that integrates the results of many individual research results in order to define the overall practical utility of a given method as well as to identify moderating factors that make a method effective.

Metacognition   The operating system of the brain that is responsible for setting learning goals, determining optimal learning strategies, and monitoring progress.

Methods   A psychologically active ingredient of a lesson or course that promotes learning. Some examples include examples, practice exercises, analogies, and feedback.

Mnemonic visual   A graphic designed to implant retrieval cues that will aid recall of information.

Modality principle   A proven instructional principle stating that complex visuals are understood more efficiently when explanatory words are presented in an audio modality rather than when presented in a written modality. Because working memory includes separate processing areas for visual and auditory information, using the auditory mode along with the visual makes most efficient use of limited working memory resources.

Modes   Three fundamental elements for communicating new content and instructional methods. Includes text, graphics, and audio.

Near transfer   Knowledge and skills that are applied in more or less the same way each time they are used. Refers to routine tasks such as logging into email or starting an automobile. Also called procedural tasks.

New virtual classroom   Instructor-led synchronous computer-mediated learning environments attended by participants online at the same time but in different locations. Typically includes options to show slides, multimedia, and computer applications, transmit instructor and participant audio, text chat, and other interactions such as polling. Also referred to as synchronous e-learning and remote instructor training.

Open-ended questions   Items that solicit responses that are unique and constructed by the learner. Asking participants to explain their answers or express an argument for a position are two examples.

Organizational visual A graphic that shows qualitative relationships among content. A tree diagram is a common example. Also called organizational graphic.

Pacing The rate at which information is delivered and the source of control of information delivery rate. Instructor-paced is typical of instructor-led events, whereas learner-paced is typical of asynchronous media such as books or asynchronous e-learning.

Packaging The surrounding elements external to the virtual classroom event itself that position the event for success. Includes elements such as pre-letters, handouts, and facilitator training.

Polling A virtual classroom facility that allows participants to respond to a multiple-choice question. Depending on the virtual classroom tool, responses can be hidden, shown next to each participant's name, or aggregated into bar graphs.

Principle-based tasks Tasks performed by adapting guidelines to varying contexts of the work environment. Some examples include making a sales presentation or designing training. These tasks require workers to use judgment to apply guidelines to new situations. Also called far-transfer tasks.

Problem-based learning (PBL) A form of guided discovery in which a course or lesson begins with a work-relevant problem or task and learning is fostered as participants solve the problem or complete the assignment. PBL uses an inductive approach to learning.

Procedural tasks A task made up of steps that are performed more or less the same way each time. Procedures are also called near-transfer tasks.

Processes A flow of activities that involve multiple entities, individuals, or organizations. A description of how things work. Some examples include how brakes work, the hiring process, and how blood circulates in the body.

Producer   An expert in virtual classroom technology who can help new instructors develop and facilitate their events.

Project-based learning   Instructional environments that require participants to engage in real-world problems or tasks. Contrast with case-based learning.

Psychological function   The mental process or processes a graphic or graphic element may support during the learning process. For example, an arrow would support attention to specific visual features.

Receptive architectures   Learning environments characterized by dissemination of information with limited or no opportunities for overt learner participation. A typical lecture and a documentary video are two examples of receptive designs.

Redundancy principle   Learning is more inefficient when sources of information are duplicated and hence risk overloading working memory. A common example is narration of on-screen text used to explain a complex visual. The audio and visual expression of words is redundant and is proven to depress learning.

Rehearsal   The mental processing of new information in working memory that results in the integration of new information with existing activated knowledge to form new mental models stored in long-term memory. Effective practice exercises lead to productive rehearsal.

Relational visual   A graphic intended to summarize quantitative data, such as a bar chart or a pie chart.

Remote instructor-led training   A form of distance learning that is usually synchronous and instructor-paced. The virtual classroom is one type of remote instructor-led training. May also be called remote live training.

Representational visual   A graphic that is intended to depict an object. A screen capture or an equipment photograph are two examples.

Seductive detail	Information related to the topic but irrelevant to the learning objective included to add interest. Because such information may distract learners, often learning is depressed. See also Las Vegas instruction.
Segmented content	Organization of lessons in which supporting concepts are presented prior to lesson tasks or process stages. Contrast with integrated content.
Social learning	Instructional environments that promote learning in the presence of others, such as in pairs or in small groups. See also collaborative learning.
Social presence	The degree to which various media features mediate interpersonal communication and thus allow participants to feel connected to others. Face-to-face learning environments are high in potential for social presence compared to print media, which are low in potential social presence.
Split attention	The dividing of limited mental resources among related content items or facilities that results in distraction or extra effort invested to integrate the materials. Using the chat window for a private unrelated discussion during a virtual classroom training event is an example.
Sponge learning	Instructional environments that are instructor-centered. The instruction dumps content in the hope that learners will absorb it. These environments have few interactive opportunities. See also receptive architecture.
Structured argumentation	A form of collaborative learning in which small teams take different perspectives on an issue, prepare a product that explains and supports their perspective, and present it to other teams.
Supporting knowledge	Information usually in the form of concepts and facts needed for learners to apply steps or guidelines to complete tasks.
Surface features	The outward appearance or features of graphics, such as whether they are an animation or line drawing.

Synchronous e-learning	Computer-mediated learning environments in which multiple geographically dispersed participants are engaged at the same time in an instructional event. Also called virtual classroom or remote live training.
Task deliverable	The desired end product and process of a problem-based learning lesson. Should mirror best-practice products and processes from the work environment.
Task input	Data learners will need relevant to their problem assignment in problem-based learning to enable them to create the task deliverable. Also called case-supporting data. Should mirror the types of case data that would be accessible in the work environment.
Transfer of learning	The retrieval and application of new knowledge that has been stored in long-term memory during training later when needed in the workplace.
Transformational visual	A graphic used to show changes or movement in objects over time or space. A demonstration of how to interact with computer software is a common example.
Trigger event	An initiating assignment or event that introduces learners to a project or case at the start of a problem-based learning lesson.
Virtual classroom	Synchronous computer-mediated learning environments with facilities for visualization, instructor and participant audio, and participant responses via polling and chat, among others. Some commonly used virtual classroom tools include Acrobat Connect Professional, Elluminate, Centra, Live Meetings, and Web Ex. See also new virtual classroom and synchronous e-learning.
Web-cam	A camera that allows projection of images from the instructor or participant's computer sites during a virtual classroom event.

White board   A facility in the virtual classroom interface that allows projection of slides as well as drawing or typing by the instructor and participants.

Working memory   A central element of human cognition responsible for active processing of data during thinking, problem solving, and learning. Working memory has a limited capacity and storage duration for information.

REFERENCES

Beishuizen, J., Asscher, J., Prinsen, F., & Elshout-Mohr, M. (2003). Presence and place of main ideas and examples in study texts. *British Journal of Educational Psychology, 73*, 291–316.

Bernard, R. M., Abrami, P. C., Lou, Y., Borokhovski, E., Wade, A., Wozney, L., Wallet, P. A., Fixet, M., & Huang, B. (2004). How does distance education compare with classroom instruction? A meta-analysis of the empirical literature. *Review of Educational Research, 74*(3), 379–439.

Burgess, J.R.D., & Russell, J.E.A. (2003). The effectiveness of distance learning initiatives in organizations. *Journal of Vocational Behavior, 63*, 289–303.

Cerpa, N., Chandler, P., & Sweller, J. (1996). Some conditions under which integrated computer-based training software can facilitate learning. *Journal of Educational Computing Research, 15*(4), 345–367.

Clark, R. C. (2005). Harnessing the virtual classroom. *Training & Development, 59*(11), 41–45.

Clark, R. C. (2007). *Developing technical training* (3rd ed.). San Francisco, CA: Pfeiffer.

Clark, R. C. (2003). *Building expertise* (2nd ed.). San Francisco, CA: Pfeiffer.

Clark, R. C., & Lyons, C. (2004). *Graphics for learning.* San Francisco, CA: Pfeiffer.

Clark, R. C., & Mayer, R. E. (2003). *e-Learning and the science of instruction.* San Francisco: Pfeiffer.

Clark, R. C., Nguyen, F., & Sweller, J. (2006). *Efficiency in learning.* San Francisco: Pfeiffer.

Cohen, E. G. (1994). Restructuring the classroom: Conditions for productive small groups. *Review of Educational Research, 64*(1), 1–35.

Dolezalek, H. (2005). The 2005 industry report. *Training, 42*(12), 14–28.

Fletcher, J. D., & Tobias, S. (2005). The multimedia principle. In R. E. Mayer (Ed.), *The Cambridge handbook of multimedia learning* (pp. 229–245). New York: Cambridge University Press.

Foshay, W. R., Silber, K. H., & Stelnicki, M. B. (2003). *Writing training materials that work.* San Francisco, CA: Pfeiffer.

Galvin, T. (2003). 2003 industry report. *Training, 40,* 21–45.

Gunarwardena, C. N., & Zittle, F. J. (1997). Social presence as a predictor of satisfaction within a computer-mediated conference environment. *The American Journal of Distance Education, 11,* 8–26.

Harp, S. F., & Mayer, R. E. (1997). The role of interest in learning from scientific text and illustrations: On the distinction between emotional interest and cognitive interest. *Journal of Educational Psychology, 89,* 92–102.

Harp, S. F., & Mayer, R. E. (1998). How seductive details do their damage: A theory of cognitive interest in science learning. *Journal of Educational Psychology, 90,* 414–434.

Hegarty, M. (2005). Multimedia learning about physical systems. In R. E. Mayer (Ed.), The *Cambridge handbook of multimedia learning.* New York: Cambridge University Press.

Hegarty, M. (2004). Dynamic visualization and learning: Getting to the difficult questions. *Learning and Instruction, 14,* 343–351.

Hegarty, M., Narayanan, N. H., & Freitas, P. (2002). Understanding machines from multimedia and hypermedia presentations. In J. Otero, J. A. Leon, & A. C. Graesser (Eds.), *The psychology of science text comprehension.* Mahway, NJ: Lawrence Erlbaum Associates.

Hill, J. R., Wiley, D., Nelson, L. M., & Han, S. (2004). Exploring research on internet-based learning: From infrastructure to interactions. In D. H. Jonassen (Ed.), *Handbook of research for educational communications and technology* (2nd ed.). Mahwah, NJ: Lawrence Erlbaum Associates.

Hmelo-Silver, C. E. (2004). Problem-based learning: What and how do students learn? *Educational Psychology Review, 16*(3), 235–266.

Hofmann, J. (2004a). *Live and online: Tips, techniques, and ready-to-use activities for the virtual classroom.* San Francisco, CA: Pfeiffer.

Hofmann, J. (2004b). *The synchronous trainer's survival guide.* San Francisco, CA: Pfeiffer.

Hung, W. (2006). The 3C3R model: A conceptual framework for designing problems in PBL. *The Interdisciplinary Journal of Problem-Based Learning, 1*(1), 55–77.

Jonassen, D. H., Lee, C. B., Yang, C. C., & Laffey, J. (2005). The collaboration principle in multimedia learning. In R. E. Mayer (Ed.), *The Cambridge handbook of multimedia learning.* New York: Cambridge University Press.

Jonassen, D. H. (2004). *Learning to solve problems.* San Francisco, CA: Pfeiffer.

Kamin, C., O'Sullivan, P., Deterding, R., & Younger, M. (2003). A comparison of critical thinking in groups of third-year medical students in text, video, and virtual PBL case modalities. *Academic Medicine, 78*(2), 204–211.

Kirschner, P. A. (2005). Technology-based collaborative learning: A European perspective. *Educational Technology, 45,* 5–7.

Kobayashi, K. (2005). What limits the encoding effect of note-taking? A meta-analytic examination. *Contemporary Educational Psychology, 30,* 242–262.

Long, K. K., & Smith, R. D. (2004). The role of web-based distance learning in HR development. *Journal of Management Development, 23*(3), 270–284.

Lou, Y., Abrami, P. C., & d'Apollonia, S. (2001). Small group and individual learning with technology: A meta-analysis. *Review of Educational Research, 71,* 449–521.

Mayer, R. E. (2001). *Multimedia learning.* Cambridge, UK: Cambridge University Press.

Mayer, R. E. (2005a). Principles for managing essential processing in multimedia learning: Segmenting, pretraining, and modality principles. In R. E. Mayer (Ed.), *The Cambridge handbook of multimedia learning.* New York, NY: Cambridge University Press.

Mayer, R. E. (2005b). Principles for reducing extraneous processing in multimedia learning: Coherence, signaling, redundancy, spatial contiguity, and temporal contiguity principles. In R. E. Mayer (Ed.), *The Cambridge handbook of multimedia learning* (pp. 229–245). New York: Cambridge University Press.

Mayer, R. E. (2005c). Principles of multimedia learning based on social cues. In R. E. Mayer (Ed.), *The Cambridge handbook of multimedia learning* (pp. 229–245). New York: Cambridge University Press.

Mayer, R. E., & Gallini, J. K. (1990). When is an illustration worth ten thousand words? *Journal of Educational Psychology, 82*(4), 715–726.

Mayer, R. E., & Jackson, J. (2005). The case for coherence in scientific explanations: Quantitative details can hurt qualitative understanding. *Journal of Experimental Psychology: Applied, 11*(1), 13–18.

Mayer, R. E., Sims, V., & Tajika, H. (1995). A comparison of how textbooks teach mathematical problem solving in Japan and the United States. *American Educational Research Journal, 32,* 443–460.

Moreno, R., Mayer, R. E., Spires, H. A., & Lester, J. C. (2001). The case for social agency in computer-based teaching: Do students learn more deeply when they interact with animated pedagogical agents? *Cognition and Instruction, 19*(2), 177–213.

Newby, T. I., Ertmer, P. A., & Stepich, D. A. (1995). Instructional analogies and the learning of concepts. *Educational Technology Research and Development, 43*(1), 5–18.

Newman, M. (2003). A pilot systematic review and meta-analysis on the effectiveness of problem-based learning. Cited in J. R. Savery (2006), Overview of problem-based learning: Definitions and distinctions. *The Interdisciplinary Journal of Problem-Based Learning, 1*(1), 9–20.

Ochoa-Alcantar, J. E., Borders, C. M., & Bichelmeyer, B. A. (2006). Distance training. In J. A. Pershing (Ed.), *Handbook of human performance technology* (3rd ed.). San Francisco, CA: Pfeiffer.

Piolat, A., Olive, T., & Kellogg, R. T. (2005). Cognitive effort during note taking. *Applied Cognitive Psychology, 19,* 291–312.

Pulichino, J. (2005). The synchronous e-learning research report 2005. The eLearning Guild Research. Accessed October 2005 at www.eLearningGuild.com.

Renkl, A. (2005). The worked-out examples principles in multimedia learning. In R. E. Mayer (Ed.), *The Cambridge handbook of multimedia learning* (pp. 229–245). New York: Cambridge University Press.

Savery, J. R. (2006). Overview of problem-based learning: Definitions and distinctions. *The Interdisciplinary Journal of Problem-Based Learning, 1*(1), 9–20.

Stonebraker, P. W., & Hazeltine, J. E. (2004). Virtual learning effectiveness: An examination of the process. *The Learning Organization, 11*(3), 209–225.

Tallent-Runnels, M. K., Thomas, J. A., Lan, W. Y., Cooper, S., Ahern, T. C., Shaw, S. M., & Lee, X. (2006). Teaching courses online: A review of the research. *Review of Educational Research, 76*(1), 93–135.

Tindall-Ford, S., Chandler, P., & Sweller, J. (1997). When two sensory modes are better than one. *Journal of Experimental Psychology: Applied, 3*(4), 257–287.

Titsworth, B. S., & Kiewra, K. A. (2004). Spoken organizational lecture cues and student note taking as facilitators of student learning. *Contemporary Educational Psychology, 29,* 447–461.

Valaitis, R. K., Sword, W. A., Jones, B., & Hodges, A. (2005). Problem-based learning online: Perceptions of health science students. *Advances in Health Sciences Education, 10,* 231–252.

Wang, A. Y., & Newlin, M. H. (2002). Predictors of performance in the virtual classroom: Identifying and helping at-risk cyber-students. *T.H.E. Journal, 29*(10), 21–28.

Wenger, E., Pea, R., Brown, J. W., & Heath, C. (1999). *Communities of practice: Learning, meaning, and identity.* Cambridge, UK: Cambridge University Press.

Woodward, A. (1993). Do illustrations serve an instructional purpose in U.S. textbooks? In B. K. Britton, A. Woodward, & M. Binkley (Eds.), *Learning from textbooks: Theory and practice.* Mahway, NJ: Lawrence Erlbaum Associates.

ABOUT THE AUTHORS

Ruth Colvin Clark, Ed.D., has focused her professional efforts on bridging the gap between academic research on instructional methods and application of that research by training and performance support professionals in corporate and government organizations. Dr. Clark has developed a number of seminars and has written six books, including *e-Learning and the Science of Instruction, Building Expertise,* and *Efficiency in Learning,* that translate important research programs into practitioner guidelines.

A science undergraduate, she completed her doctorate in instructional psychology/educational technology in 1988 at the University of Southern California. Dr. Clark is a past president of the International Society of Performance Improvement and a member of the American Educational Research Association. She was honored with the 2006 Thomas F. Gilbert Distinguished Professional Achievement Award by the International Society for Performance Improvement and is an invited *Training Legend* Speaker at the ASTD 2006 International Conference. Dr. Clark is currently a dual resident of Southwest Colorado and Phoenix, Arizona, and divides her professional time among speaking, teaching, and writing. For more information, consult her website at www.clarktraining.com.

Ann Kwinn, Ph.D., is partner and director of e-learning for Clark Training. In the past nineteen years, Dr. Kwinn has designed and managed the development of over thirty e-learning programs and consulted on others, receiving three CINDY awards and *Multimedia Producer* magazine's Top 100 Producers award. She holds a Ph.D. in instructional technology from USC, was a research fellow at ETS, and taught at UC Irvine Dr. Kwinn has written many articles and book chapters and has presented at several conferences. She is the designer of Clark's e-Learning Producer seminar and is co-author with Bill Brandon, Karen Hyder, Ron Miazga and Matthew Murray of the online book, *The eLearning Guild's Handbook on Synchronous eLearning.*

INDEX

System Requirements

PC with Microsoft Windows 98SE or later

Mac with Apple OS version 8.6 or later

Using the CD with Windows

To view the items located on the CD, follow these steps:

1. Insert the CD into your computer's CD-ROM drive.

2. A window appears with the following options:

   Contents: Allows you to view the files included on the CD-ROM

   Software: Allows you to install useful software from the CD-ROM

   Links: Displays a hyperlinked page of websites

   Author: Displays a page with information about the author(s)

   Contact Us: Displays a page with information on contacting the publisher or author

Help: Displays a page with information on using the CD.

Exit: Closes the interface window

If you do not have autorun enabled, or if the autorun window does not appear, follow these steps to access the CD:

1. Click Start -> Run.

2. In the dialog box that appears, type d:‹<\\><\\>›start.exe, where d is the letter of your CD-ROM drive. This brings up the autorun window described in the preceding set of steps.

3. Choose the desired option from the menu. (See step 2 in the preceding list for a description of the options.)

In Case of Trouble

If you experience difficulty using the CD-ROM, please follow these steps:

1. Make sure your hardware and system configurations conform to the system requirements noted earlier under "System Requirements."

2. Review the installation procedure for your type of hardware and operating system. It is possible to reinstall the software, if necessary.

To speak with someone in Product Technical Support, call 800-762-2974 or 317-572-3994 Monday through Friday between 8:30 A.M. and 5:00 P.M. Eastern time. You can also contact Product Technical Support and get support information through our website at www.wiley.com/techsupport.

Before calling or writing, please have the following information available:

- Type of computer and operating system
- Any error messages displayed
- Complete description of the problem

It is best if you are sitting at your computer when making the call.

Pfeiffer Publications Guide

This guide is designed to familiarize you with the various types of Pfeiffer publications. The formats section describes the various types of products that we publish; the methodologies section describes the many different ways that content might be provided within a product. We also provide a list of the topic areas in which we publish.

FORMATS

In addition to its extensive book-publishing program, Pfeiffer offers content in an array of formats, from fieldbooks for the practitioner to complete, ready-to-use training packages that support group learning.

FIELDBOOK Designed to provide information and guidance to practitioners in the midst of action. Most fieldbooks are companions to another, sometimes earlier, work, from which its ideas are derived; the fieldbook makes practical what was theoretical in the original text. Fieldbooks can certainly be read from cover to cover. More likely, though, you'll find yourself bouncing around following a particular theme, or dipping in as the mood, and the situation, dictate.

HANDBOOK A contributed volume of work on a single topic, comprising an eclectic mix of ideas, case studies, and best practices sourced by practitioners and experts in the field.

An editor or team of editors usually is appointed to seek out contributors and to evaluate content for relevance to the topic. Think of a handbook not as a ready-to-eat meal, but as a cookbook of ingredients that enables you to create the most fitting experience for the occasion.

RESOURCE Materials designed to support group learning. They come in many forms: a complete, ready-to-use exercise (such as a game); a comprehensive resource on one topic (such as conflict management) containing a variety of methods and approaches; or a collection of like-minded activities (such as icebreakers) on multiple subjects and situations.

TRAINING PACKAGE An entire, ready-to-use learning program that focuses on a particular topic or skill. All packages comprise a guide for the facilitator/trainer and a workbook for the participants. Some packages are supported with additional media—such as video—or learning aids, instruments, or other devices to help participants understand concepts or practice and develop skills.

- *Facilitator/trainer's guide* Contains an introduction to the program, advice on how to organize and facilitate the learning event, and step-by-step instructor notes. The guide also contains copies of presentation materials—handouts, presentations, and overhead designs, for example—used in the program.

- *Participant's workbook* Contains exercises and reading materials that support the learning goal and serves as a valuable reference and support guide for participants in the weeks and months that follow the learning event. Typically, each participant will require his or her own workbook.

ELECTRONIC CD-ROMs and web-based products transform static Pfeiffer content into dynamic, interactive experiences. Designed to take advantage of the searchability, automation, and ease-of-use that technology provides, our e-products bring convenience and immediate accessibility to your workspace.

METHODOLOGIES

CASE STUDY A presentation, in narrative form, of an actual event that has occurred inside an organization. Case studies are not prescriptive, nor are they used to prove a point; they are designed to develop critical analysis and decision-making skills. A case study has a specific time frame, specifies a sequence of events, is narrative in structure, and contains a plot structure—an issue (what should be/have been done?). Use case studies when the goal is to enable participants to apply previously learned theories to the circumstances in the case, decide what is pertinent, identify the real issues, decide what should have been done, and develop a plan of action.

ENERGIZER A short activity that develops readiness for the next session or learning event. Energizers are most commonly used after a break or lunch to stimulate or refocus the group. Many involve some form of physical activity, so they are a useful way to counter post-lunch lethargy. Other uses include transitioning from one topic to another, where "mental" distancing is important.

EXPERIENTIAL LEARNING ACTIVITY (ELA) A facilitator-led intervention that moves participants through the learning cycle from experience to application (also known as a Structured Experience). ELAs are carefully thought-out designs in which there is a definite learning purpose and intended outcome. Each step—everything that participants do during the activity—facilitates the accomplishment of the stated goal. Each ELA includes complete instructions for facilitating the intervention and a clear statement of goals, suggested group size and timing, materials required, an explanation of the process, and, where appropriate, possible variations to the activity. (For more detail on Experiential Learning Activities, see the Introduction to the *Reference Guide to Handbooks and Annuals*, 1999 edition, Pfeiffer, San Francisco.)

GAME A group activity that has the purpose of fostering team spirit and togetherness in addition to the achievement of a pre-stated goal. Usually contrived—undertaking a desert expedition, for example—this type of learning method offers an engaging means for participants to demonstrate and practice business and interpersonal skills. Games are effective for team building and personal development mainly because the goal is subordinate to the process—the means through which participants reach decisions, collaborate, communicate, and generate trust and understanding. Games often engage teams in "friendly" competition.

ICEBREAKER   A (usually) short activity designed to help participants overcome initial anxiety in a training session and/or to acquaint the participants with one another. An icebreaker can be a fun activity or can be tied to specific topics or training goals. While a useful tool in itself, the icebreaker comes into its own in situations where tension or resistance exists within a group.

INSTRUMENT   A device used to assess, appraise, evaluate, describe, classify, and summarize various aspects of human behavior. The term used to describe an instrument depends primarily on its format and purpose. These terms include survey, questionnaire, inventory, diagnostic, survey, and poll. Some uses of instruments include providing instrumental feedback to group members, studying here-and-now processes or functioning within a group, manipulating group composition, and evaluating outcomes of training and other interventions.

Instruments are popular in the training and HR field because, in general, more growth can occur if an individual is provided with a method for focusing specifically on his or her own behavior. Instruments also are used to obtain information that will serve as a basis for change and to assist in workforce planning efforts.

Paper-and-pencil tests still dominate the instrument landscape with a typical package comprising a facilitator's guide, which offers advice on administering the instrument and interpreting the collected data, and an initial set of instruments. Additional instruments are available separately. Pfeiffer, though, is investing heavily in e-instruments. Electronic instrumentation provides effortless distribution and, for larger groups particularly, offers advantages over paper-and-pencil tests in the time it takes to analyze data and provide feedback.

LECTURETTE   A short talk that provides an explanation of a principle, model, or process that is pertinent to the participants' current learning needs. A lecturette is intended to establish a common language bond between the trainer and the participants by providing a mutual frame of reference. Use a lecturette as an introduction to a group activity or event, as an interjection during an event, or as a handout.

MODEL   A graphic depiction of a system or process and the relationship among its elements. Models provide a frame of reference and something more tangible, and more easily remembered, than a verbal explanation. They also give participants something to "go on," enabling them to track their own progress as they experience the dynamics, processes, and relationships being depicted in the model.

ROLE PLAY A technique in which people assume a role in a situation/scenario: a customer service rep in an angry-customer exchange, for example. The way in which the role is approached is then discussed and feedback is offered. The role play is often repeated using a different approach and/or incorporating changes made based on feedback received. In other words, role playing is a spontaneous interaction involving realistic behavior under artificial (and safe) conditions.

SIMULATION A methodology for understanding the interrelationships among components of a system or process. Simulations differ from games in that they test or use a model that depicts or mirrors some aspect of reality in form, if not necessarily in content. Learning occurs by studying the effects of change on one or more factors of the model. Simulations are commonly used to test hypotheses about what happens in a system—often referred to as "what if?" analysis—or to examine best-case/worst-case scenarios.

THEORY A presentation of an idea from a conjectural perspective. Theories are useful because they encourage us to examine behavior and phenomena through a different lens.

TOPICS

The twin goals of providing effective and practical solutions for workforce training and organization development and meeting the educational needs of training and human resource professionals shape Pfeiffer's publishing program. Core topics include the following:

 Leadership & Management

 Communication & Presentation

 Coaching & Mentoring

 Training & Development

 E-Learning

 Teams & Collaboration

 OD & Strategic Planning

 Human Resources

 Consulting